"There are so many forever recipes in this book. *The Korean Vegan* is a gentle reset toward vegan cookery that is so well crafted, it makes exclusively plant-based Korean cooking seem obvious. It is also a proud and complicated journey of an immigrant family. As I cooked through *The Korean Vegan*, I marveled at the skill of this chef and was astounded by her talent as a writer. This book belongs in every kitchen in America."

—Tiffani Faison, chef and *Top Chef* finalist

"Come for the veganized Korean recipes, which will inspire you in the kitchen and delight your taste buds (the Tteokbokki Arrabbiata and Kkanpoong Tofu will change your life). Stay for Joanne's poetic stories about family and culture that will move you to tears. "

—Nisha Vora, creator of Rainbow Plant Life and author of *The Vegan Instant Pot Cookbook*

"Stunningly beautiful in every way. This book will make you fall in love instantly with the author, her culture, her family, and Korean cuisine. I couldn't recommend it more."

—Kim-Julie Hansen, founder of Best of Vegan and author of *Vegan Reset*

the korean
vegan
cookbook

AVERY

An imprint of Penguin Random House

New York

the Korean vegan cookbook

Reflections and Recipes *from* Omma's Kitchen

JOANNE LEE MOLINARO

AVERY

an imprint of Penguin Random House LLC
penguinrandomhouse.com

Library of Congress Cataloging-in-Publication Data

Names: Lee Molinaro, Joanne, author.
Title: The Korean vegan cookbook: reflections and
    recipes from Omma's kitchen / Joanne Lee Molinaro.
Description: New York: Avery, Penguin Random House
    LLC, 2021. | Includes index.
Identifiers: LCCN 2020057487 (print) |
    LCCN 2020057488 (ebook) |
    ISBN 9780593084274 (hardcover) |
    ISBN 9780593084281 (ebook)
Subjects: LCSH: Cooking, Korean. | Vegetarian cooking. |
    LCGFT: Cookbooks.
Classification: LCC TX724.5.K65 L48 2021 (print) |
    LCC TX724.5.K65 (ebook) | DDC 641.59519—dc23
LC record available at https://lccn.loc.gov/2020057487
LC ebook record available at https://lccn.loc.
    gov/2020057488
p.   cm.

Printed in China
10 9 8 7 6 5 4 3 2 1

Book design by Ashley Tucker

To 엄마 and Daddy,
whose stories I treasure.

And to my grandmothers,
who I hope are proud of me.

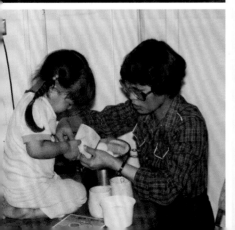

CONTENTS

INTRODUCTION 9

THE KOREAN VEGAN 17

THE KOREAN VEGAN PANTRY 23

1 THE BASICS 34

2 BBANG (빵 • Breads) 54

3 BANCHAN (반찬 • Side Dishes) 76

4 KIMCHI AND SALADS 109

5 SOUPS AND STEWS 141

6 NOODLES AND PASTAS 165

7 BAR AND STREET FOODS 194

8 MAIN DISHES 228

9 SWEETS 274

THE LEES IN KOREA 320

ACKNOWLEDGMENTS 325

INDEX 329

INTRODUCTION

SLURPING.

Cautious, but unapologetic.

My father sips a spoonful of the still-bubbling *doenjang chigae* from the worn *ddukbaegi* sitting not quite at the center of the table.

Dinner always begins with the *"clink"* of my father's steel chopsticks against a small porcelain plate of *banchan*, maybe some pickled mung beans or a saddle of kimchi. My brother and I knock our spoons against the sides of our ceramic bowls, which are filled with pearly mounds of rice. My mother plucks a single mung bean from the same small plate my father started with, the silvery chimes of her chopsticks floating toward our low kitchen ceiling.

I can hear the patter of Hahlmuhnee's[*] bare feet as she paces from the stove to the kitchen table and loads our *bapsang* with a basket of fresh *kennip*, chilies, and squash from the backyard garden, each a different shade of green, a plate bearing a whole roasted fish, and a pitcher of dark-amber, ice-cold corn tea. The worn, ellipse-shaped table we all sit around bears crayon graffiti and wads of gum on its underside but boasts a colorful assortment of more than a dozen *banchan*.

My spoon and chopsticks remain untouched. Nothing tempts me. Not the *doenjang chigae*, the chilies I'd picked for Hahlmuhnee that morning, or the mung beans my parents favored. This is not what they eat on TV or what the kids at school eat with *their* families. Why couldn't Hahlmuhnee just make spaghetti once in a while?

---

[*] Grandmother.

9

Hahlmuhnee

With a grimace, Hahlmuhnee seats herself next to me, finally resting her stiff joints. She reaches for a *kennip* so dark it looks almost blue, and places it in her open palm. She dabs a pea-size bit of *ssamjang* into its heart with the tips of her chopsticks. She adds a spoonful of rice before wrapping it up like a small gift she then brings to her mouth. She turns to me, her mouth still agape while she feeds herself, and gives me an inquiring look, as if asking, "Why aren't you eating?" While chewing, she spreads another large *kennip*—so big it extends past her long fingers. Once more, she deposits a bit of *ssamjang* right in the center, adds a spoonful of still-steaming rice, and smoothly wraps the *kennip* into a neat green bundle, but this time, presses it toward my mouth.

I part my lips.

The clinks and scrapes and chews and slurps continue for a quarter of an hour, maybe twenty minutes. The mole on Hahlmuhnee's chin seems to pulse as she chews another *kennip* wrap. My mother's pale, angular face remains expressionless, preoccupied, as she brings another spoon of rice to her thin lips. My father closes his eyes as he continues to eat, while my little brother's cheeks are barely visible behind his bowl.

There was predictability in our family's reunion at the end of each day. There was also the serenity that attends the sounds of sustenance. As children of war, scarcity and hunger were embedded in my parents' bones long before I began to complain about our lack of McDonald's at the dinner table. As a result, talking was discouraged during mealtime. Eating was a serious business that demanded undivided attention. I don't remember any pleasantries like "What happened at school today?" or "How was work, honey?" We didn't spill our guts during dinner—we filled them.

Sometimes I would help Hahlmuhnee prepare the *banchan* for dinner. We'd sit on the floor of our foyer with Daddy's day-old Korean newspapers spread out and a mountain of raw mung between us. The tails of the sprouts created the appearance of a tangle of blond hair against the black-and-white print, as Hahlmuhnee's silver tooth caught rays of sunlight streaming through the screen door.

From left to right: my father, Hahlmuhnee, and my uncle

Once, she shyly counted out the beans we were trimming in Japanese: *ichi, ni, sahn, shi.* I started copying her: *ichi, ni, sahn, shi.* She counted to ten, stopped abruptly, and admonished me severely, "It's not good to speak Japanese. It's dangerous to speak Japanese." And this is how I learned, for the first time, that there are secrets buried in our family story, ones that Hahlmuhnee thought were too dangerous to say out loud.

I wouldn't know this for years yet, but both my parents were born in North Korea—though it was simply "the northern region" of Korea when they were born. My paternal grandfather had settled in the north as a teenager, after running away from home when he was thirteen years old to avoid an arranged marriage with the daughter of a wealthy family. He managed to get through the Maebong mountain range to arrive at Hamhung, where he eventually found a job as a miner—270 miles from his father's home. According to family legend, on his way he encountered a tiger, the mythical creature of Korean folklore.

From left to right: my aunt, Hahlmuhnee, my youngest uncle, and my second uncle

After a brief stint as a coal miner, my grandfather enlisted with the Japanese Imperial police force. Working for the Japanese government allowed him to keep a tidy home with plenty of food on the table, and it even earned him at least the appearance of respect. However, Korea had suffered under the brutal thumb of Japanese rule for decades, and the word *traitor* lingered on many people's lips when they saw my grandfather's uniformed figure. These "behind the hand" whispers grew into full-blown jeers toward the end of World War II, when the days of Japan's foothold on Korea grew numbered.

On the night before what's known to the Korean people as Victory Over Japan Day, leaving behind my grandmother and my newborn father, my grandfather slipped onto the bed of a pickup truck carrying dozens of Japanese police officers destined for Seoul. Staying north would have meant certain death, but fleeing didn't absolve him—or his family—of the sins of betrayal.

A few months later, in 1946, my father passed through the 38th parallel—what would one day become the hurried man-made "boundary" between North and South Korea—swaddled on my grandmother's back. She cupped handfuls of swamp water to his

*Hahlmuhnee taught me
how to swing*

lips to keep him from crying, to avoid alerting the Communist soldiers guarding the undefined border between what would soon be two halves of a divided peninsula. Once they passed undetected, Hahlmuhnee carried my father through the mountains, where my father claims they, too, encountered a tiger, before arriving in South Korea to join her husband.

My mother's parents were both born in North Korea in a small village called Hwang Hae Do. My *omma*† was born in Ongjin in 1949, just a few years after the close of World War II, Korea's emancipation from Japan, and my father's long trek into South Korea. Omma was nearly a year old the morning of June 25, 1950, when the North Korean armed forces were engaged by the ROK (Republic of Korea) on the outskirts of her home. My mother's village was deemed a crucial chess piece in the Korean War, and the Battle of Ongjin was the opening move. Amid a hailstorm of missiles and the crackling roll of tanks, the people of Ongjin, my grandparents included, evacuated; and by that afternoon, Ongjin's sleepy homes were replaced by thick columns of smoke.

*Omma, Seoul Hahlmuhnee,
and a dumpling*

Eventually, my mother's parents were able to get passage across the Yellow Sea on a US Navy ship. They disembarked in South Korea and started their lives as refugees, living in the basement of the home of a wealthy villager and scrounging through the soil for forgotten sweet potatoes.

None of these stories were shared at the dinner table. I didn't know my parents were from North Korea until I was in college, and even then, it was one of those facts about my family's history that I swept under the rug or conveniently ignored when North Korea became a point on the "Axis of Evil," or when my friends just assumed, "*Your* family is from *South* Korea, right? Not the

---

† Mother.

Mandatory family photo

North?" It was easier to nod my head than to delve into the sordid details of my traitorous grandfather or the destitution that comes with the ravages of war. But, even though these histories never surfaced, my parents' stories brought a latent urgency to dinnertime as we communed at the table each day.

Over the years, the setting of our family's ensemble and the shape of our dining table changed as we moved from our tiny one-story ranch house in Skokie, Illinois, to a three-story home in the North Shore—at one point, my mother replaced our old wood table with a smaller, elegant glass one with curved brass legs. My brother and I couldn't mark it with so much as a fingerprint without incurring my mother's wrath. But for most of my life, and subject to few exceptions, our attendance at the dinner table was mandatory. And as a result, that dining table bore witness to some of my family's greatest joys and deepest grief.

Sometimes, I would bound into my seat at the table, buoyed by an A+ on my geometry test or by the news I'd landed the lead in the school musical. And sometimes, my father would crack open his eyelids for a moment, point at the rice kernels dotting my brother's

My little brother and me

T-shirt, and joke, "Are you saving that for lunch?" And then he'd laugh long and hard, while my brother and I looked questioningly at Omma for an explanation of Daddy's joke.

Grief, on the other hand, slowed the tempo.

My father's mother, or "Hahlmuhnee," moved in with us when my little brother was born. The day she died, my maternal grandmother—whom we referred to as "Seoul Hahlmuhnee" because she emigrated to the United States from Seoul—came to stay with us, to help my parents as they dealt with the arrangements, though, truth be told, my father did little more than allow himself to be shifted from one sofa to the next. At one point, I sat next to him, asked him if he was okay. His face was gray and he stared straight

My father in Vietnam

ahead for several minutes, as if I weren't even there. All of a sudden, his voice, hoarse and shaky, began, "You know? Your grandmother"—he paused, collecting his breath—"she held my hand and prayed for me"—he halted again—"when I went to Vietnam."

I knew next to nothing about my dad's service in the Vietnam War, other than the fact that he'd been there. Later, I'd learn he'd been a translator during the war. "It was snowing really hard that day," he continued softly. "I got on the train. I opened the window and stuck my hand out. Your grandmother, she held my hand and started praying. And then"—he stopped again—"the train, when it started to move away, your grandmother . . ." He squeezed his eyes shut for a moment. "Your grandmother, she ran along, with the train, still holding my hand and praying."

I could see Hahlmuhnee then, could hear her voice, the same one I'd listened to whispering prayers deep into the blue interiors of the bedroom I'd shared with her. I imagined how that voice chased after my father straight into the jungles of Vietnam and wrapped itself around him, head to foot, like a talisman.

Daddy remained sitting cross-legged on the love seat in the living room for several minutes, without saying anything more. At dinner-

time, Seoul Hahlmuhnee gently nudged him to the kitchen, so that he could assume his place at our dining table. All of us were seated while my grandmother shuffled around us, bringing bowls of rice and plates of *banchan* to the table. The sound of her bare feet was decidedly different from Hahlmuhnee's.

I ducked my head to start eating the bowl of rice Seoul Hahlmuhnee placed in front of me but watched my father as he slowly picked up his spoon. I let out a small sigh of relief—eating not only meant that we could all resume our part in "normalcy," but that Daddy would finally snap out of the waking dream he'd been having all day.

Suddenly, his spoon clattered. My father let out a guttural,

Hahlmuhnee and me

hiccupping sob as he brought his hands up to his face. For a moment—for what seemed like an hour—we all just sat there, because we didn't know how to respond to this wild breach in protocol.

Slowly, Seoul Hahlmuhnee stepped toward him and, unimaginably, placed her wrinkled, walnut hands on those heaving shoulders.

"Shhhhh . . . Shhhhhh. . . . You have to be strong now. It's not good to cry so hard. You have to be strong."

My father stopped crying. My grandmother sat down.

The clink of chopsticks resumed.

THE KOREAN VEGAN

I STARTED MY BLOG IN 2016, WITH AN EYE TOWARD sharing vegan versions of Korean recipes while preserving the details that sometimes get stripped in the rush to bring Korean recipes to the masses. For example, the method my aunt used to pickle cabbage for kimchi involves a special choreography, and you won't find it on other food blogs or in YouTube videos. I learned it by asking questions: "Why do you drop the knife through the cabbage instead of just cutting it on a cutting board?" "Why do you have to fold the top cabbage leaf over the rest of them?" and "Why does it matter where you get the cabbage from?" These are the kinds of secrets that breathe life into a recipe but may disappear over time.

In 2017, about a year after I had started my blog, I also began to share my family's immigrant experience, because I realized that my love of the food I grew up eating was inextricably tied to their journey in the United States. While I didn't know my parents' stories when I was growing up, as I grew older, I started to understand the importance of collecting and chronicling them—just like I would with recipes.

The recipes I share online and in this book are all plant based. Veganism remains extremely rare in Korean culture. But, after thirty-seven years of eating meat, dairy, and eggs, I made the decision to exclude animal products from my diet. For some, this commitment is an easy choice. For me, it was a huge deal. Many of the foods I grew up eating—*samgyupsahl* (grilled pork belly), *jjajangmyun* (black bean noodles), and *bulgogi* (grilled flank steak)—were about as un-vegan as you could get. Though I'd never eaten a very meat-heavy diet, I still

associated those foods with who I was, and I was terrified that going vegan meant losing my "Korean-ness."

And yet, I was surrounded by fresh vegetables throughout my childhood. Seoul Hahlmuhnee transformed our typical suburban backyard into a mini-farm, filled with tomatoes as fat as your face after a ramen binge and lime-green *hobbahk* (Korean squash) nestled in the wings. Small chili plants lined the perimeter—we'd split the chilies open until the seeds bit into our hands. In September, we would climb the massive pear tree, pick what we could reach, and wander back into the house with fingers and lips sticky with autumn. And at the far end of the yard was my grandmother's pride and joy: dozens of tall, graceful stalks of perilla leaves that turned their heart-shaped faces to the sun like a troupe of ballerinas.

Though we would have fish every now and again, meals consisted largely of rice, fresh veggies from the backyard, and a variety of other small meatless dishes, or *banchan*, that my grandmother would prepare. Meat was very rarely on the dinner table—Hahlmuhnee considered meat an unnecessary indulgence, reserved for special occasions.

Like many of her generation in North Korea, my *hahlmuhnee* grew

Chunjinam Hermitage

up a rice kernel away from starvation. During the Korean War, she watched the faces of her children—my mom and her sister—turn gray from hunger. The whole country was on fire, and it seemed all they had to eat were the ashes. On the run, she could no longer dig into the soil and plant the meals that would fill their bellies.

Is it any wonder, then, that the very first thing she did when my parents finally bought a piece of land of their own in Skokie was to plant the hibiscus cutting my grandfather carried on his lap during the long plane ride from Korea? She spent the next decade tilling, sowing, and tending our backyard until the

Onggi at Chunjinam Hermitage

majority of our meals came from ingredients she'd grown herself.

I visited South Korea during the summer of 2019, hoping to see some of the places that remained so vivid to Seoul Hahlmuhnee until she passed away. While I was there, I had the opportunity to meet with the renowned Buddhist monk and cook Jeong Kwan sunim, who has become famous in the food world. Jeong Kwan sunim is the OG Korean vegan— she excludes all animal products from her cooking and maximizes flavor by preparing dishes with richly brewed soy sauces and other *jiangs* (sauces) made from soybeans that have been fermenting in *onggi* (massive clay fermenting pots) for decades. Her food has been described as perhaps the most exquisite on Earth.

I was appropriately intimidated to visit Jeong Kwan sunim at her home in the Chunjinam Hermitage, which is tucked into a crevice of Baegam Mountain. When I told her about my mission to "veganize" Korean food and my Instagram account and blog, she listened politely, her large round eyes sparkling with something akin to amusement. As she explained, Korean plant-based eating is not a new idea. Korean temple food, the cuisine prepared by Korean Buddhist monks, has been around for more than a thousand years, predating Korean BBQ and bibimbap.

Chunjinam Hermitage

For Jeong Kwan sunim, her refusal to eat meat is an extension of her life's philosophy, which is to do as little harm as possible to the planet, to animals, to one another, and to oneself. As she explained, "When you do harm to others, you do harm to yourself." Gesturing to the dark soil beneath the blades of grass as we tramped through her garden, she said, "When you hurt the earth, you hurt yourself." Gripping my elbow, she continued, "When you hurt someone else, you hurt yourself." She then added, "It's impossible to do *no* harm—when you pull something out of the ground to eat it, you will hurt the ground. But the idea is to do the *least* harm, so that you do the least harm to yourself."

Chunjinam Hermitage

Jeong Kwan sunim's gentle but powerful message—*do less harm*—resonated with me on a very basic level because, ultimately, for me, being vegan is about leaving a smaller footprint on the planet, healing my body after decades of disordered eating, and knowing that my meals involve as little animal suffering as possible.

The question I get asked the most is whether I miss meat. It may seem strange, but the one food I missed for a long time was SPAM. I never really loved the taste or texture, but I missed what those little sodium bombs *meant* to me. I remember fighting with my little brother over who got the last pink chunk swimming in a pot of *chigae* (stew). To be honest, we loved it partly because SPAM, like the ham all the other kids ate between two slices of white bread and the hot dogs my mother chopped into our spaghetti, was an *American* food. At least, to us.

Fishing for SPAM in a pot of spicy kimchi stew is a uniquely Asian American experience. One of the last nonvegan meals I had was a kimchi *chigae* at my favorite Korean bar, packed with hunks of extra

Chunjinam Hermitage

SPAM. It marked me as a card-carrying member of the Korean diaspora, a child of immigrants, with stories built on war, poverty, racism, and courage, because SPAM, in some strange, beautiful way, signified that we had made it. We had survived. And survival, we'd learned, was something we never took for granted.

This was a club I didn't want to be ousted from simply because I'd decided to stop eating meat. And perhaps that's why I found myself in Omma's kitchen so often after I went vegan. Though I could no longer spar for SPAM, I could learn how to make kimchi *chigae*—starting with making kimchi all the way to preparing the stew—from the closest

My first birthday party

link I had to a heritage I could never physically don. There was no plane in the world that could fly me to North Korea, but my mother's words and her food could transport me to a place as close to it as possible.

What I've learned by collecting and sharing these recipes is that what really matters isn't whether the food tastes exactly the way your grandmother made it but how it makes you feel. For me, the recipes in this book remind me of the garden in the backyard of our Skokie house, the deep wrinkles in my grandmother's hands. They remind me of my mother's perseverance, my father's laughter.

They remind me of home.

THE KOREAN
VEGAN PANTRY

THROUGHOUT THIS COOKBOOK, YOU WILL SEE REFER-ences to ingredients I use on almost a daily basis. Some of these will look familiar to you: garlic, onions, potatoes. Others, however, may look decidedly *unfamiliar*. I know what you're thinking—*I'll just substitute!* While I admire your resourcefulness, the truth is, a lot of these recipes simply won't taste the same or even come out right if you use substitutes. So, while I know you're itching to make that *jjajangmyun* dish, be sure you know the difference between "black bean sauce" and "*fermented* black soybean sauce" first! Trust me. *Jjajangmyun* isn't going to taste right if you try to make it with a can of black beans.

A word on measurements—the majority of the measurements in this book are listed in standard forms of volume (e.g., cups, table-spoons, teaspoons, etc.). When it's more convenient to measure a particular ingredient in weight (for example, dried pasta), however, I've listed the ingredients in ounces. For recipes that require more precision (e.g., breads and baked desserts), I've included metric measurements.

Finally, I've included allergen information for each recipe:

- "GF" means it's naturally gluten-free.

- "GFO" means there's a gluten-free option (e.g., using gluten-free soy sauce).

- "NF" means it's nut-free.

SOY SAUCE

Soy sauce is deeply misunderstood. Due to concerns about soy, as well as the bad mass-produced versions out there, people are starting to think they need to replace soy sauce with something "healthier." One notable vegan Twitter account called soy sauce "an overpriced and trashy adaptation of tamari sauce." Of course, the obvious flaw in this tweet (which the account immediately retracted after a couple of thoughtful replies) is that tamari sauce *is* soy sauce. Like marinara or barbecue sauce, there are a variety of different ways soy sauce can be prepared, which speaks to not just its complexity but also its history.

Soy sauce is, as the name suggests, a sauce made out of soybeans. Originating in China, soy sauce has been around for over two thousand years. It is simply absurd to think, then, that there can be only one or two different kinds of soy sauce. There are literally *hundreds* of variations of soy sauce. In fact, in Korea (where soy sauce has been around since 57 BCE), the Korean Ministry of Food and Drug Safety mandates that every bottle of soy sauce for sale be categorized into one of four categories: (a) naturally brewed, (b) blended, (c) hydrolyzed acid, and (d) flavored. But even within these four categories, there are dozens of varieties that can make things very confusing.

So, here's where I come out on soy sauce:

• Stick to naturally brewed soy sauce as much as possible.

• Read the labels carefully—many soy sauces include unusual (or nonvegan) ingredients to "enhance" flavor or consistency, like anchovy broth or high fructose corn syrup. I prefer soy sauces with shorter ingredients lists: water, soybeans, salt, wheat, spirits (which are not added but occur as part of the fermentation process).

• Experiment with different kinds of soy sauce for different dishes. For example, *guk-ganjang*, which translates to "soup soy sauce," is excellent for flavoring broths and stews, as the name suggests. *Guk-ganjang* is made from simply boiling the liquid that is left over from fermenting soybeans into *doenjang* (discussed later!). It has a cleaner and more concentrated flavor than most commercial soy sauces and therefore has a lighter color. Throughout this book I will reference it as "light soy sauce," but the "light" refers to the color, not the sodium level. In fact, this "light" soy sauce is saltier than regular soy sauce, and so, with this one, less is often more!

• Finally, allergic to soy? I got you. Coconut aminos offer a great substitute for soy sauce!

MY FAVORITE BRAND: Sempio Yukinong Organic Soy Sauce

GLUTEN-FREE CORNER: Most Korean soy sauces use wheat in the fermentation process, and so they are not gluten-free. However, tamari (Japanese soy sauce) is usually not made with wheat and so is gluten-free (though I've seen even some bottles of soy sauce with the "tamari" label made with wheat—make sure to check the labels!).

STORAGE: I keep my soy sauce in the pantry because I can usually go through a bottle in a couple of weeks. If you'd like to make yours last longer (6 months), stick it in the fridge.

DOENJANG

Doenjang is fermented soybean paste. The traditional variety of *doenjang* was actually a by-product of soy sauce brewing. *Doenjang* usually consists of soybeans, salt, water, and spirits (again, not added but occurring during the fermentation process); like soy sauce, mass-produced versions have a whole host of other ingredients that are, in my opinion, unnecessary. The fewer the ingredients you read on the label, the better. More important, though, certain "flavored" varieties of *doenjang* may contain nonvegan items, like anchovies and even beef broth.

Doenjang is one of those ingredients I'm sometimes afraid to use when I'm cooking for people who are new to Korean cuisine. It doesn't look very appetizing and it smells rather pungent. However, drop a spoonful of this stuff (and that's really all you need) into a pot of hot veggie broth or a pan of sautéed vegetables and you will soon be asking yourself why *doenjang* hasn't always been a part of your pantry.

I often describe *doenjang*'s flavor as an intense miso. Miso is similar to *doenjang* as it, too, is derived from fermenting soybeans. However, miso is fermented with a different method to offer a slightly milder, more delicate flavor. That said, if you enjoy the umami of miso, you will likely very much appreciate *doenjang*.

MY FAVORITE BRAND: Sempio Togeul Doenjang

GLUTEN-FREE CORNER: Many brands of *doenjang* use wheat for thickening; therefore, make sure to check labels to find something gluten-free. Sempio Togeul Doenjang is naturally gluten-free.

STORAGE: Keep *doenjang* in the fridge and it will last for months.

GOCHUJANG

Gochujang has become the new "it" condiment in the cool kids' culinary scene. With the advent of bibimbap (for which *gochujang* serves as the sauce that binds the *bibim* or "mixed" ingredients), *gochujang* is now becoming as prevalent as sriracha or salsa (and provides an excellent kick for your tacos). But what actually is *gochujang*?

Gochujang literally translates into "chili" (*gochu*) "sauce" (*jang*). Like *doenjang* (and so many other Korean ingredients), its base consists of fermented soybeans, but dried Korean chilies are added to give it that fiery punch in the gut (literally). In terms of flavor, I often liken it to a really spicy ketchup, since most varieties contain sweeteners. In terms of texture, it looks and feels a lot more like tomato paste than ketchup, as it is often thickened with either rice or wheat flour.

How *spicy*? Here is a handy-dandy metric for *gochujang* hotness measured in GHU (Gochujang Hot-Taste Units). Most *gochujangs* are in the 45–75 GHU range.

GHU	HOTNESS
>100	Burn your tongue off hot
75–100	"I need a hose" hot
45–75	Gettin' sweaty hot
30–45	"Hey that's got some kick!" hot
<30	"Didn't you say spicy?"

MY FAVORITE BRAND: Chung Jung One Sunchang Gochujang

GLUTEN-FREE CORNER: As mentioned above, some brands use wheat flour as a thickener. However, many brands, including Chung Jung One, have gluten-free varieties made with glutinous rice flour.

STORAGE: Keep *gochujang* in the fridge and it will last for months.

JJAJANG

The word *jjajang* (sometimes referred to as *choonjang*) comes from a Chinese word that means "fried sauce." It is the essential ingredient for making the ever-popular *jjajangmyun* (black bean noodles). However, subbing in your regular black beans in a *jjajangmyun* recipe will result in a very different dish. The paste consists of fermented black soybeans, sweeteners, and a thickener (usually wheat flour). You can use the paste, which is quite dense and salty, as a condiment for veggies (my father likes to dip raw onions or pickled daikon radishes in the paste as a premeal snack), but it is mostly used to make a sauce for the noodles.

MY FAVORITE BRAND: Assi Black Bean Jjajang

GLUTEN-FREE CORNER: Unfortunately, there are no gluten-free brands for *jjajang*.

STORAGE: Keep *jjajang* in the fridge and it will last for months.

SESAME OIL

As the name suggests, sesame oil is derived from sesame seeds. Like soy sauce, there are numerous different varieties of sesame oil; however, the kind used in the Korean kitchen is made from toasted sesame seeds and is therefore darker than the cold-pressed variety (cold-pressed is made from raw sesame seeds). Some people use sesame oil for cooking, but toasted sesame oil has a lower smoke point than its cold-pressed counterpart. Thus, I use it more often for seasoning or combine it with extra-virgin olive oil (which has a higher smoke point). Sesame has an intense, velvety flavor that largely goes to waste when it is burned off during cooking (in my opinion). Accordingly, many recipes call for ½ to 1 teaspoon of sesame oil right at the end of cooking in order to bind the flavors together with the fat in the oil while imparting the rich aroma.

MY FAVORITE BRAND: Chung Jung One

GLUTEN-FREE CORNER: Naturally gluten-free!

STORAGE: Keep sesame oil in the pantry for up to 6 months.

GOCHUGARU

Gochugaru translates into "pepper" (*gochu*) "powder" (*garu*). Made out of bright red Korean chilies, the flakes are used to season numerous Korean recipes, most notably *gochujang* and kimchi. Although the literal translation of *garu* is "powder," *gochugaru*'s texture varies, much like salt. It can come in a very fine powder (almost like flour) or as flakes. The *gochugaru* I use is the "flake" kind, since the finer stuff is mostly for making *gochujang*.

As with *gochujang*, the spice level of *gochugaru* depends upon the chilies themselves. Many brands label their *gochugaru* as "*maewoon*" (very spicy) or "*duhl-maewoon*" (less spicy), though often these are labeled in Korean. Just ask your friendly Korean grocer for a little help to pick out a brand that's not too spicy for you.

A word on subbing: The question I get asked the most about *gochugaru* is whether it can be subbed. In my opinion—no. There are decent substitutes for soy sauce (coconut aminos) and *doenjang* (miso), but I have yet to sample a spice that tastes quite like *gochugaru*. Moreover, most spices are ground too fine to provide the correct texture. Instead of trying to find a substitute for *gochugaru*, you're better off subbing with *gochujang*, which will, at least, have the right flavor profile.

MY FAVORITE BRAND: Tae-Kyung Gochugaru

GLUTEN-FREE CORNER: Naturally gluten-free!

STORAGE: I keep a little bit of *gochugaru* in my pantry for everyday use. The rest of it I store in the fridge, which will maintain freshness for 3 to 6 months, or even in the freezer to maximize freshness for up to 1 year.

DASHIMA

Perhaps the word is out on seaweed, but *dashima* (kelp) has been my secret weapon for flavor since going vegan. Many vegans still rely mostly on fungi as a way to add umami to their Asian cooking, but for me, a sheet of dried kelp reigns supreme for flavor.

A stroll through the seaweed aisle at an Asian grocery store will introduce you to dozens of different textures, cuts, and varieties of these sea plants. *Dashima* typically comes in large dried sheets (not to be confused with *undaria*, which looks like shriveled-up strips of seaweed), though some brands have started to cut them up into smaller pieces. Many traditional Korean kitchens (including my mom's!) use anchovies for flavor, but in my experience, *dashima* offers a more delicate reminder of the sea.

I usually use only one large sheet (cut into smaller pieces to fit into my pot) for a vat of vegetable stock. So, you don't need a lot if you're cooking a stew for only two or three people. One important tip is that if you cook *dashima* for too long, it can go bad. I once boiled the stuff for several hours and it made my soup bitter and slimy (yuck!). I therefore "fish" (pun intended!) mine out after 30 to 45 minutes if I'm making a big batch (like Vegetable Broth, page 43) or after only 10 to 15 minutes for a small pot (like Soondooboo Chigae, page 157).

MY FAVORITE BRAND: Chung Jung One

GLUTEN-FREE CORNER: Naturally gluten-free!

STORAGE: Keep *dashima* in the fridge to maximize flavor and it will last indefinitely.

DRIED MUSHROOMS

Just because I like *dashima* does not mean it's the only game in town when it comes to flavor. I keep a bag of huge dried shiitake mushrooms in my pantry at all times. Not only do they make one of the best bases for a plant-based broth (just submerge a handful in a quart of cold filtered water for a few hours), but when reconstituted, these mushrooms are meaty and juicy and explode with flavor.

A few tips on cooking with shiitake mushrooms:

- Go with dried over fresh. Trust me. Not only do the dried ones pack more flavor, they are usually larger and more uniform in size.

- Choose the ugly ones. The ones with pockmarks and "blemishes" on their heads are much more flavorful than the pristine ones. I have no idea why, but after years of trying out all sorts of shiitake mushrooms, I've always had the best luck with the uglier ones.

- Most dried shiitake mushrooms still have a stem—be sure to slice these off before cooking with them (no need to slice them off if just making a broth).

MY FAVORITE BRAND: Assi

GLUTEN-FREE CORNER: Naturally gluten-free!

STORAGE: Keep shiitake mushrooms in the pantry. Because they are dried, they will last indefinitely.

PLANT MILK

Plant milk isn't typically thought of as a traditional Korean ingredient, but you'd be surprised how much we use it. I've been drinking soy milk (or *dooyoo*, as it's sometimes called in Korean) since I was little, as soy milk is viewed as just a tasty beverage, not as an alternative milk. Not surprisingly, there are hundreds of different varieties of soy milk at Asian grocery stores, ranging from plain unsweetened versions to some soy milks that taste more like milkshakes.

While soy milk remains *my* go-to for most of my recipes, I've tried all kinds of milks since going vegan, including almond milk, cashew milk, hazelnut milk, coconut milk, rice milk, and oat milk. All of these milk options will work in the recipes in this book. ***However, soy and oat milk are the best options for baking because of their higher protein content.*** I've noticed that when I use soy or oat milk (in lieu of a nut milk) my baked goods come out richer and bouncier. However, these differences will only be noticeable to someone who's spent too many hours in the kitchen experimenting with different kinds of milk—not to the average person with a sweet tooth who just wants a slice of cake!

MY FAVORITE BRAND: Sahmyook Soy Milk

GLUTEN-FREE CORNER: Naturally gluten-free!

STORAGE: Keep it in the fridge.

GARRAETTEOK (Rice Cakes)

Garraetteok are a kind of rice cake made out of a rice flour paste that is steamed and shaped into tubes, discs, and sometimes, small spheres. *Garraetteok* remind me a lot of pasta. They taste like gnocchi, only a little chewier. *Garraetteok* are typically used in only savory recipes, like *tteokguk* (rice cake soup) or the wildly popular street food *tteokbokki* (spicy rice cakes). Because they are made with just rice, *garraetteok* are naturally gluten-free.

You can find *garraetteok* in the frozen foods aisle, as well as in or near the prepared foods section at the Korean grocery store. Fresh *garraettoek* are usually delivered from a local Korean bakery each morning, and I would highly recommend getting your hands on the fresh version if you can. They are much easier to cook with and taste delicious plain. If you cannot find fresh *garraettoek*, frozen *ttoek* will work nearly as well—you just need to microwave it until it thaws before using.

MY FAVORITE BRAND: Fresh from a local Korean bakery

GLUTEN-FREE CORNER: Naturally gluten-free!

STORAGE: Keep it in the fridge for up to 1 week or in the freezer for longer.

PAHT (Sweet Red Bean Paste)

Dessert was not a big thing in my family. It usually consisted of sliced fresh fruit (like Korean pears, apples, oranges, melon, or persimmon). On special occasions, we would have rice cake (a different kind, not the *garraetteok* discussed earlier), usually stuffed with sweet red bean paste. In the summertime, my parents would treat us to *pahtbingsoo*, shaved ice topped with sweet red beans. Thus, I grew up believing that Korean desserts always had *paht*—sweet red bean paste.

The red beans are also referred to as adzuki beans. You can certainly make your own red bean paste, but for convenience, I buy a few cans when I'm at my local Asian grocery store. Just be sure to check the labels, as some of them contain dairy as a thickener. The beans are sweetened with sugar, but if you make your own, you can sweeten them with maple syrup, agave, or a sweetener of your choice.

MY FAVORITE BRAND: Sura

GLUTEN-FREE CORNER: Naturally gluten-free!

STORAGE: Keep it in the pantry until it's opened and then store it in the fridge, where it will stay good for a few days.

LIQUID EGG REPLACER

We have truly come a long way in terms of vegan substitutes. When I first adopted a plant-based diet in 2016, the only egg replacers I saw were powders designed primarily to serve as substitutes for eggs in baked recipes. I always preferred using flax eggs (i.e., flaxseeds plus water) or aquafaba (canned chickpea liquid) for my muffins and cakes, but have you ever tried frying a flax egg or aquafaba? Take my word for it—you don't want to. Although I wasn't much of an egg person before I went vegan, I did miss my mom's *gyerranmari* every once in a while, so when liquid egg replacers came on the scene in 2018, I was game. I busted out the nonstick pan and spatula, and before I knew it, I had a perfectly rolled omelet. Still, I knew that some vegan products could look the part but never ever taste the part. I popped a sliced roll into my mouth and my mind was inalterably blown. It tasted exactly like my mom's *gyerranmari*. It was like a door that I assumed would remain closed for the rest of my life was thrown wide open. Throughout this book, you will see what came of it when I walked through that door.

MY FAVORITE BRAND: JUST Egg

GLUTEN-FREE CORNER: JUST Egg is gluten-free; however, be sure to check the labels of other brands.

STORAGE: Keep it in the refrigerator until opened, after which it is good for about 1 week.

the BASICS

The word *bap* in Korean translates literally to "rice." However, because every Korean meal (and I mean *every* meal, including breakfast) almost always contains rice (with the occasional exception of a noodle-based meal), the term *bap* can also refer to "meal." So, "I need more *bap*, please" translates to "I need more rice," while "Let's eat *bap*!" translates to "Let's eat!" even if there is no rice in the meal (e.g., you're eating noodles). This chapter will cover what I call the "basics," including the most basic recipe of all, *bap*. In addition, you'll see staples that appear on most Korean menus and dining tables, and sauces and other components I use in recipes in later chapters.

APPA AND RICE

When my grandfather was thirteen years old, he ran away from home to avoid marrying the young girl his father had selected for him. When he came back to his father's house a decade later with a wife and son, my grandfather was given a small plot of land filled with stones—hardly the rich acres of soil inherited by his brothers.

Determined not to let his father break his spirit, my grandfather concluded that while he may not have the land to grow his own rice, he had the wits to broker the sale of everyone else's. So, every five days, at the crack of dawn, the village merchants, my grandfather, and his eldest son—my father—loaded into the back of a pickup truck, together with whatever wares they hoped to sell that day. Sometimes, the nearest market was fifty miles away, and my father, just nine years old, would be jostled like a sack of potatoes for over an hour before starting a full day of work.

My father's job was simple but crucial. Once he and my grandfather reached the market, he ran as fast as his legs could carry him, sometimes for miles, and greeted the rice farmers hoping to sell an individual bag of rice or two, before they were swarmed by other rice traders like my grandfather. According to my dad, the key was to be the first buyer the farmers saw because it was always that first greeting that set the terms of the rice trade for the rest of that day. He would then lead the farmers back to his father to strike a bargain. His father, in turn, sold all the bags of rice accumulated throughout the day to one or maybe two rice distributors for a modest profit. Thus, between my father's legs and my grandfather's brains, according to my dad, "Finally, [they] could escape from poverty."

Every time I make rice (which is nearly every day), I think of one

Daddy and me at college graduation

Daddy and me at his college reunion at Yonsei University

of the biggest fights I ever had with my father. He had tasked me with making rice one day after school, and angry that the chore had fallen to me and not my brother, I was sloppy. I didn't rinse the rice even once, paid little attention to how much water I'd added, and threw it in the rice cooker before returning to whatever I was doing. A couple of hours later, my dad called me down to the kitchen, which was never a good sign. Warily, I trudged downstairs, and as soon as my feet hit the kitchen tiles, he turned to me with the rice in hand. I could see the whites of his eyes—something that happened only when he was about to blow a gasket.

"What is this?" he hissed at me. He was holding the rice container in one hand, while he pawed at the rice with a plastic rice paddle.

"What . . . ? It's the rice," I answered.

"Why did you make it like this? It's too DRY!" He roared the last word and hurled the rice container and the paddle into the sink. "No one can eat this!"

My brother and his friends were all witnesses to my father's "rice rage," and thus this episode has been permanently installed as part of the Lee Family Canon of stories. Of course, it's funny to think about it now, even as I compulsively rinse the rice over and over until the water runs clear and press my palm against the grains to check how much water I need to add or remove. And perhaps it's the reason I always feel a tiny dart of joy when I crack open the lid of the rice cooker or *dolsot* to find an exquisite pot of rice—not too dry and not too mushy.

Just perfect.

MUSHROOM DASHI

MAKES 4 CUPS

DIFFICULTY: Easy
ALLERGENS: GF, NF

6 large or 7 medium dried
shiitake mushrooms

I used to think that "dried" foods could never ever be as flavorful as the fresh stuff. I was wrong. After I began shopping at a Korean grocery store myself (instead of relying on my mom!), I learned there are dozens and dozens of varieties of mushrooms that you can't ever find "fresh" here in the United States. I also discovered that soaking the mushrooms in some cold water for a few hours creates an incredibly rich and flavorful stock, while also providing a handful of beautiful, plump, reconstituted mushrooms to use in a recipe. This dashi works great for mushroom *juuk* (or mushroom risotto), any *chigae*, or as a base for *tteokbokki*. I now have massive bags of dried mushrooms in my pantry, along with a mason jar or two of mushroom dashi in my fridge at all times.

1. Submerge the dried mushrooms in 4 cups cold filtered water for at least 4 hours at room temperature.

2. Scoop out the reconstituted mushrooms and save them for future use. They are just as good as, if not better than, regular "fresh" mushrooms for soups, stews, stir-fries, and a variety of recipes throughout this book!

3. Pour the dashi through a fine-mesh sieve or cheesecloth into a storage container. The dashi will keep in the refrigerator for up to 1 week. Freeze for any future use.

BAP (밥 · Rice)

1 cup short-grain
 brown rice

1 cup short-grain sweet
 brown rice

2 tablespoons black
 glutinous rice

½ cup pearled barley

You may be thinking, "I know how to make rice, I don't need a recipe for this one." Yes, basic rice is pretty easy to make, even if you don't have a fancy rice cooker (mine talks to me in Korean). But step into the grains aisle of any Korean grocery store and you will find row after row of different colors, brands, sizes, and types of rice, with rice bags as large as you are. You will instantly appreciate just how critical rice is to Korean cuisine.

My parents make rice every single day. It's as much a part of the morning routine as a pot of coffee is for most Americans. It's not surprising, then, that perfectly fluffy and plump rice is a foregone conclusion for those who've been making it every single day for their entire lives. However, "perfect rice" is not to be taken for granted by the uninitiated.

This is my favorite "everyday rice"—the kind of rice I like to make in my rice cooker before heading out to the office, so that it's warm and perfect when I get home to start dinner.

1. Rinse the dry rice grains and pearled barley under hot water (as hot as you can bear) multiple times until the water is no longer cloudy. Drain as much excess water as possible.

2. Place the clean rice and barley in a small pot or rice cooker with 3 cups water. If you are using a rice cooker, set the cooker to the "mixed grain" option and cook for 45 to 65 minutes (the time will vary based on your rice cooker). If you are not using a rice cooker, with the lid on, bring the pot of rice to a boil over medium-high heat (you need to keep an eye on this). As soon as the water comes to a boil, reduce the heat to a simmer and cook for 15 minutes with the lid slightly askew to allow a sliver of steam out.

3. Fluff the rice using a fork or a rice paddle. Replace the lid and cook until all the moisture has been cooked off and the rice is tender (but not mushy), about 15 minutes.

VEGETABLE BROTH

MAKES 6 CUPS

DIFFICULTY: Easy
ALLERGENS: GF, NF

2 tablespoons sesame oil

2 carrots, roughly chopped

1 stalk celery, roughly
chopped

3 cloves garlic, unpeeled

2 white onions, unpeeled
and roughly chopped

4 green onions, untrimmed
and roughly chopped

1 russet potato, roughly
chopped

½ cup roughly chopped
daikon radish, unpeeled

2 large or 3 small dried
shiitake mushrooms

2 large or up to 4 small
dried porcini mushrooms

7 to 8 leaves light-colored
cabbage

1 large sheet dashima
(see page 29),
broken into smaller
pieces to fit your pot

1 tablespoon black
peppercorns

My mother makes the most velvety, delicious broths. No matter how many expensive cartons of stock or broth I would buy from fancy markets, I could never achieve the rich "welcome to my home" taste of my mother's soups. Thankfully, she shared some of her secrets, and my aunts and I used them to create an incredible vegetable broth that is perfect for stews and soups. It's best to make several batches of this and freeze it, so you NEVER have to resort to store-bought stock again! This recipe is referenced throughout the book in numerous other recipes. However, if you find you have run out, feel free to substitute store-bought vegetable broth in a pinch.

1. In a large soup pot, heat the sesame oil over medium heat. Add the carrots, celery, garlic, onions, potato, daikon, dried mushrooms, cabbage leaves, and dashima to the pot and cook for 2 minutes.

2. Add 12 cups of water and the peppercorns and bring to a boil over medium-high heat. Reduce the heat to low and simmer for 30 minutes.

3. Remove the dashima and let the broth simmer until reduced by half, about 3 hours.

4. Discard the vegetables and pour the stock through a fine-mesh sieve or cheesecloth to strain out any bits and pieces.

NOTES
Be sure to clean all the vegetables thoroughly, because you will be keeping the peels on many of them.

OMMA'S KOREAN BBQ SAUCE

MAKES 3 CUPS

DIFFICULTY: Easy

ALLERGENS: GFO, NF

½ red onion, cut into chunks

3 scallions, trimmed

8 to 9 cloves garlic, peeled

1 cup soy sauce

¼ cup brown rice syrup (or your preferred sweetener)

2 tablespoons rice vinegar

2 tablespoons mirin

½ cup rough-chopped Korean pear or apple

½ cup rough-chopped red bell pepper

1 knob fresh ginger

1 teaspoon sesame oil

1 teaspoon freshly ground black pepper

¼ cup Mushroom Dashi (page 39) or water

2 tablespoons potato starch

One of the very first things my mother ever taught me to make in the kitchen was her Korean barbecue marinade—that is, the liquid gold you soak your meats and vegetables in before grilling them. It is absolutely bursting with umami and garlicky goodness, and I like to keep a jar on hand at all times. It's so simple to make, and I often use it in place of soy sauce for many recipes. While it's great as a marinade, you can also use it as a base for a sauce that is delicious with hearty dishes like Mushroom Galbi (page 237) or Bulgogi (page 235). "Sauce-ifying" the marinade is very easy, and I have jars of the sauce version in my refrigerator at all times, too!

1. In a high-powered blender, combine the red onion, scallions, garlic, soy sauce, brown rice syrup, rice vinegar, mirin, Korean pear, bell pepper, ginger, sesame oil, and pepper and blend until smooth and frothy.

2. Transfer the marinade to a medium pot and bring to a boil over medium-high heat. Cook the liquid until reduced by about one-third, about 10 minutes.

3. In a small bowl, stir the mushroom dashi into the potato starch to create a slurry. Gradually stir the slurry into the cooking marinade and continue stirring until the sauce thickens.

4. Once the sauce has thickened, remove it from the heat and let it cool (allowing it to thicken a little more). Once cooled, store it in the refrigerator for use in the next several days or freeze it for future use.

"FISHY" SAUCE

MAKES 1½ CUPS

DIFFICULTY: Easy

ALLERGENS: GFO, NF

1½ cups soy sauce

4 large or 6 small dried shiitake mushrooms

4 handfuls fresh enoki mushrooms

2 shallots, roughly chopped

4 cloves garlic, peeled

5 (2-inch) squares of dashima (see page 29)

2 tablespoons mirin

2 tablespoons balsamic vinegar

2 tablespoons rice vinegar

2 teaspoons black peppercorns

For me, the biggest stumbling block to going vegan as a Korean was kimchi. How does one make kimchi without fish sauce? The truth is, kimchi tastes just as good without fish sauce if it's done right. While fish sauce provides some flavor, it also facilitates fermentation. So, the trick to making kimchi without fish sauce is extra time. When I was playing around with my kimchi recipes, I came up with my own "fishy" sauce to add that subtle umami punch. Like regular fish sauce, a little goes a long way, so use with caution!

1. In a medium saucepan, combine 3 cups water, the soy sauce, shiitakes, oyster mushrooms, shallots, garlic, dashima, mirin, balsamic vinegar, rice vinegar, and peppercorns. Bring to a boil over medium-high heat. Reduce the heat and simmer for 1 hour.

2. Discard the vegetables and continue to simmer the sauce until it reduces by half, about 1 hour.

3. Pour the sauce through a fine-mesh sieve or a cheesecloth and into a container to remove the small bits. Store in the refrigerator for up to 6 months or freeze for future use.

SPICY SOY SAUCE DRESSING

MAKES 1½ CUPS

DIFFICULTY: Easy

ALLERGENS: GFO, NF

1 cup soy sauce

2 tablespoons gochugaru (see page 28)

3 to 4 cloves garlic, minced

2 scallions, chopped

¼ cup finely diced red onion

1 shishito pepper or jalapeño, sliced

1 Fresno pepper, sliced

2 tablespoons brown rice syrup or maple syrup

1 tablespoon rice vinegar

1 tablespoon mirin

1 teaspoon freshly ground black pepper

½ teaspoon ground turmeric

There is nothing more satisfying than coming home after a long day of work and whipping up a dish that looks and tastes like you've been slaving away in your kitchen all afternoon. This insanely flavorful dressing is the magic potion that makes it possible. It only takes 15 minutes to put together, and it lasts in the refrigerator for weeks. Not only can you use this dressing as a dipping sauce for your favorite savory dishes, you can pour a little bit over beans, vegetables, or even a bowl of rice, or use it to braise tofu. You'll have yourself something that looks and tastes fancy, but could not be simpler.

In a small bowl, whisk together the soy sauce, gochugaru, garlic, scallions, red onion, shishito pepper, Fresno pepper, brown rice syrup, rice vinegar, mirin, black pepper, and turmeric. Store in a covered container in the refrigerator for up to 1 month. Shake well before serving.

SPICY GOCHUJANG DRESSING

MAKES ½ CUP

DIFFICULTY: Easy

ALLERGENS: GFO, NF

¼ cup gochujang
  (see page 26)
1 teaspoon yellow mustard
1 tablespoon mirin
1 tablespoon rice vinegar
1 tablespoon maple syrup
1 tablespoon soy sauce

Omma (my mom) always complains that I don't give her enough advance notice when I drop in to say hello. To her, "proper" advance notice is about one week, as this is how much time she apparently needs to prepare a decent meal for me and my husband. The last time we came by, she plated some steamed broccoli drizzled with the most delicious spicy red sauce, while complaining "I have no *banchan*! You gave me no time to make anything!" My husband and I made fine work of the broccoli (it was gone in about 5 minutes). While we put on our shoes and said our good-byes, Omma rattled off the ingredients to her "I had no time to make anything" sauce. The very next day, I made some steamed asparagus and this dressing was the perfect accompaniment!

1. In a small bowl, whisk together the gochujang, mustard, mirin, vinegar, maple syrup, and soy sauce. Add 1 tablespoon of water and continue to stir. If the sauce is still too thick (it should be the consistency of a salad dressing), add 1 more tablespoon of water and stir.

2. Store in a covered container in the refrigerator for up to 1 month.

BORICHA
(보리차 · Cold Barley Tea)

SERVES 6 TO 8

DIFFICULTY: Easy

ALLERGENS: NF

16 ounces pearled barley

Growing up, our "water" was a tawny-colored drink my grandmother called *boricha*, or "barley tea." In Korean, the word for water (*mool*) is often used interchangeably with *boricha*, and for a long time, I assumed that everyone drank *boricha* as water, too. It wasn't until I had some friends over after school and one of them asked for some apple juice while pointing to the cold pitcher of *boricha* in my fridge that I realized that my "water" might be a little different. *Boricha* has enough punch not to qualify as straight water, but it isn't quite strong enough to be served as an iced tea when you have guests over. It's as common as rice or kimchi in a Korean household.

1. In a large cast-iron or heavy-bottomed pot, spread the barley in a single layer (you may have to do this in batches). Toast over medium heat, stirring to avoid burning, until the barley turns a dark brown color, about 25 minutes.

2. If done in batches, return all the barley to the pot. Add 8 cups filtered water. Increase the heat to medium-high and bring to a boil. Reduce the heat and simmer for 3 to 4 more minutes.

3. Set a sieve over a pitcher and pour the barley tea into the pitcher. Discard the toasted barley. Store in the refrigerator and serve with ice on especially warm days.

2

BBANG
(빵 · Breads)

Relatively speaking, bread is a recent addition to the Korean diet. Although it was introduced to Korea in the nineteenth century by Catholic missionaries ("bread of life"), it wasn't until the Japanese occupation during the first half of the twentieth century that bread became more prevalent in Korean cuisine. Even then, bread was always viewed as a luxury item, like bananas or milk, and today you'll rarely, if ever, see a bread item in a traditional Korean restaurant. That said, you'll see dozens of bakeries sidling up to coffee shops in a single city block of Seoul and other large urban areas in South Korea these days, brimming with pastries, cakes, and every imaginable iteration of *bbang* you can dream up. This chapter includes bread recipes for beginners and experts alike. They are all delicious.

OMMA IN THE US

My mother emigrated from South Korea to the United States in her early twenties. Omma arrived in the "land of dreams" with whatever clothes she could stuff into a duffel bag, some rice, toothpaste, soap, and the money she'd been saving up for two years in Korea—a total of $800.

Aiming to secure a position at a hospital in Chicago while studying for her boards, she rented a one-bedroom flat for ninety-nine bucks a month up in Lakeview. Small, cramped, and rife with code violations, she slept with all her appendages firmly within the confines of the bed she shared with her roommate, to avoid whatever it was that made the scurrying sounds on the creaking wooden floors every night.

Omma's nursing school graduation

She'd never lived so close to a lake before. So, she found herself wandering over to Lake Shore Drive often, perhaps after a grueling session of hitting the books or when she was hungry and didn't have money for food. And other times, she would head to the lake when she was bored and was not in the mood to talk to her roommate, simply to watch the foam curling up onto the shore like a furtive but welcoming smile.

She went to school twice a week to learn English while also attending nursing school to take her boards. Attempting to pass the nursing exams was itself a challenge, but doing so in a language with which she was only superficially familiar was a lot like trying to navigate the Grand Canyon without a compass. She pored over those books each night until the Roman letters swam together like a family of crawling ants and the hunger pangs she couldn't quite satisfy shrouded her wits.

On the afternoon of the test results, she called her father on the pay phone around the corner from the apartment.

"Daddy, I failed."

She thought of the roll of money she'd brought with her on the day she left for the States, how her father had cautioned her to save half of it just in case she needed to buy a ticket home, how she had spent almost all of it on the assumption—the *presumption*—that she would pass her exams and secure a full-time job to pay for her rent, a pair of new nursing shoes, and, eventually, an airplane ticket for her father. She would have to return home, empty-handed.

Her father comforted her the best he could through the static of an international phone call and told her that she was not a failure, that of course she could come home. But then, he said something different:

"But, Sunny . . . if you come home now, you might regret it for the rest of your life."

Tough words to hear with little more to her name than the loose change she fingered in her right coat pocket. Omma hung up the phone and turned east, toward Lake Michigan.

It was a typical winter day in Chicago—impossibly sunny while being brutally cold. There were few people brave enough to face the biting wind that ripped off the lake. Omma, both hands in her pockets, set one foot in front of the other along the lakefront path, wondering where she could gather the funds to survive another round of exams—and even then, how she could pass them when she'd already failed.

Slowly, a figure emerged from the periphery. A small, old woman, her frail supine body stooped in submission to the cold. Gripping the handful of quarters, dimes, and nickels she had in her right pocket, Omma rounded her narrow shoulders and watched the toes of her shoes, as they sidled closer and closer to the edge of the lake. She had no money to give away and wanted to avoid the inevitable entreaty.

Sure enough, a pair of wrinkled upturned hands appeared

beneath my mother's nose. The old woman was short but still a little taller than Omma. Her skin was deeply creased and her hair was gritty and gray, but her blue eyes were clear and probing. All she had on was a light spring jacket.

"Ma'am, do you have a dollar for a cup of coffee? It's so cold," she inquired.

Omma felt for the loose coins in her pocket. She fingered their ridged edges, the worn copper of pennies and the thicker and smooth faces of quarters, as if she were fingering the words her father had delivered to her on the pay phone just minutes earlier.

She pulled her hand out of her pocket and poured the change right into the wrinkled palms, which were beginning to turn chapped and red. The air was unforgiving, and Omma started to bring her hand back to the warmth of her coat pocket, but not before the old lady snatched it up into her own. They were like ice.

The wrinkled lady with the beautiful blue eyes didn't say "Thank you" or "God bless" or "Have a lovely day" that afternoon. She said something else—something that my mother would never forget. Something that she would one day repeat to her American daughter:

"You're going to pass that test."

DOLSOT BBANG
(돌솥빵 · Stone Pot Bread)

MAKES 1 LOAF

DIFFICULTY: Easy

ALLERGENS: NF

2½ cups (350g)
   all-purpose flour

1 tablespoon sugar

1 teaspoon salt

½ teaspoon instant
   (rapid-rise) yeast

1¼ cups (300g) warm
   water (between 100°F
   and 110°F)

A *dolsot* or *ddukbaegi* is like the Korean version of a Dutch oven. It's a smaller pot (usually designed for 2 to 4 servings of stew or rice) carved out of agalmatolite or made out of earthenware, which keeps food sizzling and scorching hot long after it comes off your stove. The *dolsot* is often associated with the popular Korean dish bibimbap. Bibimbap is usually served in a regular bowl, but *dolsot bibimbap* is served in the *dolsot*, so that the rice is still crackling at your table (kind of like when you order fajitas or tandoori).

I had seen so many simple recipes for making bread in a Dutch oven, and so I came up with this bread recipe using a traditional Korean *dolsot* for my mom and my aunts. They all believe that I am some bread-making goddess because of all the different breads I whip up every weekend. This recipe requires few ingredients, needs minimal kneading, and bakes up in the same pot they use for a *chigae* (like *kimchi chigae*) and bibimbap. Of course, if you don't have a *dolsot*, you can certainly substitute with your Dutch oven!

1. In a large bowl, mix together the flour, sugar, salt, yeast, and water using a wooden spoon until a dough forms. Using your hands, knead the dough gently in the bowl for 2 to 3 minutes.

2. Place the dough on a clean surface and rinse out the bowl with warm water. Dry the bowl and mist it with a little cooking spray. Place the dough back in the bowl, cover it with plastic wrap or a lid, and set it aside in a warm place until the dough has doubled in size, about 1 hour.

3. Punch down the dough to release the gas. Once more, knead the dough for about a minute inside the bowl and then shape it

recipe continues

into a ball (use a little flour on your hands if the dough is sticky). Re-cover the bowl and set it aside until it has doubled in size, 35 to 45 minutes.

4. Meanwhile, preheat the oven to 400°F. Place a medium dolsot in the oven to preheat.

5. Remove the dough from the bowl and place it on a sheet of parchment paper. Knead for about 1 minute and then shape it into a ball.

6. Carefully remove the hot dolsot from the oven. Holding both ends of the parchment paper (with the dough balanced in between), gently cradle and place the dough into the dolsot.

7. Cover the pot, place it in the oven, and bake until the bread is a lovely brown color, 45 to 50 minutes.

PERILLA LEAF FOCACCIA

SERVES 8

DIFFICULTY: Medium

ALLERGENS: NF

2¼ teaspoons active dry
    yeast

1 tablespoon sugar

1 cup (240g) warm water
    (between 100°F and
    110°F)

2½ cups (350g)
    all-purpose flour

1 teaspoon salt

½ cup (65g) extra-virgin
    olive oil

2 cloves garlic, minced

3 to 4 perilla leaves,
    cut into ribbons,
    plus 3 to 4 small whole
    leaves for topping

Coarse sea salt,
    for sprinkling

When I was little, my grandmother would often send me to the backyard to pick perilla leaves. They grew on stalks nearly as tall as I was on a small plot of rich soil behind our home. I was always so proud when I came back to the kitchen with a T-shirt full of leaves as big as my face. Perilla leaves are easy to grow in your yard or even in a small urban garden on your patio. Though they look like large mint leaves, they are tender and mild, with notes of sesame. I love using them for salads and in this focaccia.

1. In a small bowl, mix together the yeast, sugar, and warm water. Set it aside until the mixture starts to foam, about 10 minutes.

2. Meanwhile, in a medium bowl, combine the flour, salt, ¼ cup of the olive oil, the garlic, and perilla ribbons.

3. Slowly pour the yeast mixture into the flour. Using a wooden spoon (or chopsticks), stir the mixture together until a dough forms. Using your hands, knead the dough for about 5 minutes. You can do this in the bowl or you can remove the dough and knead it on a floured surface.

4. Wash and rinse the bowl with warm water. Mist it with a little cooking spray and return the dough to the bowl. Cover the bowl with plastic wrap or a lid, and set it aside somewhere warm until it has doubled in size, about 1 hour. Punch down the dough to release excess gas. Re-cover the bowl with plastic wrap or a lid, and set it aside somewhere until it has doubled in size, about 45 minutes.

recipe continues

5. Punch down the dough to release excess gas. Knead it for another minute or so. Add the remaining ¼ cup olive oil to a medium pan (I use a cast-iron pan, but you can also use a 9-inch baking pan).

6. Place the dough into the oiled pan and use the fingers of both hands to spread and press the dough so that it stretches to the edges of the pan. Flip the dough over and repeat, creating the trademark "dimpling" of focaccia. Cover the pan with a dry kitchen towel and let it sit for another 20 minutes.

7. Meanwhile, preheat the oven to 425°F.

8. When the dough is ready to bake, sprinkle generously with sea salt and top with a few whole perilla leaves. Bake until golden brown, about 26 minutes.

PAHT BBANG
(팥빵 · Red Bean Paste Bread)

MAKES 2 LOAVES

DIFFICULTY: Medium

ALLERGENS: NF

1 cup (240g) warm water (between 100°F and 110°F)

½ cup (120g) plant milk, warmed (between 100°F to 110°F), plus 3 tablespoons plant milk

1 tablespoon sugar

4 teaspoons active dry yeast

4 cups (560g) bread flour

½ tablespoon salt

⅓ cup (43g) extra-virgin olive oil

3 cups (927g) paht (sweet red bean paste)

1 tablespoon maple syrup

Coarse sea salt, for sprinkling

1 tablespoon toasted sesame seeds

This is a delicious braided challah made with a little sweet red bean paste, or *paht*. Because the red beans are not too sweet, they pair nicely with the stiff, tight crumb of challah. I like to sprinkle the top with a little sea salt and sesame seeds to really highlight the nutty sweetness of the beans.

1. In a small bowl, mix together the water, the warmed ½ cup plant milk, the sugar, and yeast. Set aside until the mixture begins to foam, about 10 minutes.

2. In a large bowl, combine the flour, salt, and olive oil. Add the yeast mixture and begin stirring with a wooden spoon until a dough begins to form.

3. Remove the dough from the bowl and place it on a floured surface. Knead the dough with your hands for about 5 minutes. Shape the dough into a ball and place it in a medium bowl. Cover it with plastic wrap or a lid and set it aside in a warm place until doubled in size, about 1 hour.

4. Preheat the oven to 400°F. Line two baking sheets (or one very large baking sheet) with parchment paper.

5. Punch down the dough to release the gas. Knead the dough for 2 minutes and then shape it into a ball. Divide the dough into two equal portions. Place one portion of the dough back into the bowl and re-cover.

6. Divide the remaining portion of dough into 3 equal pieces. On a floured surface, use a rolling pin to roll one piece of the dough into a 10 × 7-inch rectangle. Position the dough so that it is horizontal (i.e., so a long side is facing you).

recipe continues

7. Spoon ½ cup of the paht onto the dough and use the back of a spoon or an offset spatula to spread it out like peanut butter over a piece of bread, leaving a ½-inch border along the edges.

8. Starting at a long side, roll the dough up into a log and seal the edges and the ends by pinching them off. Repeat with the remaining portions of dough, until you have three stuffed ropes (½ cup of paht for each rope).

9. Lay the three stuffed ropes side by side on the lined baking sheet. (This way, you don't have to transfer the braided dough before placing it in the oven.) Bring the tops together and pinch them, so they are sealed to each other. Then, begin to braid the ropes gently, but as tightly as you can, by bringing the left rope over the middle rope, the right rope over the middle rope, and repeating until you arrive at the bottom. Pinch the ends to seal. Set the braided dough aside and cover it with a kitchen towel.

10. Repeat steps 6 through 9 with the other half of the dough to make the second loaf.

11. Allow the second loaf to sit under a kitchen towel for another 10 minutes (I have not noticed an appreciable difference in the two braids, even though the first one has already proofed while I was braiding the second).

12. Meanwhile, in a small bowl, mix together the remaining 3 tablespoons plant milk and the maple syrup.

13. Brush the milk "wash" over the surface of the loaves. Sprinkle the loaves with sea salt and the sesame seeds.

14. Place the baking sheets in the oven and bake until the bread is golden brown, about 50 minutes. Remove them from the oven and allow them to cool for approximately 15 minutes on a wire rack.

SEAWEED SESAME BAGELS

MAKES 8 BAGELS

DIFFICULTY: Medium

ALLERGENS: NF

1⅓ cups (315g) warm water (between 100°F to 110°F)

2¼ teaspoons active dry yeast

1 tablespoon sugar

3½ cups (480g) bread flour

1 tablespoon barley malt powder or brown sugar

2 teaspoons fine sea salt

1 sheet roasted seaweed, divided in half

1 tablespoon maple syrup or brown rice syrup

1 tablespoon plant milk (I prefer nut milk)

2 tablespoons extra-virgin olive oil

1 tablespoon toasted sesame seeds

1 tablespoon coarse sea salt, for topping

Hi. My name is Joanne and I am addicted to carbs. When I started baking my own bread, it was like a whole new world opened up to me. I no longer needed to depend upon the local bakery for my fix—I could simply supply my own yeasty deliciousness! The inspiration for this recipe came from my mother's little sister (my *eemo*). While chewing on a piece of my homemade focaccia, she whispered, "This would be so good with some *gim* [roasted seaweed]." The following week, I decided to bake up some bagels and throw a little seaweed in the dough, just for her. How'd they turn out? Let's just say, these are now something I need to bake every time she comes over!

1. In a small bowl, mix together the very warm water, yeast, and sugar. Set it aside until the yeast begins to foam on top, about 10 minutes.

2. In a stand mixer fitted with the dough hook, combine the bread flour, malt powder, and the fine sea salt. Begin mixing on low to combine the dry ingredients. Slowly pour in the yeast mixture and allow the mixer to continue mixing until a dough starts to form.

3. Knead the dough on medium-low speed for about 4 minutes. Then, continue to knead on high speed for about 4 more minutes. Remove the dough from the mixer—it will be pretty tough and dry.

4. On a floured surface, continue kneading by hand until the dough smooths into a ball, about 2 minutes. Place the dough in a clean bowl, cover it with plastic wrap or a lid, and set it aside in a cool and dry place until it has doubled in size, 1 hour to 1½ hours.

5. Punch down the dough to release the gas. Using kitchen shears, snip each half of the sheet of seaweed into thin strips. Reserve half of

recipe continues

the strips for topping and sprinkle the other half over the top of the bagel dough. On a floured surface, knead the dough to incorporate the seaweed and create a ball. Return the dough to the bowl, cover it, and set it aside until it doubles in size, another 45 minutes.

6. Preheat the oven to 450°F.

7. Punch down the dough again and shape it into a ball. Divide the dough into 8 equal portions. Working with one portion at a time, keep the other portions in the bowl with a lid to keep them from drying out. Roll the dough into a ball. Then, pinch the center of the ball with your thumb and index or middle finger. Gently stretch the hole in the middle of the dough until it is about 1 inch in diameter. The hole will seem too large, but the bagel will shrink while baking. Repeat with the remaining pieces of dough. Place them on a baking sheet and cover with a dry kitchen towel. Let rest for 15 minutes.

8. In a large pot, combine 8 cups water and the maple syrup and bring to a boil over high heat. Drop the bagels into the boiling water (do not crowd the pot—you may have to do this in batches) and allow the bagels to cook on each side for 1 minute. Remove from the water and return them to the baking sheet.

9. In a small bowl, mix together the plant milk and 1 tablespoon of the oil. In another small bowl, toss together the sesame seeds, the remaining seaweed strips, and remaining 1 tablespoon oil.

10. Brush the milk "wash" onto the tops of the boiled bagels and sprinkle with the sesame/seaweed mixture. Sprinkle with the coarse sea salt.

11. Transfer the bagels to the preheated oven and bake until the bagels are firm and browned, about 13 minutes. Allow the bagels to cool on a wire rack for 5 minutes before enjoying.

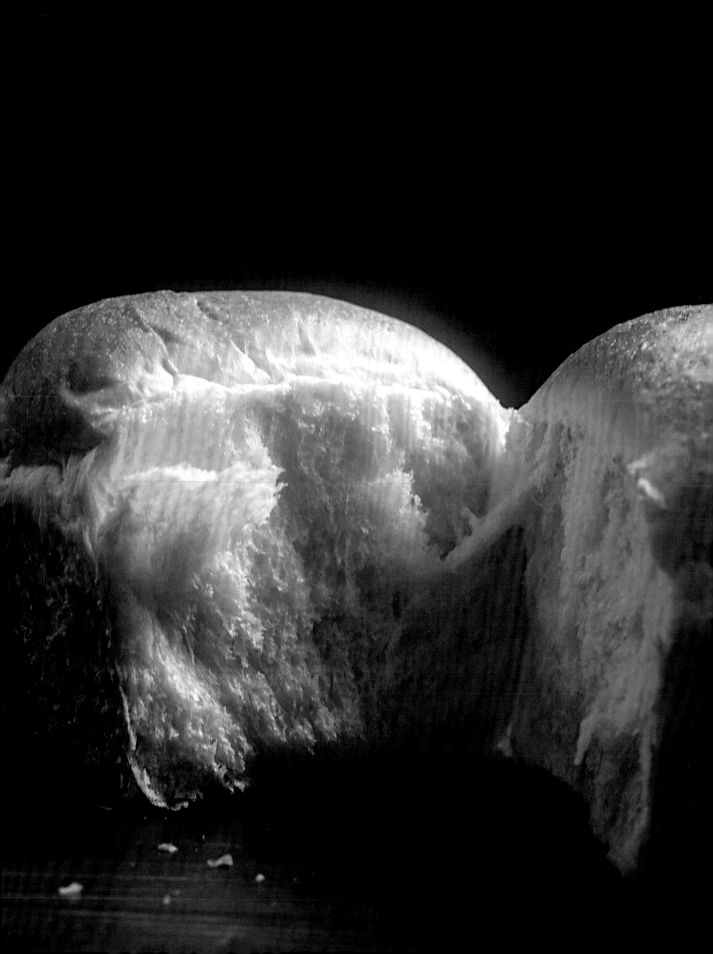

MILK BREAD

MAKES 1 LOAF

DIFFICULTY: Practice
makes perfect

ALLERGENS: NF

FOR THE TANGZHONG

⅕ cup (24g) bread flour

FOR THE DOUGH

2¾ cups (383g) bread
flour

⅕ cup (40g) sugar

2¾ teaspoons (7g) soy
milk powder

2¼ teaspoons (7g) instant
(rapid-rise) yeast

1½ teaspoons (8g) salt

¾ teaspoon (3g) baking
powder

⅓ cup (72g) plant milk

5 tablespoons (33g)
aquafaba (canned
chickpea liquid)

2⅓ tablespoons (33g)
vegan butter

FOR THE GLAZE

3 tablespoons plant milk

1 tablespoon maple syrup

Before I became vegan, one of my favorite places to visit was a Korean bakery. Korean bakeries are unlike any other bakeries in the United States. You walk in and the first thing you notice is the sheer variety of breads, pastries, cakes, cookies, and other yummies sitting quietly in their little compartments, like books that are waiting to be devoured. Unlike American bakeries, Korean bakeries often carry breads you really can't find anywhere else—like milk bread. Milk bread, as the name suggests, typically contains a lot of milk to give it that buttery, spongy texture. Here, I use soy milk (though any plant milk will do), along with soy milk powder, which helps provide the richness of the original. I also use aquafaba (canned chickpea liquid) to give the bread some "spring." One of the unique aspects of baking milk bread is the starter, or "tangzhong." Tangzhong is a simple mixture of warm water and flour over low heat. When added to the bread dough, it allows the flour to retain more water, resulting in a much more tender bread that stays soft for longer than your average loaf. This is one of the more advanced bread recipes in the book, but you will be so proud of yourself when your homemade milk bread comes out of the oven!

1. Prepare the tangzhong: In a nonstick saucepan, combine the flour and ½ cup (118g) water. Set over medium-low heat and begin stirring with a silicone spatula. Continue stirring until the mixture becomes a very smooth paste, with no lumps, about 10 minutes. Remove from the heat and scrape it into a small container. Refrigerate for at least 3 hours and up to 24 hours. Remove from the refrigerator and allow it to sit at room temperature for 1 hour before using.

2. Make the dough: In a stand mixer fitted with the dough hook, combine the flour, sugar, soy milk powder, yeast, salt, and baking

recipe continues

powder. On low speed, mix everything together to avoid clumps of baking powder. Add the plant milk, aquafaba, and tangzhong. Mix on medium until the dough begins to form, about 2 minutes.

3. Add the vegan butter and resume mixing on high for 10 to 12 minutes. The dough should be smooth, bouncy, and a little sticky.

4. Shape the dough into a nice round ball (you can use gloves or flour your hands to handle the dough) and place it in a bowl misted with cooking spray or greased with vegan butter. Cover the bowl with a lid or plastic wrap and set it aside in a warm place until the dough has doubled in size, 1 hour to 1½ hours. When you poke the dough with your index finger, it should leave a clean hole that does not readily bounce back.

5. Punch down the dough to release the gas. Divide the dough into three equal portions. Work with one portion at a time (keep the other two underneath a towel or plastic wrap to prevent them from drying out). On a floured surface, knead the dough gently by folding the dough in half, flipping it over, and folding it in half once more. Then, use both hands to shape the piece into a compact ball, taking care to handle the dough as little as possible. Repeat with the remaining two portions of dough and set them all aside underneath a towel until they have grown slightly (not doubled), another 15 to 20 minutes.

6. Lightly grease a 9 × 5-inch nonstick loaf pan. Again, working with one piece of the dough at a time, use a rolling pin to flatten the ball into a long oval about 8 × 4 inches. Position the dough vertically (i.e., with a short end facing you). Fold the top half of the dough down toward the middle of the oval. Fold the bottom half up to meet the top folded half (like an envelope). Press the ends together with the heel of your hand.

7. Turn the entire piece of dough 90 degrees clockwise. Starting from the bottom edge, roll the dough up into a very thick log. Gently place the roll in the greased loaf pan, seam-side down. Repeat

with the remaining two pieces of dough. Cover the loaf pan with a kitchen towel and let the dough rest until it rises enough to peek over the edge of the loaf pan, about 40 minutes. Do not allow it to rest too long; the dough should be firm to the touch, not fragile, when it is ready to glaze and bake.

8. Meanwhile, preheat the oven to 355°F.

9. Make the glaze: In a small bowl, mix together the plant milk and maple syrup. Once the dough has finished proofing, gently brush the top of the bread with the glaze.

10. Transfer to the oven and bake until the top is golden brown, about 45 minutes. Remove from the oven and allow the bread to cool in the pan for 15 minutes. Gently remove from the pan with an offset spatula or a small knife and let it cool on a wire rack before serving.

NOTES

As this is an advanced bread recipe, the measurements are intentionally precise and, therefore, a scale is highly recommended.

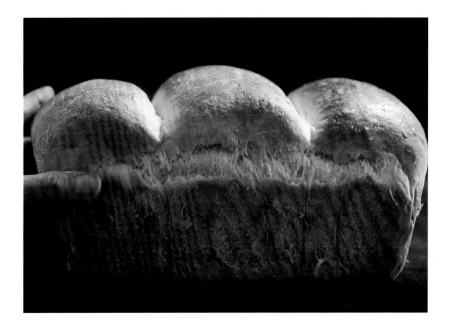

3

BANCHAN
(반찬 · Side Dishes)

One of the hallmarks of a Korean dining table is the number of *banchan*, or side dishes. I think of basically everything that isn't a bowl of rice as a "side dish," since rice is often the center of the meal. Rice is usually served with numerous (sometimes over a dozen) *banchan*, ranging from kimchi to rich "entree"-type dishes like a stew or Korean barbecue. You will almost never see a meal with any fewer than three small *banchan*. The challenge, of course, is making all these side dishes. Though they are usually quite simple and involve only a handful of ingredients, coming up with three or more of them (my mom usually has at least five for her exasperated "I didn't do anything because you gave me no notice that you were dropping by" meals) can take a lot of time. Now, if you've got a particularly slow Sunday coming up, you can try making a whole bunch of them at once. But most Korean cooks will stagger their preparation. How do they stay good, you ask? Well, the vast majority of *banchan* are pickled and, in fact, some of them are not designed to be eaten immediately (like kimchi!). In most Korean restaurants, almost all menu items will include a plethora of *banchan* in your meal ticket, without any additional cost. A noodle dish, however, will often come with very few *banchan* (usually just kimchi). Do not be fooled by the small size of these dishes. They not only pack incredible flavor, they can take days and weeks to prepare since there are so many of them!

OMMA AND SWEET POTATOES

After my mother's family crossed the 38th parallel when my mother was about a year old, they landed in a small valley along the southern fringe of South Korea called Suk Bong Rhee, Chun La Namdo. They were referred to as "Korean War refugees."

They were homeless. My grandparents traveled from house to house, begging for scraps of food and a place to sleep for the night. When they were lucky, they dug up leftover vegetables from recently harvested fields to supplement their daily meal of watery porridge.

Eventually, my grandfather was able to find a job as a janitor at a local middle school. He was good with his hands—he made kites for my mom and whittled toys for the neighborhood children. They were always poor, though.

Still, my mother remembers her childhood with great fondness. Poverty and war are powerful, yes. But so is the taste of fresh berries picked by your own hand along the ridge of a mountain lumbering over the hot months of summer like a drowsy silverback. Or the smell of barley heads snipped off their willowy bodies and roasted over an open flame beneath a blanket of preening stars. Her favorite, though, has always been sweet potatoes.

"You know, when I eat these sweet potatoes . . ." My mother has a way of saying her words in English as if they are too big for her mouth. She cuts them up into small pieces—"poe-tae-toes."

". . . when I eat these sweet potatoes, it always makes me remember when I was a little girl," she recounts one day while slicing up the bright orange yam I had just taken out of the toaster oven. My mother rarely comes by my house, but I am sick and she insisted on bringing me a vat of radish soup. To this day, my mother's soup is my cure-all. As a nurse, it's her way of showing affection and care (the

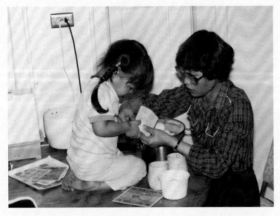

word she often used instead of the awkward-sounding "love").

"Why?"

"Because," she starts, while holding out a gooey orange morsel. "Because," she reiterates, "these were the best food."

"What do you mean, the 'best food'?" In my mind, the list of "best foods" included French fries, Chicago-style deep-dish pizza, donuts. It did not include sweet potatoes.

"When we were refugees . . ." she answers between mouthfuls, expertly peeling the skin off another stringy piece, before popping it into her mouth.

"Wait. When you guys got to South Korea?" I ask. I realize that I actually know very little about my mother's childhood. Other than the few snatches of conversation I managed to overhear over the years,

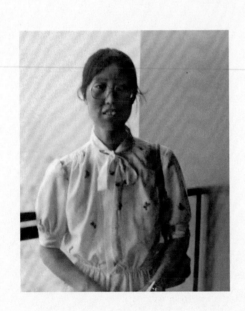

most of what I "know" is nestled between Wikipedia and myth. This was the first I'd ever heard her talk about what it was like shortly after escaping North Korea.

"Mm-hmmm," she says from inside another mouthful. "We had nothing. Nothing. So, the people in that village, they would harvest these," holding up what remains of her potato in my face, "and then give us what they had left over. And we would eat them just like this," she finishes, while sucking her fingers. And I believe her, more than I've ever believed anything else she's ever said to me, because she isn't looking at me when she explains these things. My 4-foot 11-inch, 90-pound mother is too busy cleaning her plate.

"And then, afterwards, I would run over to the field and dig up whatever I could find, you know, just a small piece," then she shows me the underside of her hand, which has been her sign for "tiny" for as long as I can remember. "That was the way we lived back then."

She pauses to look up at me.

"That's why, when I retire, I want to serve. I want to serve that village. They were so good to us."

BINDAETTEOK
(빈대떡 · Mung Bean Pancakes)

SERVES 8 TO 10

DIFFICULTY: Easy

ALLERGENS: GFO, NF

2 cups dried peeled split mung beans

1 cup mung bean sprouts

1 cup Baechu Kimchi (page 117) plus 2 tablespoons kimchi liquid

8 to 10 scallions, cut into 2- to 3-inch lengths

3 to 4 cloves garlic, thinly sliced

5 to 6 fresh shiitake mushrooms, stems discarded, caps thinly sliced

2 teaspoons soy sauce

1 tablespoon sesame oil

½ teaspoon salt

1 teaspoon freshly ground black pepper

2 tablespoons egg replacer (preferably JUST Egg), plant milk, or aquafaba (canned chickpea liquid)

2 tablespoons extra-virgin olive oil

Spicy Soy Sauce Dressing (page 49), for serving

Bindaetteok is something we grew up eating all the time, and as a result, I sort of took it for granted. It wasn't until college (when Omma's cooking was scarce) that I became excited about seeing it on the menu of a restaurant on campus or even in the prepared foods section of a local Korean grocery store. What sets *bindaetteok* apart from other Korean pancakes is the texture—it's made out of mung beans instead of flour, and therefore, neither the batter nor the finished product is smooth. Rather, it has the mouthfeel of a potato pancake. You can purchase mung beans already dried and peeled, so that all you have to do is soak them to make them soft enough to blend into a thick batter.

1. Soak the dried mung beans in cold water until softened, about 4 hours. Drain and set aside.

2. Meanwhile, in a large pot of boiling water, blanch the mung bean sprouts for 1 to 2 minutes, then run them under cold water to stop the cooking process. Transfer the mung beans to a large bowl, add the kimchi (without the liquid), scallions, garlic, mushrooms, soy sauce, and sesame oil and marinate for at least 30 minutes (but no more than 4 hours).

3. In a blender, combine the soaked mung beans, the salt, black pepper, egg replacer, kimchi liquid, and up to 1 cup water. Blend until a slightly orange batter forms (it should be like oatmeal). If your blender is not large enough to accommodate all the mung beans at once, work in batches.

4. Pour the batter into a large bowl and mix half of the marinated vegetables into the batter.

recipe continues

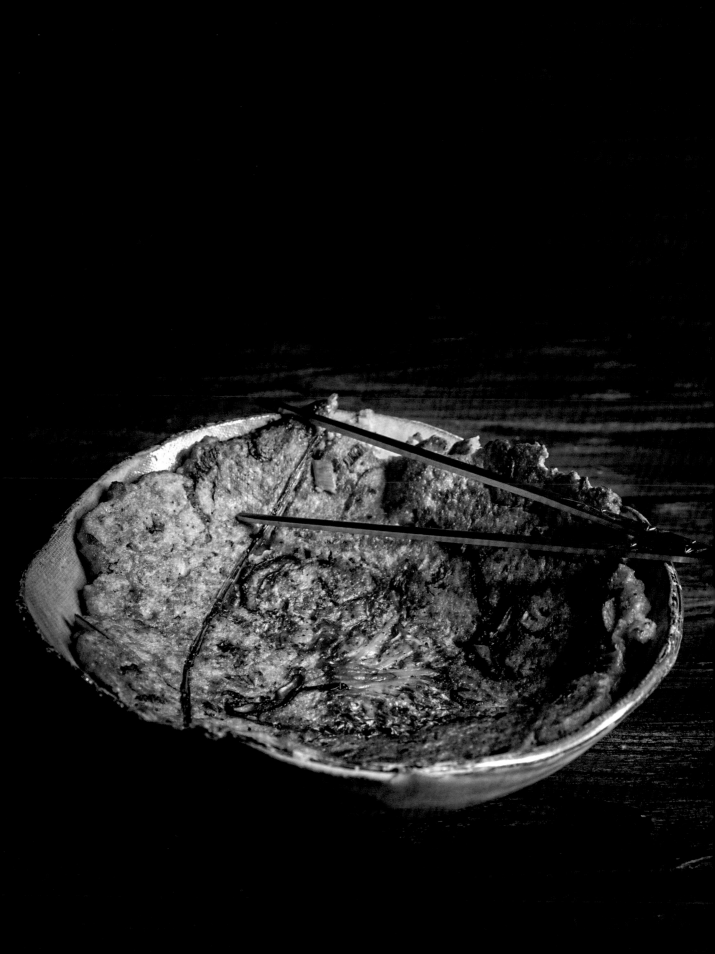

5. In a large nonstick skillet, heat 1 tablespoon of the olive oil over medium heat. Spread a piece of the marinated kimchi, 4 to 5 pieces of scallion, and a couple slivers of garlic and mushrooms in the pan. Then spoon 3 to 4 tablespoons of the batter over the vegetables in the pan. Cook until the bottom is golden brown, about 2 minutes. Flip the pancake and cook until both sides are evenly cooked, an additional 2 minutes. Continue to make more pancakes, adding extra oil as necessary.

6. Serve with the spicy soy dressing.

KALE MOOCHIM
(케일 무침 · Dressed Kale)

2 cups chopped kale
   (see Note)
1 tablespoon doenjang
   (see page 25)
½ teaspoon freshly ground
   black pepper
1 tablespoon sesame oil
1 tablespoon sesame seeds

One of the mainstay *banchan* of the Korean table is spinach *moochim*, or "dressed" spinach. The spinach is parboiled and mixed with a little *doenjang* and sesame oil. A simple, incredibly nutritious, and delicious dish that—like many Korean recipes—is designed to stay good for a very long time. Unfortunately, I'm not a spinach fan. I much prefer a sturdier green, one that retains some structure even when things get boiling hot, so I switched out the spinach for kale and voilà: kale *moochim*.

1. Set up a large bowl of ice and water. In a large pot, bring 4 cups of water to a boil. Drop the kale into the boiling water for 2 minutes. Transfer the kale to the ice bath to stop the cooking.

2. Drain the kale, wrap it in a large kitchen towel, and squeeze out the excess liquid (this is the hardest and most annoying part of the recipe, but it's necessary).

3. Place the kale in a bowl, add the doenjang, black pepper, sesame oil, and sesame seeds and mix everything together, preferably by hand.

NOTES
I like using the stems for the extra fiber whenever I cook my kale; however, feel free to use only the leaves here if you want a more uniform texture.

ROASTED DOENJANG-GLAZED ONIONS

SERVES 8 TO 12

DIFFICULTY: Easy

ALLERGENS: GFO, NF

2 large white onions, sliced into ⅓-inch-thick rings

Salt and freshly ground black pepper

2 tablespoons extra-virgin olive oil

2 tablespoons doenjang (see page 25)

1 teaspoon white wine vinegar

I have a secret. Her name is Deborah. She is one of my dearest friends, and she has a treasure trove of simple recipes designed to make anyone fall in love with vegetables. While I was visiting her home over the summer, she sliced up a couple of gorgeous white onions that she picked up at her favorite farmers' market. She drizzled them with a little oil and sprinkled them with some thyme, salt, and pepper. They came out of the oven about 40 minutes later and I kid you not, I ate them like they were deep-fried onion rings. When I got home, I decided to *doenjang* them up a bit, and this glorious *doenjang*-glazed onion was born. Enjoy them over a salad, on a sandwich, or just plain. They are THAT good.

1. Preheat the oven to 475°F. Line a large baking sheet with parchment paper.

2. Place the sliced onions in a large bowl and season them with salt and pepper.

3. In a small bowl, mix together the olive oil, doenjang, and vinegar until smooth. Add the dressing to the large bowl of onions and mix with your hands or a large spoon until the onions are evenly coated.

4. Arrange the onions on the lined baking sheet. Do not overcrowd the baking sheet—use two baking sheets if necessary.

5. Transfer the onions to the oven and roast for 25 minutes. Flip the onions and cook until they are golden brown, 10 to 15 minutes longer.

HOBBAHK JEON
(호박전 · Battered Squash)

During the height of summer, my *hahlmuhnee*'s garden in my childhood backyard would be littered with squash. Some of them were squat and round, about the size of my brother's face, and others were long, like zucchini. The most memorable aspect of Korean squash is the color—they are bright green, almost fluorescent. When my aunt brings me some from her garden, I feel like she is gifting me with a basket of sparkling peridot. Korean squash is also less watery and therefore stands up well to heat (without getting mushy). *Hobbahk jeon* is another simple and healthy dish you can add to your Buddha bowl, bibimbap, or salad, or just enjoy by itself.

1. Using 1 teaspoon of the salt, salt each side of the squash and set them aside on paper towels for 15 minutes. Flip and allow the squash to sit for an additional 15 minutes. This will draw out excess liquid from the squash. Pat them dry before using.

2. In a small bowl, combine the plant milk and vinegar (this is vegan buttermilk).

3. In a separate shallow bowl, mix the pepper, potato starch, turmeric, and the remaining 1 teaspoon salt.

4. Dip the squash slices into the vegan buttermilk and then coat them with the potato starch mixture. Tap the excess potato starch off and place the squash slices on a plate.

5. In a large nonstick skillet, heat 1 tablespoon of the olive oil over medium-high heat. When the oil is hot, add a layer of squash. Do not crowd the pan (you may have to work in batches; add more oil as necessary). Cook until browned, 3 to 4 minutes. Flip the squash and cook until both sides are browned, an additional 2 to 3 minutes. Enjoy with spicy soy dressing.

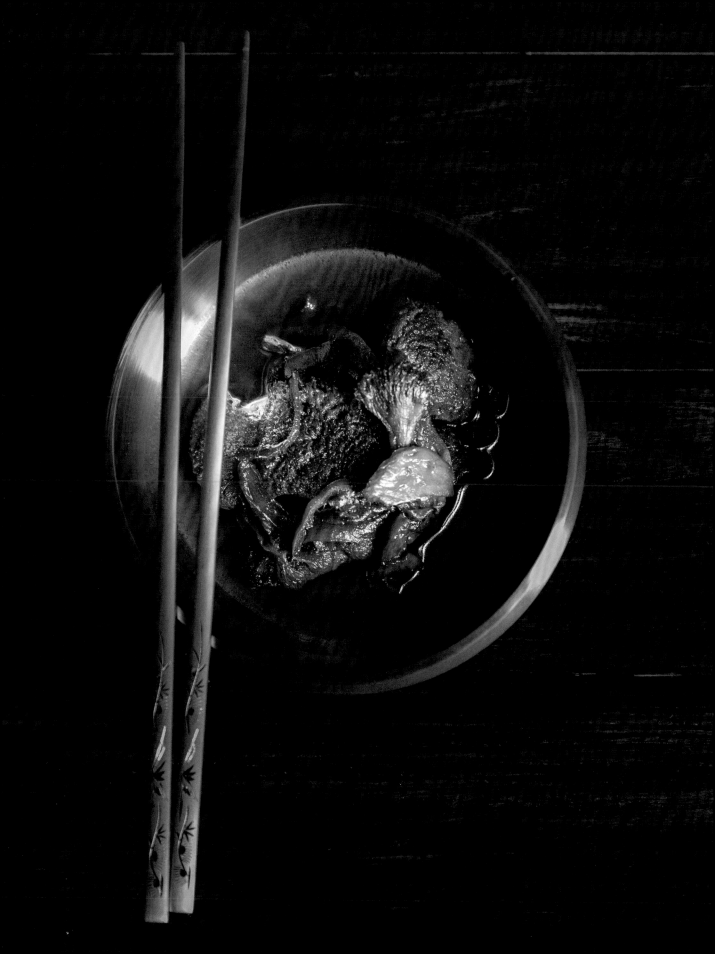

BRAISED LION'S MANE MUSHROOMS

SERVES 4 TO 6

DIFFICULTY: Easy
ALLERGENS: GFO, NF

3 heads lion's mane mushroom

2 tablespoons extra-virgin olive oil

½ medium onion, julienned

2 scallions, white part only, chopped

7 cloves garlic, thinly sliced

2 to 3 Korean green chilies, cut into large pieces

½ teaspoon freshly ground black pepper

4 tablespoons soy sauce

2 tablespoons soup (light) soy sauce

3 tablespoons maple syrup

3 tablespoons mirin

½ cup Mushroom Dashi (page 39) or water

My family and I discovered the lion's mane mushroom at a local restaurant. There were chunks of what I thought was meat in my soup, and I almost sent it back, before the waiter explained, "No, no, that's mushroom!" We were amazed. The following day, I was elated to find some of these puffy-looking fungi at our local farmers' market. I came home and decided to braise them, just as I would *jang jorim*, or braised beef flank, which is a very traditional Korean *banchan*. The best part about traditional *jang jorim* is that the meat falls apart after stewing in the braising liquid, which is exactly what the lion's mane mushroom does in this recipe.

1. Cut the lion's mane mushroom into 2- to 3-inch chunks. In a medium skillet, heat the olive oil over medium-high heat. When the oil is hot, add the mushroom chunks to the pan and lightly sear, 2 to 3 minutes on each side.

2. Add the onion, scallion whites, garlic, and chilies and stir-fry the vegetables together with the mushrooms, until the onions begin to soften, about 2 minutes. Sprinkle with the black pepper.

3. Deglaze the pan with both kinds of soy sauce, maple syrup, and mirin. Add the dashi and bring to a boil. Reduce the heat and simmer the mushrooms in the braising liquid until they are nearly falling apart, 2 to 3 minutes.

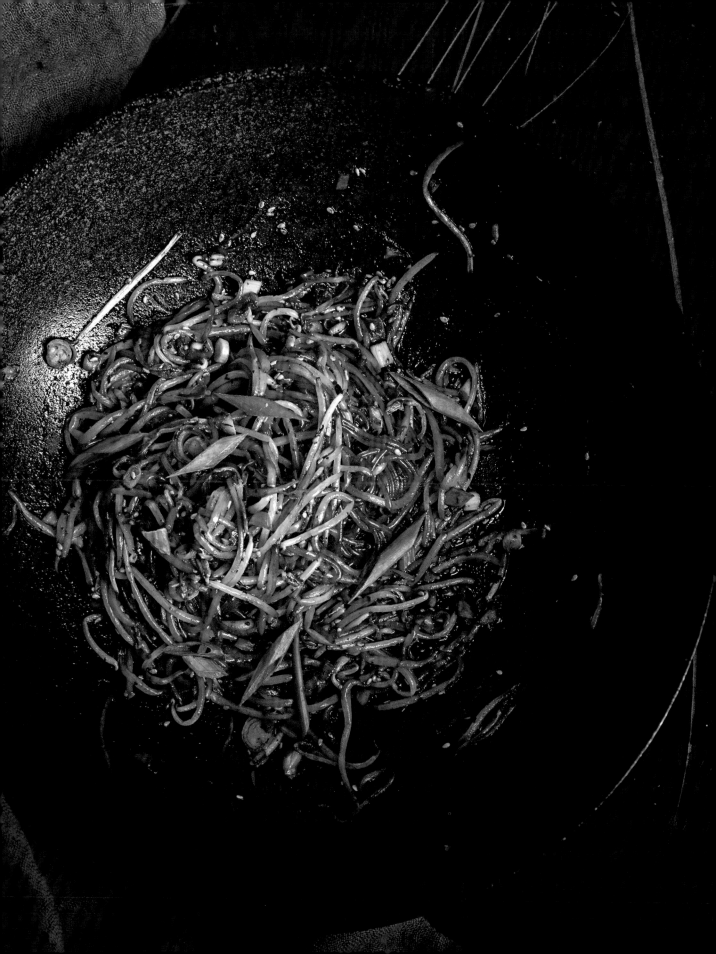

STIR-FRIED MUNG BEAN SPROUTS

SERVES 2

DIFFICULTY: Easy

ALLERGENS: GFO, NF

2½ ounces (70g) sweet
  potato vermicelli
  (about 1 handful)

2 tablespoons extra-virgin
  olive oil

1 tablespoon plus
  1 teaspoon sesame oil

½ onion, julienned

3 cloves garlic, minced

3 cups mung bean sprouts

½ teaspoon salt

½ teaspoon freshly ground
  black pepper

1 tablespoon gochugaru
  (see page 28)

2 tablespoons soy sauce

1 tablespoon rice vinegar

1 teaspoon maple syrup

I've never really liked "sprouts." I assiduously remove them from my salads or sandwiches and never really understood their appeal. They taste too . . . "sprout-y" for me. But, I was watching one of my favorite Korean dramas (*Itaewon Class*) when I realized that I had actually grown up eating sprouts, though they are not the kind you see in Western cuisine (i.e., the kind you see topping a sandwich). I've been eating bean sprouts my whole life! I love mung bean sprouts and soybean sprouts. Stir-frying them, just like they did on an episode of *Itaewon Class*, is not only delicious, it's super easy.

1. Soak the vermicelli in a large bowl of warm water while you bring 4 cups water to a boil in a medium pot. When the water is boiling, add the noodles and cook them until they are springy, about 8 minutes. Drain the noodles in a colander and run cold water over them until they are no longer too hot to touch. Set the noodles aside.

2. In a large nonstick skillet, heat the olive oil and 1 tablespoon of the sesame oil over medium-high heat. When the oils are hot, add the onion and garlic and sauté until the onion turns translucent and the garlic starts to brown, 2 to 3 minutes.

3. Add the mung bean sprouts, salt, and pepper and continue to sauté all the vegetables for another 3 to 4 minutes.

4. Add the gochugaru, soy sauce, vinegar, and maple syrup. Stir all the vegetables until they are evenly coated. Cover the pan, reduce the heat to low, and cook for an additional 2 minutes.

5. Uncover and add the cooked vermicelli noodles. Stir until the noodles are fully incorporated. Drizzle with the remaining 1 teaspoon sesame oil right before serving.

DOTORI MUK
(도토리묵 · Acorn Jelly) WITH BLACKBERRY DRESSING

SERVES 4

DIFFICULTY: Easy

ALLERGENS: GFO

FOR THE JELLY

½ cup ground acorn

FOR THE DRESSING

¼ cup blackberries, fresh or frozen

1 tablespoon water or fresh lemon juice

4 to 5 tablespoons Spicy Soy Sauce Dressing (page 49), to taste

FOR THE SALAD

3 perilla leaves, julienned

¼ cup julienned carrot

¼ cup julienned cucumber

¼ cup julienned red onion

1 scallion, thinly sliced

¼ cup Baechu Kimchi (page 117), chopped into 1-inch pieces

¼ cup fresh blackberries

1 sheet roasted seaweed, cut into small strips

FOR SERVING

1 teaspoon chili threads, for garnish (see Note)

1 teaspoon sesame oil

1 tablespoon sesame seeds

My grandmother loved *dotori muk*. As soon as we'd enter her tiny little apartment, we would see trays and trays of it sitting on every empty scrap of counter space and even the window ledges. Where other grandmothers put apple pies to cool, mine set acorn jelly. Her *dotori muk* was absolutely a labor of love. She would pound and grind the acorn flesh, remove the tannins, and get them to "gel" the old-fashioned way. Lucky for the rest of us, you can find ground acorn in Asian grocery stores. All you have to do is add water and heat. Thank goodness, because this Korean delicacy is one you don't want to miss!

1. Make the jelly: Line a 9-inch square baking pan with two sheets of parchment paper so that they hang over all four sides.

2. In a small pot, combine the ground acorn and 3 cups water. Set over medium-high heat and stir with a wooden spoon until the mixture comes to a boil. Reduce the heat and continue cooking for 9 to 12 minutes, stirring as it thickens, to avoid lumps.

3. Pour the mixture into the lined baking pan and let it sit at room temperature until cooled, about 1 hour. Then refrigerate the pan until the mixture sets (i.e., hardens into a jelly), at least 4 hours.

4. Make the salad dressing: In a small saucepan, combine the blackberries and water and bring to a boil over medium-high heat. Reduce to a simmer and cook for 15 minutes. Strain the mixture

recipe continues

through a sieve set over a small bowl. Add the spicy soy dressing and stir.

5. Remove the acorn jelly from the pan by gently flipping the pan over a cutting board. Cut the jelly into desired sizes and shapes (you can do cubes, batons, squares, etc.). Place about ¾ cup acorn jelly in each of four bowls.

6. Make the salad: In a separate small bowl, mix the perilla leaves, carrot, cucumber, red onion, scallion, kimchi, blackberries, and seaweed.

7. To serve: Gently set the salad over the acorn jelly. Drizzle with the dressing and garnish with the chili threads, sesame oil, and sesame seeds.

NOTES

Chili threads are, as the name suggests, extremely thin strips of dried chili. The threads are made from dried Yidu chilies, which are named after the region from which they are sourced.

GYERRANMARI
(계란말이 · Korean-Style Omelet)

SERVES 1

DIFFICULTY: Medium
ALLERGENS: GF, NF

1 cup egg replacer
(preferably JUST Egg)

½ teaspoon salt

Pinch of black salt
(optional; see Notes)

½ teaspoon freshly ground
black pepper

1 scallion, chopped

2 tablespoons finely diced
red bell pepper

2 tablespoons finely diced
red onion

1 tablespoon extra-virgin
olive oil

I was not an egg person growing up. The only eggs I'd eat were either boiled until the yolks were green or fried until the edges were black. However, on occasion, my mom or grandmother would have some leftover egg strips after making *kimbap* (Korean-style rolls that look like maki or sushi rolls) and for whatever reason, I found those to be delicious. Until I went vegan, whenever I got hungry for a small snack or just felt depressed or cranky, my mom would fry me up some *gyerranmari*, or a simple Korean-style omelet. I realize now that I miss the comfort it gave me more than I miss the food itself. But vegan ingredients have come a long way in the past couple of decades, and thanks to egg replacers, my mom is once again able to hand me a plate of sunshine the next time I get a case of the blues.

1. In a small bowl (or a measuring cup with a spout), mix the egg replacer, salt, black salt (if using), black pepper, scallion, bell pepper, and onion with a fork or small whisk.

2. In a small nonstick skillet (see Notes), heat ½ tablespoon of the oil over medium-high heat. Slowly pour half of the "egg" mixture into the pan—enough to reach the edges of the pan. When the edges start to pull away and the mixture starts to bubble (kind of like a crepe or pancake), use a silicone spatula to begin pulling the edges away all the way around. You can also gently shake the pan to loosen it from the pan.

3. Slowly, using your spatula, lift up the edge of the right side of the egg and begin rolling it toward the left (just like you would roll

recipe continues

a sheet of wrapping paper) until almost the entire egg is rolled up. Pull the egg roll back to the right edge of the pan (where you started rolling).

4. Add a little more oil to the pan and pour half of the remaining egg mixture into the empty area of the pan (i.e., the left side of the pan) so that the mixture meets the very end of the rolled egg, creating a seamless sheet of egg. Cook and roll up as above.

5. Repeat steps 2 and 3 until all the egg mixture has been used.

6. Remove the egg roll when it is completely cooked on the outside. It should be roughly 4 to 5 inches long. Slice the roll crosswise into ½-inch-thick pieces.

NOTES

Himalayan black salt contains sulfurous compounds that give the salt a lightly "eggy" scent. It is often sold as kala namak. Adding it to your egg replacer will make your vegan egg even more indistinguishable from the original!

I use a rectangular (5½ × 7-inch) Japanese tamagoyaki pan, but you can also use a small skillet. Just be sure it's a good nonstick.

For a demonstration of how to make *gyerranmari*, please head over to The Korean Vegan's website (https://thekoreanvegan.com /egg-sushi/).

DOOBOO JEON
(두부전 · Tofu Cakes)

MAKES 8 CAKES

DIFFICULTY: Easy

ALLERGENS: GF, NF

1 (16-ounce) block firm tofu, pressed (see Note)

¼ cup finely diced carrot

3 fresh shiitake mushrooms, stems discarded, caps diced

2 scallions, chopped

1 teaspoon salt

½ teaspoon freshly ground black pepper

3 tablespoons egg replacer (preferably JUST Egg; see Note)

1 tablespoon potato starch

Vegetable oil, for frying

Spicy Soy Sauce Dressing (page 49), for serving

I've tried just about every diet out there, including the low-carb diet (call it by whatever name you want). When I was low-carb, my aunt used to make me these "tofu cakes" that were flourless. When I went vegan and asked her if she could still make them for me, she shook her head, laughed, and said, "No, because it needs egg." With all the new egg replacers out there, this is no longer an impediment; but, even without any egg replacer, it's so easy to make these vegan versions of my aunt's delicious tofu cakes!

1. In a large bowl, mix together the tofu, carrot, mushrooms, scallions, salt, pepper, 1 tablespoon of egg replacer, and the potato starch until the mixture is pretty mushy. Divide the mixture into 8 portions and shape them into round "nuggets."

2. In a very large nonstick skillet, heat enough oil to lightly coat the surface of your pan over medium-high heat. Place the remaining egg replacer in a small bowl. Before adding the nuggets to the pan, dip them into the bowl of egg replacer until they are evenly coated. Drop them onto the pan and cook until they are all evenly browned, about 2 minutes per side. Serve with spicy soy dressing.

NOTES

Pressing tofu is necessary to remove excess liquid. Place the block of tofu (you can cut it in half horizontally as well) on a flat surface lined with a kitchen towel. Place another towel over the top of the tofu. Place cookbooks, a heavy pot, or a heavy pan on top of the tofu for 15 to 30 minutes.

If you don't have egg replacer, you can substitute 1 tablespoon plant milk in the tofu mixture and then use a mixture of 2 tablespoons plant milk, 1 teaspoon potato starch, and ¼ teaspoon ground turmeric for dipping the cakes into before frying.

KKENIP BUCHIMGAE
(깻잎 부침개 · Perilla Leaf Pancakes)

**MAKES 12 TO
16 MEDIUM
PANCAKES**

DIFFICULTY: Easy

ALLERGENS: GFO, NF

2 cups all-purpose flour
(see Note)

½ cup potato starch

½ tablespoon garlic
powder

½ tablespoon onion
powder

1 teaspoon salt

1 teaspoon freshly ground
black pepper

½ Korean squash or
regular zucchini,
julienned

1 carrot, julienned

4 to 5 perilla leaves,
julienned

1½ cups ice-cold water

12 to 16 small perilla
leaves, whole

4 to 5 scallions, julienned

Vegetable oil, for frying

Spicy Soy Sauce Dressing
(page 49), for serving

When I announced to my family that I was going vegan, my mother was especially worried. She wondered whether I would get enough protein (surprise!), if this was a symptom of my never-ending quest to be "skinny" (she was onto something there . . .), and how I could possibly keep up with my running eating nothing but vegetables. But mostly, she was panicked about what the heck she would cook for me when I came over.

She soon discovered how easy it was to make *buchimgae*, or pancakes typically made with seafood, without the shrimp or oysters. Simply add water to the flour mix and a bunch of vegetables for a quick batter. Omma makes a huge batch whenever we come over and saves some in the freezer for unannounced visits. I now do the same for myself, you know, for those unannounced cravings that occur around 10:17 p.m.

1. In a large bowl, combine the flour, potato starch, garlic powder, onion powder, salt, pepper, squash, carrot, and julienned perilla leaves. *Do not add the whole perilla leaves or scallions.*

2. Add the cold water to the bowl and stir. You should have a fairly thick and rough batter, but if it's too thick to work with, add more ice water, 1 tablespoon at a time, until you arrive at a consistency that's thicker than regular pancake batter but not as thick as biscuit batter.

3. In a nonstick skillet, heat enough oil to coat the pan over medium-high heat. Before pouring in any batter, throw a few scallions onto the pan, as well as one whole perilla leaf. *Then* pour

recipe continues

1 ladle (about ¼ cup) of batter over the top of the scallions and perilla leaf, so that they are completely covered.

4. Cook for about 3 minutes. Flip the pancake and cook until both sides are evenly browned, an additional 2 minutes. Repeat to make more pancakes.

5. Serve with spicy soy dressing.

NOTES

Gluten-free flours work very well with this recipe; however, because of the additional moisture in the batter often caused by gluten-free flours, fry the pancakes at a lower temperature so they have more time to "dry out" without burning.

GAMJA JORIM
(감자조림 · Braised Potatoes)

SERVES 4

DIFFICULTY: Medium

ALLERGENS: GFO, NF

4 medium Yukon Gold potatoes, cut into bite-size chunks

2 tablespoons extra-virgin olive oil

½ cup chopped red onion

3 cloves garlic, minced

¼ cup chopped red bell pepper

2 to 3 Korean green chilies or jalapeños, chopped

2 tablespoons brown sugar or maple syrup

1 tablespoon brown rice syrup or maple syrup

3 tablespoons soy sauce

1 cup Vegetable Broth (page 43) or water

½ tablespoon sesame oil

½ teaspoon freshly ground black pepper

1 teaspoon toasted sesame seeds

This is hands down one of my favorite recipes on the planet. I never met a potato I didn't want to marry, and this particular recipe includes all the flavors I grew up loving. My aunt shared this dish with me when I first went vegan, and now it is on the menu at practically every family gathering. And let me tell you, she never makes enough! Now, the trick with this dish is all about timing. If you cook the potatoes too long, they will become mushy. If you don't cook the potatoes long enough, they will be too hard. Somehow, my aunt always manages to hit that sweet spot—the potatoes are nice and firm on the outside, while being irresistibly tender on the inside. I will say, one of the things to avoid is using russet or Idaho potatoes—those turn to mush no matter how attentive you are! Stick to the waxier varieties and that'll give you a leg up. I like to spoon these potatoes with some of the sauce right onto a bowl of rice. The trickle-down effect is absolutely delicious!

1. Submerge the potatoes in cold water for 10 to 15 minutes to remove excess starch. Pat dry.

2. In a large skillet, heat the olive oil over high heat. When the oil is hot, add the potatoes and cook for 4 to 5 minutes, until the potatoes begin to brown.

3. Add the onion, garlic, bell pepper, and chilies and sauté all the vegetables for another 2 minutes. Add the brown sugar and brown rice syrup and toss the vegetables to make sure they are all evenly coated.

recipe continues

4. Deglaze the pan with the soy sauce. Add the vegetable broth and bring to a boil, then reduce the heat, cover, and cook the potatoes until almost fork-tender, another 15 minutes, while intermittently lifting the lid off the pan to spoon some of the braising liquid over the tops of the potatoes. If the braising liquid disappears before the potatoes are fully cooked, simply add 2 to 3 tablespoons of additional broth.

5. When the potatoes are nearly fork-tender, take the lid off the pan. At this point, the braising liquid should be reduced to an almost glaze-like consistency. Continue to cook the potatoes for an additional 2 minutes, until fully fork-tender.

6. Do not stir the potatoes too much once they are cooked. Add the sesame oil, black pepper, and sesame seeds before serving.

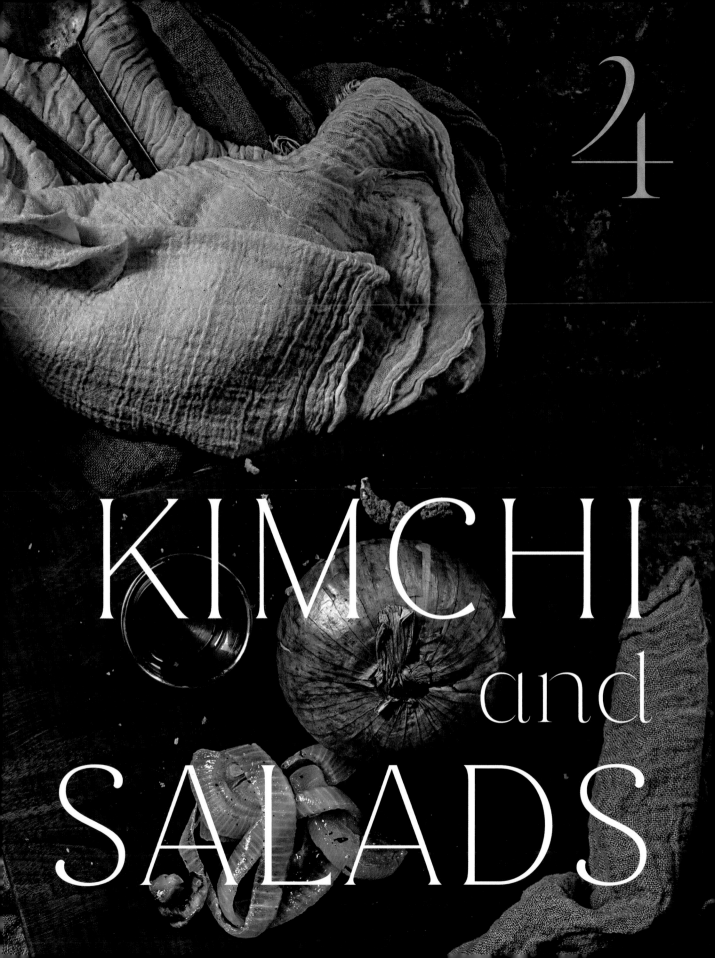

4

KIMCHI and SALADS

Many people see the word *kimchi* and immediately think of fiery-looking cabbage. While cabbage kimchi is definitely the most typical of kimchis, it is not the only kind of kimchi out there. In fact, there are hundreds of different kinds of kimchi—so many varieties that one could write a whole book on just kimchi! And originally, kimchi was not red at all. At its roots, kimchi is more about preservation than spice. Chilies were added to kimchi only a few hundred years ago. Prior to that time, kimchi was just a pickled vegetable.

While Korean cuisine is extremely vegetable centric, "salad" is not a typical item at a Korean meal. Most vegetables are pickled, and fresh vegetables are usually dipped in sauce as you would with crudités or used as a wrap for Korean barbecue (like lettuce wraps). That said, many Korean ingredients—like *doenjang* (see page 25) or *gochujang* (see page 26)— are perfect for dressings, and they've inspired me to eat more salads!

HAHLMUHNEE AND KIMCHI

"Sun Young, the key to delicious kimchi is the *kimchi byung*." Hahlmuhnee motioned to the line of spotless mason jars that sat quietly against the garage wall. "Do you see how clean they are? Hahlmuhnee spent all day yesterday emptying and scrubbing them, so that we could pack a fresh new batch of kimchi today."

I walked over to the *kimchi byungs* that Hahlmuhnee had lined up side by side. Just yesterday, they were slopped over with the garish red of chili and stank of old fish. Somehow, Hahlmuhnee had whisked them clean, and today I could see my reflection in the glass. The jars were the large industrial-size kinds with plastic white lids that took both my hands to unscrew.

I bent down and squatted in front of one them, unscrewed the lid, and took a whiff.

"Hahlmuhnee! They still smell like rotten fish!" I unscrewed the lid of the next jar, and it too smelled of yesterday's kimchi.

"Pfftt. Of course they do. That is the secret to the best kimchi," Hahlmuhnee muttered. Her silver tooth glinted as she grimaced when she sank her arms into the large bucket of cabbage, chili powder, and salt. Hahlmuhnee never used the big rubber gloves Omma used when she made kimchi, and soon, she was up to her elbows in what anyone else might have guessed was a very violent crime. She began pouring and rubbing a thick red paste into each individual cabbage leaf as she continued:

"Tomorrow's kimchi is tastier, Sun Young, because it is brined by yesterday's kimchi. The older the *kimchi byung*, the more delicious the kimchi. You see those *kimchi byungs* that Hahlmuhnee cleaned yesterday? I've had those *kimchi byungs* since before you were born. I brought them with me from my home village in Korea. What you are smelling is the salt from the ocean by my home, the garlic I fermented inside a bit of cheesecloth I buried one foot below the dirt, where it was cool, the *gochugaru* your grandfather would bring home on days he and your father had done well at our fruit stand."

Hahlmuhnee held a small scarlet piece of cabbage between her fingers. "So, when you eat this kimchi next week, you will not only be eating the kimchi from yesterday, but you will also be eating a tiny little bit of the kimchi I packed for your father's lunchbox when he was your age. You must remember this when you are packing kimchi for your family one day."

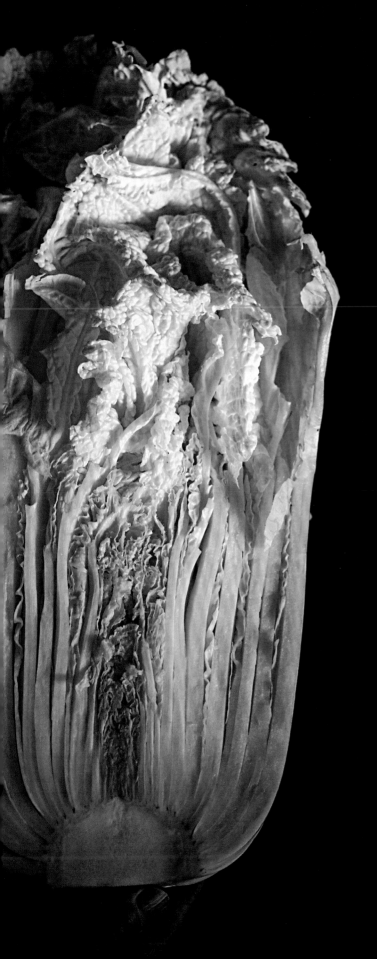

KIMCHI BASICS

No matter what kind of vegetable you use, there are usually three parts to making kimchi: (a) the first pickling, (b) the broth/paste, and (c) the fermentation. Kimchi requires some level of initial pickling. This can be for as little as 15 minutes or up to 24 hours in some cases. This preliminary pickling process will determine the texture of your kimchi. The broth or paste that you make for your kimchi will, of course, impact the flavor and spice level (if you are making a spicy kimchi). And finally, the last stage is fermentation. Some kimchis are not designed to be fermented for too long but are supposed to be eaten immediately, while others taste good only after the mixture has been sitting out for several days.

While I'd like to tell you that there are bright-line rules regarding salting, saucing, and fermenting, like many things in life, the rules of kimchi are, well, "bendy." For example, how long you should soak your cabbage in brine will depend upon how fresh that cabbage is to begin with, how large it is, and even where it was grown. The amount of chili powder you use to make the sauce will depend upon how spicy that chili powder is and how much heat you can handle. I find the final stage of kimchi-making—the fermentation—to be the most subjective. I like my kimchi ripe but not too ripe. My cousin, on the other hand, likes hers practically rancid. To each her own, right?

CUCUMBER KIMCHI
(오이김치)

SERVES 6 TO 8

DIFFICULTY: Easy
ALLERGENS: GF, NF

1 pound Korean cucumbers, Kirby pickling cucumbers, or Persian (mini) cucumbers

3 tablespoons coarse sea salt

2 to 4 tablespoons gochugaru (see page 28)

¼ cup julienned red onion

2 tablespoons sugar

2 tablespoons rice vinegar

2 tablespoons mirin

Cucumber kimchi was the first kimchi I ever learned to make because it's so easy. It's a great way to dip your toe into the pool of pickled Korean vegetables, if you're a little intimidated to try cabbage or radish kimchi. Not only that, it's an excellent garnish for your salads, sandwiches, and, of course, on rice. The lovely thing about this recipe—like all kimchis!—is that you can make a bunch in advance (double or triple the recipe!) and serve it for weeks! My grandmother had a huge jar of cucumber kimchi in her fridge at all times that she used throughout the year. As a result, her *bapsang* (dining table) always delivered multiple different kimchis at every meal!

1. Cut the cucumbers into ¼-inch-thick discs and place them in a very large bowl. Add the salt and stir the cucumbers so that they are evenly coated. Set them aside for 15 minutes.

2. Check on your cucumbers. By this time, there should be some liquid collecting at the bottom of the bowl. Stir the cucumbers around a little so that the cucumbers on the bottom are now on the top and vice versa. Set them aside for another 15 minutes.

3. Drain off the liquid and rinse the cucumbers thoroughly to eliminate excess salt. Pat them dry with a kitchen towel. Place them back in the large bowl.

4. Add the gochugaru (2 to 4 tablespoons depending on your spice threshold), red onion, sugar, vinegar, and mirin. Stir the cucumbers until they are evenly coated.

5. Store the cucumber kimchi at room temperature for 2 to 3 days for a quicker "pickling" and then place it in the refrigerator to enjoy for several weeks.

BAECHU KIMCHI
(배추김치 · Napa Cabbage Kimchi)

MAKES I HALF-
GALLON JAR

DIFFICULTY: Hard

ALLERGENS: GFO, NF

2 large heads napa
cabbage

½ cup kosher salt or coarse
sea salt

FOR THE PASTE

2 tablespoons sweet white
rice flour

2 tablespoons brown rice
syrup or maple syrup
(I prefer brown rice
syrup)

¼ cup minced garlic

1 knob fresh ginger, sliced

½ onion, roughly chopped

¼ cup Persimmon Puree
(page 285) or roughly
chopped Korean pear
or apple

¼ cup "Fishy" Sauce
(page 47) or soy sauce

1 tablespoon dashima
powder (see Note)

1 cup gochugaru
(see page 28)

1 cup julienned daikon
radish

½ cup julienned carrots

3 to 4 scallions, cut into
1½-inch lengths

1 cup 2-inch lengths garlic
chives

My *wehsoongmoh* (my uncle's wife) bent over the silver bowl, which was so wide she couldn't link her hands around its rim if she'd had to. She fished out one scarlet piece of cabbage and began wrapping it like a small package.

"It is important not to let the gas out, Sun Young, because that is what's going to make the kimchi taste delicious. So you have to take one leaf and wrap the rest together, tight and neat, just like this," she said, as she presented what looked all too much like a beating heart, resting in her hands.

"Where did you learn this? Who taught you this?" I asked, thinking of all the YouTube videos I'd watched on kimchi-making and how none of them had ever mentioned this technique.

"You know, I lost my mother when I was very young. I used to watch her in the kitchen. And when she died, all of a sudden, all those memories came back to me. Because I missed her."

1. Rinse both heads of cabbage under cold water and pat them dry. Trim off the bottom stubs (if any) of the cabbage heads. With a large sharp knife, starting at the butt of the cabbage head, create a 2-inch slit down the middle. With your hands, use the slit to tear the rest of the cabbage head right down the middle. Tearing the cabbage head (as opposed to cutting it with your knife) preserves the beautiful shape of the cabbage leaves in the middle.

2. You will now have two halves of the cabbage head. Create a 2-inch slit at the butt of each cabbage half, *but do not tear the section in half (you will do that later).*

3. Rinse all the cabbage leaves once more so that they are damp. You will now need to salt each leaf. Place the cabbage half so that

recipe continues

You can usually find *dashima* powder at a Korean grocery store. If you can't find it, though, you can always make your own by grinding a small sheet of *dashima*!

its internal leaves are facing up. Begin by sprinkling salt over the top leaf, then gently lifting that leaf up to reveal the leaf beneath it. Sprinkle with more salt, making sure to press the salt into the crevices toward the bottom (where the leaves are much thicker). Repeat this process until all the leaves are salted.

4. Place the cabbage in a humongous bowl and allow it to rest for at least 2 hours, but preferably 4 hours, turning the cabbage every 30 to 45 minutes. You will notice that over time, a reservoir of liquid will accumulate in the bowl. Baste the cabbage with this brine for additional flavor.

5. Meanwhile, make the paste: In a small pot, combine the sweet white rice flour and 1 cup water and cook over medium-high heat, stirring constantly to avoid clumping. It should come to a gentle boil in a few minutes, at which point it will begin to thicken. Add the brown rice syrup and cook for a little longer, continuing to stir, until the mixture thickens into a paste. Remove it from the heat and set aside to cool.

6. In a high-powered blender, combine the garlic, ginger, onion, persimmon puree, "fishy" sauce, and dashima powder. Blend until smooth.

7. In a large bowl, combine this garlic/ginger mixture with the cooled rice flour paste. Add the gochugaru. Stir in the julienned radish, carrots, scallions, and garlic chives.

8. After 4 hours, the cabbage should be pretty "bendy"—it should not readily snap. Rinse the cabbage heads in cold water multiple times to remove excess salt and any dirt. Now you can go ahead and tear the cabbage along the slits you placed in them earlier. You should now have 4 equal sections of cabbage per head.

9. As you did with the salt, spread a little of the kimchi paste over each leaf. You don't need to coat every last square inch of the leaf,

recipe continues

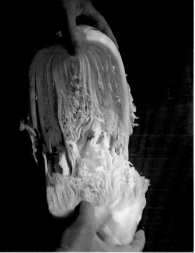

but it should be done evenly (i.e., no one leaf should get more than any other!).

10. Take one-quarter of a cabbage and place it on a flat surface so that the smaller "inner" leaves are facing up. With the exception of the widest leaf at the bottom (which you do not want to roll), roll the remaining section of the cabbage from the leafy tip down to the thicker "butt."

11. Pull the bottom leaf (which you didn't roll) up and around the rolled cabbage, so that it creates a lovely tight "package" of cabbage. Doing this will prevent additional air pockets and facilitate optimal fermentation.

12. Place the "cabbage package" into a large mason jar and press down (gently) to squeeze out any additional pockets of air. Repeat with the remaining sections of cabbage.

13. Add any leftover paste. Push down gently. You can also add a clean stone as a weight (my *hahlmuhnee* always did this) if you want to make sure it's compact.

14. Put the lid on the jar (not too tight, since the gasses released from the fermentation process could cause it to pop) and place it in the refrigerator for at least 1 week (I like waiting a full 3 weeks before enjoying). You can also leave it at room temperature for quicker (but smellier) fermentation.

15. Exercise caution when you unscrew that lid for the first time. Gas will have built up from the fermentation and if the jar is packed to the very top, it's possible the kimchi juices will overflow as soon as you crack it open. Open the lid slowly and over the sink.

GEOTJURI KIMCHI
(겉절이 · Barely Pickled Kimchi)

DIFFICULTY: Easy

ALLERGENS: GFO, NF

2 heads napa cabbage

¼ cup kosher salt or coarse
sea salt

FOR THE PASTE

2 tablespoons sweet white
rice flour

3 tablespoons brown rice
syrup or maple syrup
(I prefer brown rice
syrup)

¼ cup minced garlic

1 knob fresh ginger, sliced

½ onion, roughly chopped

¼ cup "Fishy" Sauce
(page 47) or soy sauce

¼ cup Persimmon Puree
(page 285) or roughly
chopped Korean pear
or apple

1 cup gochugaru
(see page 28)

1 cup julienned daikon
radish

½ cup julienned carrot

3 to 4 scallions, cut into
1½-inch lengths

1 cup 2-inch lengths garlic
chives

Every once in a while, I've come home after a long day at work, scooped a bit of leftover rice into my bowl, cracked open the refrigerator, and looked for the kimchi only to realize, wait. Where's the kimchi? And all of a sudden, this horrible panic wells up in my throat until I remember the three syllables that will squelch my fear: "geot-juh-ri." *Geotjuri*, or "kimchi salad," as I like to call it, is a barely pickled kimchi that takes far less time than the traditional kimchi recipes. It is designed to be enjoyed immediately after preparation, instead of several days (if not weeks) after it is mixed. In fact, if you've got some premade kimchi paste sitting around (perhaps left over from your annual kimchi-making day—what, you don't have one?), it will take you about 35 minutes from start to finish to make this fabulously refreshing kimchi recipe. So, never fear—even if you've gone through your store of kimchi, with a little bit of foresight, kimchi is never ever out of reach.

1. Pull the leaves of the cabbage heads apart. For all but the smaller inner leaves, cut each leaf into 2 or 3 smaller pieces by running the blade of a very sharp knife through the leaf while you hold it up (like running a knife through sheets of paper to cut them in half) or simply cut the leaves on a cutting board.

2. Place the cabbage pieces in a large bowl with ½ cup water and the salt. Set aside for about 30 minutes, turning the leaves a few times.

3. Meanwhile, make the paste: In a small pot, combine the sweet white rice flour and 1 cup water and cook over medium-high heat, stirring constantly to avoid clumping. The mixture should come to a gentle boil in a few minutes, at which point it will begin to thicken.

recipe continues

Add the brown rice syrup and cook for a little longer, continuing to stir, until the mixture thickens into a paste. Remove from the heat and set aside to cool.

4. In a high-powered blender, combine the garlic, ginger, onion, "fishy" sauce, and persimmon puree. Blend until smooth.

5. In a large bowl, combine this garlic/ginger mixture with the rice flour paste. Add the gochugaru. Stir in the radish, carrot, scallions, and garlic chives.

6. Pour the paste, together with the julienned vegetables, over the cabbage leaves, incorporating them with your hands so that the leaves are evenly coated.

7. Enjoy immediately after preparing. Store in the refrigerator and enjoy for up to 2 weeks longer.

MOOL KIMCHI
(물김치 · Water Kimchi)

MAKES 1 HALF-
GALLON JAR

DIFFICULTY: Easy

ALLERGENS: GF, NF

1 pound Korean radish or
daikon radish, trimmed,
peeled, and cut into
2-inch batons

2 tablespoons coarse
sea salt

¼ cup sugar

4 to 5 scallions, left whole

3 serrano peppers, halved
and seeded

½ Fuji apple or Korean
pear, cut into
¼-inch-thick slices

1 teaspoon thinly sliced
fresh ginger

4 or 5 cloves garlic, halved

In the summer, there is quite literally nothing more refreshing than a bowl of *mool kimchi*, which literally translates into "water kimchi." Think of it as a very cold soup, designed to cleanse your palate and cut through the heavier *banchan* at the dinner table. My mother brought me a jar of her homemade *mool kimchi* when I moved into my new apartment, and after several months, it still tastes just as it should—a little sweet, a little tart, and perfectly invigorating.

1. Place the radish batons in a very large bowl. Add 1½ tablespoons of the salt and mix the radish pieces until they are evenly coated with salt. Set aside for 30 minutes, until the radishes become "bendy."

2. Place the radishes in the mason jar. Add the remaining ½ tablespoon salt, the sugar, whole scallions, serranos, apple, ginger, and garlic. Stir well.

3. Pour in 4 cups water until all the contents of the jar are completely submerged. Seal the jar well and store at room temperature for 2 to 3 days.

4. After 2 to 3 days, the brine will turn a little cloudy. Taste the brine—it will be a little sour and slightly carbonated. Cut off a small piece of radish and taste to determine whether it has adequately pickled. If not, continue to store at room temperature for another 2 days.

5. Once the radishes are pickled to your preference, store them in the refrigerator. Serve cold with brine.

CHONG GAK KIMCHI
(총각김치 · Ponytail Kimchi)

MAKES I HALF-
GALLON JAR

DIFFICULTY: Medium

ALLERGENS: GFO, NF

10 to 12 baby daikon radishes, with leafy tops

½ cup kosher salt or coarse sea salt

FOR THE PASTE

2 tablespoons sweet white rice flour

2 tablespoons brown rice syrup or maple syrup (I prefer brown rice syrup)

¼ cup minced garlic

1 knob fresh ginger, sliced

½ onion, roughly chopped

¼ cup Persimmon Puree (page 285) or roughly chopped Korean pear or apple

¼ cup "Fishy" Sauce (page 47) or soy sauce

1 tablespoon dashima powder (see Note, page 119)

1 cup gochugaru (see page 28)

3 to 4 scallions, cut into 1½-inch lengths

2 cups 2-inch lengths garlic chives

Chong gak kimchi, sometimes referred to as "ponytail kimchi" because the radish leaves are kept intact and form a "tail" to the radish, is my favorite kimchi and probably one of my all-time favorite *banchan*. I could eat nothing but rice, water, and this kimchi every day for every meal for weeks without complaint. When my mom sees me yanking out radish after radish from the massive kimchi jar, she always says, with a mixture of both pride and ruefulness, "You ARE Korean!" Growing up, I tried so hard to fit in, I did everything I could to hide my "Koreanness." But, I was afraid that when I went vegan, I would never be able to eat proper kimchi again, so I immediately set out to veganize *chong gak kimchi*. As with *baechu kimchi*, it takes a little longer than normal to pickle than the nonvegan version, but it tastes JUST as good. The recipe is very similar to *baechu kimchi*; the main difference is the pre-pickling time. You also add a handful more garlic chives to the paste. That's about it!

1. Rinse the radishes under cold water. Clean and trim them by snipping off the tails at the root end (not the leafy tops) and peeling with a vegetable peeler.

2. Slice the radishes in half lengthwise, including through the stems, leaving the tops attached. If the radish is very small, you don't need to cut it in half. Rinse all of the radishes under cold water once more and place them in a large bowl.

3. Add the salt and, using your hands, make sure that all the radishes are evenly coated. Set the bowl aside for 45 minutes. Then, shift the radishes around with your hands again and let them sit for another 30 minutes.

recipe continues

4. You will notice that over time a reservoir of liquid will accumulate in the bowl. When your radishes are "bendy" (i.e., resist snapping in two), drain off the liquid and rinse the radishes multiple times under cold water to remove excess salt and any leftover dirt.

5. Meanwhile, make the paste: In a small pot, combine the sweet white rice flour and 1 cup water and cook over medium-high heat, stirring constantly to avoid clumping. The mixture should come to a gentle boil in a few minutes, at which point it will begin to thicken. Add the brown rice syrup and cook for a little longer, continuing to stir, until the mixture thickens into a paste. Remove from the heat and set aside to cool.

6. In a high-powered blender, combine the garlic, ginger, onion, persimmon puree, "fishy" sauce, and dashima powder and blend until smooth.

7. In a large bowl, combine this garlic/ginger mixture and the rice flour paste. Add the gochugaru. Stir in the scallions and garlic chives.

8. Pour the paste, together with the julienned vegetables, over the radishes, incorporating them with your hands so that the radishes and the leafy tops are evenly coated.

9. Take two halves of a radish (if they were cut in half) and bind them together by wrapping their stems around them. Place them inside a half-gallon mason jar. Repeat with the remaining radishes.

10. Place the lid on the jar and place in the refrigerator for at least 1 week.

11. Exercise caution when you unscrew that lid for the first time. Gas will have built up from the fermentation, and if the jar is packed to the very top, it's possible the kimchi juices will overflow as soon as you crack it open. Open the lid slowly and over the sink.

KALE AND RAMEN SALAD

SERVES 4

DIFFICULTY: Easy

ALLERGENS: GFO

FOR THE DRESSING

1 tablespoon gochujang

1 tablespoon maple syrup

1 tablespoon soup (light) soy sauce

½ tablespoon sunflower seed butter

1 teaspoon white wine vinegar

FOR THE SALAD

6 cups curly kale, stemmed, deribbed, and roughly chopped

2 tablespoons extra-virgin olive oil

5 or 6 fresh shiitake mushrooms, stems discarded, caps cut into ⅛-inch-thick slices

Half a (1 oz/60g) package ramen noodles, crushed (see Notes)

1 teaspoon salt

7 or 8 perilla leaves, stemmed and julienned

¼ zucchini, sliced lengthwise (see Notes)

¼ cup julienned red onion

1 scallion, chopped

2 tablespoons chopped walnuts

1 date, pitted and chopped

1 teaspoon freshly ground black pepper

"You know, it's amazing. I used to hate kale. And now it's definitely one of my top three favorite vegetables," I mused over breakfast one morning. "Then you should like more salads," was my husband's reply. I realized that my reluctance to eat salads might have something to do with their unfamiliarity. Then I had a thought: Maybe the best way to get over it would be to add ingredients from my childhood? Enter ramen noodles. This salad has toasted ramen instead of croutons and a dressing that tastes a lot like the ramen broth I grew up eating with my dad. I love it with kale, my favorite green. It's definitely a salad that I am now happy to eat all the time!

1. Make the dressing: In a small bowl, whisk together the gochujang, maple syrup, soy sauce, sunflower seed butter, and white wine vinegar until smooth and creamy.

2. Prepare the salad: Place the kale in a large bowl. Add 2 tablespoons of the dressing and, using your hands, massage the dressing into the kale. Refrigerate the dressed kale for at least 45 minutes (and up to 24 hours).

3. Meanwhile, in a medium nonstick skillet, heat the oil over medium-high heat. When the oil is hot, add the sliced mushrooms and sauté until their edges start to brown, about 5 minutes.

4. Add the crushed ramen noodles and salt to the mushrooms. Cook over medium heat until the ramen noodles also start to brown, about 7 minutes. When the noodles are crunchy (not chewy), set them aside while you assemble the remainder of the salad.

5. Take the bowl of massaged kale out of the refrigerator and add the perilla leaves, sliced zucchini (which you can roll into rosettes), red onion, scallion, walnuts, date, and black pepper.

recipe continues

6. Sprinkle the salad with the toasted ramen and mushrooms and drizzle with additional dressing to taste.

NOTES

To prepare the ramen noodles, use the handle of your knife or a mallet to crush them in an unopened bag. You only need to use half a bag for this recipe—set the remaining noodles aside for future salads.

To roll the zucchini into rosettes, you will need to slice the zucchini paper thin or use a mandolin.

PICKLED PERILLA LEAVES (깻잎)

SERVES 5 OR 6

DIFFICULTY: Easy

ALLERGENS: GFO, NF

½ cup Spicy Soy Sauce Dressing (page 49)

40 perilla leaves

My grandmother's pickled perilla leaves, or *kkenip*, were a favorite among her grandchildren, so she often made jars and jars of them that would last for several weeks. It thus became a year-round staple of our dining table, and now it can contribute to yours.

1. Add 2 tablespoons of the dressing to the bottom of a pickling container. Use a shallow container that is not too much larger than your largest perilla leaf.

2. Place a perilla leaf on the bottom of the pickling container. Spoon 1 to 2 teaspoons of the dressing over the leaf. Repeat with the remaining perilla leaves. Pour the remaining dressing over the top of the last perilla leaf.

3. Seal the lid and place the container in the refrigerator for 3 days before enjoying.

BRUSSELS SPROUT SALAD

SERVES 8

DIFFICULTY: Easy

ALLERGEN: GF, NF

½ tablespoon extra-virgin olive oil

¼ cup sliced cremini mushrooms

1 tablespoon balsamic vinegar

Pinch of salt

½ teaspoon black pepper

FOR THE DRESSING

¼ cup baba ganoush or hummus

2 teaspoons yellow mustard

2 tablespoons maple syrup

Juice of ½ lemon

¼ teaspoon garlic powder

1 teaspoon salt

1 teaspoon black pepper

1 teaspoon extra-virgin olive oil

FOR THE SALAD

10 to 12 Brussels sprouts, trimmed and thinly sliced

4 lacinato kale leaves, stemmed, deribbed, and roughly chopped

½ cup pomegranate seeds

¼ cup pumpkin seeds, toasted

¼ cup diced zucchini

½ cup cooked corn kernels

½ cup Roasted Doenjang-Glazed Onions (page 87)

Growing up, we never had salad. All our vegetables were either pickled or cooked. The concept of eating raw vegetables—mixed together—was weird and, well, unappealing. Since going vegan, though, I realized that the problem wasn't salad per se. It was just that my idea of salad was boring. Now, I love to create salads that are packed with ingredients that I enjoy with super-simple dressings (so you can't mess it up!). This Brussels sprout salad is perfect for summer, when you want something refreshing and with lots of fun texture!

1. In a small nonstick skillet, heat the olive oil over medium-high heat until hot. Add the mushrooms and cook for 3 to 4 minutes, without mixing them very much. Add the vinegar, salt, and black pepper and stir the mushrooms with a wooden spoon until they are coated evenly in the balsamic glaze. Set aside to cool.

2. Make the dressing: In a tall container, mix together the baba ganoush, mustard, maple syrup, lemon juice, garlic powder, ½ teaspoon of the salt, and ½ teaspoon of the pepper. Slowly drizzle in the olive oil while stirring the dressing with a whisk or an immersion blender. The dressing should be creamy but not too thick. Add 1 teaspoon water if it is too thick.

3. Prepare the salad: In a large salad bowl, combine the Brussels sprouts, kale, pomegranate seeds, pumpkin seeds, zucchini, and corn. Add half of the dressing. Add the remaining ½ teaspoon salt and the remaining ½ teaspoon pepper. Using your hands, mix the salad and massage the dressing into the kale leaves well. Refrigerate for about 45 minutes before serving.

4. When ready to serve, add the rest of the dressing, mix well, and top with the glazed onions.

KOREAN PEAR SLAW

SERVES 4

DIFFICULTY: Easy

ALLERGENS: GFO

FOR THE DRESSING

Juice of ½ lemon

2 teaspoons brown rice syrup, agave syrup, or maple syrup

1 tablespoon doenjang (see page 25)

1 tablespoon sesame oil

1 tablespoon water

½ teaspoon salt

½ teaspoon freshly ground black pepper

FOR THE SLAW

½ head cabbage, julienned

1 Korean pear, julienned

7 to 10 perilla leaves, julienned

½ cup julienned red onion

½ bulb fennel, plus 1 fennel stalk, chopped

2 scallions, chopped

½ teaspoon salt

½ teaspoon freshly ground black pepper

¼ cup slivered almonds

If you've ever been to a Korean restaurant or had the opportunity to dine at a traditional Korean table, you will rarely see anything resembling "salad" among the various items. The typical Korean meal consists of pickled vegetables or, at best, fresh lettuce or other large greens to use as "wraps" for grilled meat. The idea is to cut the grease of the meat while also providing complementary textures. With that in mind, this cabbage and Korean pear slaw is the perfect side dish to a backyard BBQ or to use on top of a char-grilled black bean burger.

1. Make the dressing: In a small bowl, whisk together the lemon juice, brown rice syrup, doenjang, sesame oil, water, salt, and pepper.

2. Assemble the slaw: In a large salad bowl, combine the cabbage, Korean pear, perilla leaves, red onion, fennel, and scallions. Season the slaw ingredients with the salt and pepper and add the almonds. Pour the dressing over the slaw and incorporate it well (use your hands, if you dare!). Serve immediately or make up to 1 day in advance and refrigerate.

NOTES

Scrape the seeds from the middle of the cucumber before dicing, as they will add too much liquid to the potato salad.

KOREAN POTATO SALAD WITH SCALLION AIOLI

SERVES 6

DIFFICULTY: Easy

ALLERGENS: GF, NF

FOR THE SALAD

2 Yukon Gold potatoes, chopped

1 Korean sweet potato, chopped

⅔ cup canned chickpeas

¼ teaspoon ground turmeric

½ cup diced carrot

½ cup diced seeded cucumber (see Note)

1 apple, chopped

1 tablespoon brown rice syrup or maple syrup

1 teaspoon salt

½ teaspoon freshly ground black pepper

¼ teaspoon ground white pepper

FOR THE SCALLION AIOLI

¼ cup canned chickpea liquid (aquafaba)

½ tablespoon brown rice syrup or maple syrup

1 teaspoon mirin

½ teaspoon mustard powder

1 teaspoon white wine vinegar

1 teaspoon salt

1 scallion, chopped

1 cup extra-virgin olive oil

Watching my father chopstick some potato salad at a Korean BBQ joint was always a bit of an odd experience, sort of like watching my American husband use a fork to eat kimchi. Believe it or not, potato salad is a very typical *banchan* on a Korean *bapsang*. I'm not sure how this particular dish found its way to the Korean table, but it's quite yummy and easy to veganize!

1. Make the salad: In a large pot of boiling water, cook the potatoes until they are fork-tender, about 20 minutes. Drain the potatoes, transfer them to a bowl, and set aside for a few minutes for them to dry. Mash the potatoes with a potato masher or a fork until they are lumpy (not smooth).

2. In a bowl, mash together the chickpeas and turmeric with a fork. Add to the bowl with the potatoes.

3. Add the carrot, cucumber, apple, brown rice syrup, salt, black pepper, and white pepper to the bowl with the potatoes. Mix everything together until all the ingredients are well incorporated.

4. Make the scallion aioli: Pour the chickpea liquid into a tall glass or container, wide enough to fit an immersion blender. Add the brown rice syrup, mirin, mustard powder, vinegar, salt, and scallion. Begin blending the ingredients together using an immersion blender. With the blender running, slowly pour the olive oil down the side of the container. Within about 30 seconds the liquid will emulsify into a creamy sauce. Continue to trickle in the olive oil while blending and blend until the desired thickness is achieved.

5. Spoon 5 to 6 tablespoons of the aioli into the potato salad. Incorporate the dressing with a large spoon until the potato salad is thick and well coated. Store leftover aioli in the fridge for up to 1 month.

5

SOUPS and STEWS

Some of the lesser-known dishes in Korean cuisine are the *chigaes*, which probably best translate as "stews." Normally cooked in a *ddukbaegi*, *chigae* can refer to a variety of different dishes, like *kimchi chigae* or *doenjang chigae* or *budae chigae*. Basically, any soup that is a little heartier qualifies as a *chigae*. Most Korean meals will have either a *chigae* or a *guk* (soup or broth) that you eat with rice and other *banchan*. Most *chigaes* can be turned into a *guk* by using fewer ingredients and more broth. For example, *doenjang chigae* has a lot of different vegetables and tofu, whereas *doenjang guk* has a few veggies, usually no tofu (or very sparse tofu), and lots of delicious broth. This chapter includes both *chigaes* and *guks*, and you'll soon discover how incomplete a meal feels without at least one of these!

SUN YOUNG AND TTEOKGUK

In 2018, I married my current husband, Anthony, in a beautiful deconsecrated church in Rome, Italy. Prior to that, I was a divorcée. While I joyously look forward to my future with Anthony, every now and again, certain things catapult me back to my past. To this day, when someone mentions the popular Korean dish *tteokguk*, or rice cake soup, I instantly think of the morning of January 1, 2005, just four months before my first wedding.

I had come over to my parents' home to wish them a Happy New Year and enjoy my mother's *tteokguk*. I sat across the kitchen table from my parents as Omma slid both a bowl of *tteokguk* and a card toward me. I flipped open the card. I read and reread what she had written. The card, crammed with so many words that New Year's Day, signed by both my mom and dad, boiled down to one desperate plea:

"Please don't marry this man in four months."

I smile (a little) now thinking about that morning. Because I remember how much I raged against my parents. "Love is all that matters!" I yelled, even while knowing, deep down, that my parents' doubts were legitimate. I could see from the lack of any expression on

Anthony and me in Rome, Italy; photograph by Kenny Kim

Omma's face that she disagreed. Love mattered, yes, but so did a lot of other things. A lesson she wanted to save me from, but one I was determined to learn the hard way. Daddy, on the other hand, cowed by my wrath, nodded his head in capitulation. "Okay, okay, maybe you're right. As long as you really love him . . ."

I left my parents' house without touching that bowl of *tteokguk*.

Now, whenever I prepare a bowl of *tteokguk* for anyone, I think of that morning and my mother's face, the heart she cloaked with the kind of grace that I think only mothers can master, and wonder, all over again, what might have happened if I had simply taken a spoonful of her soup.

YUKGAEJANG
(육개장 · Spicy Scallion and Fernbrake Soup)

SERVES 4

DIFFICULTY: Medium
ALLERGENS: GFO, NF

FOR THE SAUCE
¼ cup gochugaru

2 tablespoons soy sauce

1 tablespoon sesame oil

½ teaspoon maple syrup

½ teaspoon salt

1 teaspoon freshly ground
   black pepper

1 teaspoon gochujang

FOR THE SOUP
2 cups gosari
   (dried bracken)

4 or 5 dried shiitake
   mushrooms

1 teaspoon baking soda

1 cup mung bean sprouts

½ onion, julienned

12 scallions, cut into
   2- to 3-inch lengths

4 cloves garlic, minced

6 cups Vegetable Broth
   (page 43)

2-inch square of dashima
   (see page 29)

2½ ounces (70g) sweet
   potato vermicelli, cooked
   according to package
   directions (see Note)

1 tablespoon sesame oil

It never failed: Every single time we went apple picking, my *hahlmuhnee* would screech on the way home, "STOP!! GOSARI!!" My father would hit the brakes, and we'd all tumble out of the car with plastic grocery bags my grandmother had packed for just this purpose: to pick *gosari*, also known as fernbrake. Fernbrake (or bracken) is a type of wild green that grows just about everywhere, from the deep woods studding the mountains of Korea to the sides of Michigan freeways. My brother and I would stuff our grocery bags with them, and my grandmother's eyes would light up, thinking of all the different *banchan* and *chigaes* she could make. *Gosari* is also the star ingredient in one of my favorite soups growing up— *yukgaejang*, a spicy and vegetable-rich soup that is traditionally made with beef. My mother would buy cartons of *yukgaejang* from the local Korean grocery store on her way home after a long day of work. It was the perfect late-night family dinner, and this meat-free version doesn't miss a beat.

1. Make the sauce: In a small bowl, mix together the gochugaru, soy sauce, sesame oil, maple syrup, salt, and pepper. Set aside.

2. Make the soup: Soak the bracken and dried mushrooms in cold water for 1 hour (they can be in the same container).

3. Drain the bracken and mushrooms. In a small saucepan of boiling water, add the baking soda and soaked bracken and cook for about 30 minutes (this will remove the smell). Meanwhile, remove the stems from the shiitakes and slice the caps into ⅛-inch-thick pieces. Set aside.

recipe continues

4. In a small pot of boiling water, blanch the mung bean sprouts for 1 to 2 minutes. Drain and run under cold water to stop the cooking process.

5. When the bracken is tender (not mushy), combine the reserved sauce, bracken, mushrooms, sprouts, onion, scallions, and garlic and marinate for about 15 minutes.

6. Meanwhile, in a large pot, combine the vegetable broth and dashima and bring to a boil. Add the marinated vegetables along with all the marinade and cook for an additional 20 minutes, removing the dashima a few minutes early.

7. Add the cooked vermicelli noodles and drizzle with the sesame oil right before serving.

NOTES

I love adding vermicelli to *yukgaejang*. However, the problem with adding those starchy noodles to any dish is that over time, they will absorb the surrounding liquid and become fat and mushy. Therefore, add only as much as you know you will eat immediately.

TTEOK-MANDU GUK
(떡만두국 · Rice Cake Soup with Dumplings)

SERVES 4

DIFFICULTY: Easy
ALLERGENS: GFO, NF

1 tablespoon extra-virgin olive oil

1 teaspoon sesame oil

¼ cup chopped white onion

1 clove garlic, minced

2 teaspoons salt, plus more for serving

1½ cups frozen or fresh garraetteok oval discs (see page 32)

1 Yukon Gold potato, cut into half moons

3 cups Vegetable Broth, (page 43)

8 to 10 Mandoo (page 251)

Freshly ground black pepper

FOR GARNISH

Strips of Gyerranmari (page 97)

Seaweed strips

2 scallions, chopped

Tteokguk (or "rice cake soup") is one of my most requested recipes. The minute people find out I veganize Korean food, they ask, "Hey, do you have a *tteokguk* recipe?" These days, most people assume that *tteokguk* includes dumplings; but, to be accurate, *tteokguk* is, like most Korean cuisine, a rather humble soup that consists of broth and rice cakes. *Tteokguk* with dumplings makes for a more luxurious dish and is called *ttoek-mandu* (dumpling) *guk*.

Tteokguk is not only the quintessential Korean comfort food, it is a dish steeped in tradition and meaning. It is served on New Year's Day (whether you celebrate that according to the Lunar or Western calendar), and the rice cakes symbolize luck or blessings to come in a brand new and "pure" year. On every New Year's Day that I'm not with my family, I make myself a pot of *tteokguk*—not because it's "tradition," but because it reminds me of the mornings I spent with my family huddled over a piping hot bowl of soup, asking my mom for more *tteok* in my *guk*.

1. In a large pot, heat the olive oil and sesame oil over medium-high heat until hot, about 30 seconds. Add the onion, garlic, and salt and cook until fragrant, about 2 minutes.

2. Add the rice cakes and the potatoes and stir to coat evenly with oil. Add the broth and deglaze the bottom of the pot. Bring it to a boil, then reduce the heat to low and simmer until the potatoes are nearly cooked, about 15 minutes.

3. Add the mandoo (dumplings) at the very end and cook for 1 more minute. Season with salt and pepper to taste.

4. To serve, garnish with the gyerranmari, seaweed strips, and scallions.

FENNEL DOENJANG GUK
(된장국 · Fermented Soybean Soup)

SERVES 4

DIFFICULTY: Easy

ALLERGENS: GFO, NF

1 tablespoon sesame oil

½ bulb fennel, plus 1 stalk, thinly sliced

4 or 5 dried shiitake mushrooms, rehydrated and thinly sliced

1 Yukon Gold potato, diced

1 teaspoon salt

4 cups Mushroom Dashi (page 39)

2 tablespoons doenjang (see page 25)

1 (16-oz.) container medium-firm tofu, cut into ½-inch-thick slices

½ tablespoon extra-virgin olive oil

The Buddhist monk Jeong Kwan sunim not only excludes animal products from her cooking, she also avoids cooking with onions and garlic, as they overly "excite the senses" and interrupt meditation. This simple dish is inspired by Jeong Kwan sunim and doesn't rely on garlic or onions to do the heavy lifting. It is a humble but spectacularly flavored *doenjang* soup.

1. In a Dutch oven or ddukbaegi, heat the sesame oil over medium heat. Add the fennel, mushrooms, and potato. Cook until the mushrooms start to brown, 3 to 4 minutes. Stir in the salt.

2. Add the mushroom dashi and doenjang and stir until the doenjang dissolves. Reduce the heat and let the soup simmer until the potatoes are fully cooked, about 15 minutes.

3. In a nonstick pan set over medium-high heat, sear one side of the tofu slices in the olive oil for 6 to 7 minutes, until browned. Remove the tofu and divide among four bowls. Pour the broth over the tofu and serve.

SPICY DOENJANG CHIGAE (된장찌개 · Fermented Soybean Stew)

SERVES 4

DIFFICULTY: Easy

ALLERGENS: GFO, NF

1 tablespoon sesame oil

1 tablespoon gochugaru (see page 28)

¼ onion, diced

3 cloves garlic, minced

1 small potato, diced

½ cup diced zucchini

1 teaspoon salt

½ teaspoon freshly ground black pepper

3 tablespoons doenjang (see page 25)

1 tablespoon soup (light) soy sauce

2 cups Vegetable Broth (page 43)

1 (16-ounce) block medium or firm tofu, cut into bite-size cubes

2 scallions, chopped

½ jalapeño, seeded and thinly sliced

I could eat *doenjang chigae*, a stew made with fermented soybeans, every single day and never grow tired of it—as long as it's this particular recipe. Before I started cooking, I remember having dinner at a friend's house, and she served up a piping-hot bowl of *doenjang chigae*. I was excited. I spooned a good bit of it into my mouth; I immediately regretted it. Her *chigae* was watery, bland, and, in my opinion, a waste of perfectly good *doenjang*! *Doenjang chigae* is supposed to be about the *doenjang*, the fermented soybeans. I add a heaping amount and never fear I'll be accused of serving watery *chigae*!

1. In a medium ddukbaegi or Dutch oven, heat the sesame oil over medium heat. Immediately add the gochugaru and begin stirring with a wooden spoon. Make sure the gochugaru does not burn (turn dark), as it will get bitter.

2. When the gochugaru starts to bubble and froth, add the onion, garlic, potato, zucchini, salt, and pepper. Continue to cook until fragrant, about 1 minute.

3. Add the doenjang and stir until the vegetables are evenly coated. Add the soy sauce and deglaze the pot. Pour in the vegetable broth. Add the tofu and bring the stew to a boil. Reduce the heat and allow the stew to simmer until the potatoes are tender, about 20 minutes.

4. Add the scallions and jalapeño and cook for 2 more minutes before serving.

KIMCHI CHIGAE
(김치찌개 · Kimchi Stew)

SERVES 4

DIFFICULTY: Easy

ALLERGENS: GFO, NF

1 tablespoon sesame oil

1 tablespoon extra-virgin olive oil

4 scallions, white parts chopped, green parts cut into 1-inch lengths

½ cup diced onion

1 teaspoon minced fresh ginger

2 to 3 cloves garlic, minced

1 small potato, diced

2 to 3 cups sour Baechu Kimchi (page 117)

1 tablespoon gochujang (see page 26)

2 teaspoons brown rice syrup

2 tablespoons soup (light) soy sauce

2 cups Vegetable Broth (page 43)

1 (16-ounce) block medium or firm tofu, cut into ½-inch cubes

¼ cup black beans

Kimchi is a food that was designed to feed people for a very long time. Regular cabbage will go bad in a week. Kimchi, on the other hand, can feed a family for several months. Once the kimchi in your refrigerator starts to get a little TOO sour for your tastebuds, though, you know it's time to make *kimchi chigae*, or kimchi stew. It's not a good idea to try and make this with fresh kimchi—the kind you'd be happy to eat out of the jar, as the flavors will not be developed enough (or "stinky" enough!) to withstand the cooking process. This simple recipe will layer the intense kimchi flavors you love into a rich stew. Note, this recipe does include one non-traditional component—black beans! I definitely did not pick that up from my mom, but I'm always looking for ways to incorporate more beans into my diet. Enjoy with a bowl of piping-hot rice!

1. In a medium ddukbaegi or Dutch oven, heat the sesame oil and olive oil over medium-high heat. When the oil is hot, add the scallion whites, onion, ginger, garlic, and potato. Sauté the vegetables until the onions turn translucent, about 3 minutes.

2. Add the kimchi and continue to cook until it begins to caramelize, about 1 minute. Add the gochujang and brown rice syrup and stir the vegetables to evenly coat.

3. Add the soy sauce to deglaze the bottom of the pot. Add the vegetable broth and bring to a boil. Reduce the heat and simmer until the potatoes are tender, about 15 minutes.

4. Add the tofu, black beans, and the scallion greens and cook for an additional 2 minutes before serving.

SOONDOOBOO CHIGAE
(순두부찌개 · Silken Tofu Stew)

SERVES 4

DIFFICULTY: Easy

ALLERGENS: GFO, NF

1 tablespoon sesame oil

2 tablespoons gochugaru
(see page 28)

¼ onion, diced

3 cloves garlic, minced

1 small potato, diced

½ cup hobak or regular
zucchini half-moon discs
(¼ inch thick)

2 teaspoons salt

½ teaspoon freshly ground
black pepper

1 tablespoon soup (light)
soy sauce

2 cups Vegetable Broth
(page 43)

2 (16-ounce) blocks
silken tofu

2 scallions, chopped

This is the first real Korean recipe I ever learned from my mother. I had just graduated from college and my girlfriends, who were very familiar with my obsession with *soondooboo chigae*, bought me a traditional large *ddukbaegi* so I could make my favorite dish at home. Not surprisingly, it was one of the first Korean recipes I veganized when I went vegan. This recipe is really all about the silken tofu, an ingredient many people only use for smoothies. But, like all tofu, silken tofu absorbs the flavors it cooks in, and in this case, that's a fiery and smoky broth made with *gochugaru*. Silken tofu is velvety and tender, and the liquid that seeps out during the cooking process rounds out all the flavors to create a perfect accompaniment to a humble bowl of rice.

1. In a medium ddukbaegi or Dutch oven, heat the sesame oil over medium heat. Immediately add the gochugaru and stir with a wooden spoon. Make sure the gochugaru does not burn (turn dark), as it will get bitter.

2. When the gochugaru starts to bubble and froth, add the onion, garlic, potato, zucchini, salt, and pepper. Continue to cook until the onions begin to turn translucent, 2 to 3 minutes.

3. Add the soy sauce to deglaze the pot. Pour in the vegetable broth. Add the silken tofu, breaking it up gently with your spoon into large chunks (you do not want it to look curdled). Reduce the heat and simmer until the potatoes are tender, about 20 minutes.

4. Add the scallions and cook for 1 to 2 more minutes before serving.

GAMJA TANG
(감자탕 · Potato Stew)

SERVES 3 OR 4

DIFFICULTY: Medium
ALLERGENS: GFO, NF

4 cups Vegetable Broth (page 43)

1 teaspoon sliced fresh ginger

2 dried shiitake mushrooms

1 onion, julienned

1 dried red chili

2 tablespoons doenjang

4 cloves garlic, minced

2 tablespoons gochugaru

2 tablespoons gochujang (see page 26)

2 tablespoons "Fishy" Sauce (page 47) or soy sauce

¼ cup roasted wild sesame seeds (perilla seeds)

1 teaspoon sesame oil

3 Yukon Gold potatoes, halved

1 cup mung bean sprouts

2 scallions, roughly chopped

5 to 6 perilla leaves, roughly chopped

2½ ounces (70g) sweet potato vermicelli, cooked according to package directions (see Note, page 147)

1 tablespoon sesame oil

When I was growing up, my grandmother would make this dish for us very rarely. While the name *gamja tang,* or "potato stew," suggests that the majestic spud is the star of the show, in actuality the main component of *gamja tang* is a big piece of pork shoulder. I think this is why my grandmother rarely cooked this dish—pork is tricky to cook with and it often left our kitchen smelling a little . . . funky. When I decided to go plant based, I was excited to re-create this dish so that it truly lived up to its name by restoring the potato to its rightful place as the star!

1. In a medium ddukbaegi or Dutch oven, combine the vegetable broth, ginger, mushrooms, onion, chili, and doenjang. Bring to a boil, then reduce the heat and simmer until you have a lovely aromatic broth as a base for this stew, 45 minutes to 1 hour.

2. Fish out the mushrooms and slice them, then return the slices to the broth.

3. In a small bowl, mix together ½ cup water, the garlic, gochugaru, gochujang, "fishy" sauce, and wild sesame seeds.

4. Make the stew: Add the sauce, potatoes, and bean sprouts to the broth and simmer until the potatoes are tender, about 30 minutes.

5. Right before serving, add the scallions, perilla leaves, sweet potato vermicelli, and sesame oil.

NOTES

You can find dried *miyeok* at the Asian grocery store, where there is often an entire aisle devoted to laver and other seaweed products. For this recipe, you want to look for "sea mustard" or *undaria*. The seaweed will look like very skinny dark twigs. Steer clear of *dashima*—those long, thick sheets of kelp that you use for seasoning broths (like the Vegetable Broth, page 43).

MIYEOK GUK
(미역국 · Seaweed Soup)

SERVES 4

DIFFICULTY: Easy

ALLERGENS: GFO, NF

1 ounce dried miyeok or undaria (see Note)

1 tablespoon sesame oil

2 cloves garlic, minced

1 teaspoon salt, plus more to taste

½ teaspoon freshly ground black pepper, plus more to taste

1 tablespoon soup (light) soy sauce

6 cups Vegetable Broth (page 43) or water

"I saw your name on a list that the nurses gave me when I was in labor. I saw 'Joanne' and I thought, Ohhhhh . . . sounds so beautiful! What a beautiful name!" This is how my mother describes naming me when I am little, and so, I grew up thinking that this is how everyone gets their American name—off a list they give you at the hospital right before you're born.

My mother was reading a novel while giving birth to me. Perhaps that's why I love books so much.

I wonder whether anyone was there to make her a bowl of seaweed soup, or "birthday soup." It's supposed to help women who've just given birth regain their strength. Though perhaps if she was reading a book through labor, Omma simply checked out of the hospital with me in tow and made the soup herself. She has interesting tips for preparing this dish. For instance, my mother swears that frying the seaweed in a little sesame oil before adding it to the soup helps soften it, so I never skip that step.

1. In a large bowl, soak the dried seaweed in cold water for about 15 minutes to reconstitute it. Rinse the seaweed and pat dry with a kitchen towel. Using a pair of kitchen shears, cut the seaweed into bite-size pieces.

2. In a medium pot, heat the sesame oil over medium heat. Add the reconstituted seaweed and the garlic. Stir-fry the seaweed for about 3 minutes. Season with the salt and pepper. Add the soy sauce to deglaze the pot.

3. Add the vegetable broth and bring to a boil. Reduce the heat and simmer for an additional 20 minutes. Season with salt and pepper to taste.

GAMJA GUK
(감자국 · Potato and Leek Soup)

SERVES 4

DIFFICULTY: Easy
ALLERGENS: GF, NF

1 tablespoon sesame oil

2 medium Yukon Gold potatoes, julienned

¼ cup julienned leek

3 cloves garlic, minced

1 small shallot, julienned

¼ cup chopped Korean squash or regular zucchini

2 teaspoons salt, plus more to taste

1 teaspoon freshly ground black pepper, plus more to taste

4 cups Vegetable Broth, (page 43)

This is a very humble but delicious soup that my dad often makes for my mom. One day, my mom cooed into the phone, "Daddy makes the best *gamja guk*—so simple, but so, so good." I often think that this is how my best recipes come to be—they are usually inspired by what my mom tells me she and my dad are eating for dinner. I got off the phone with her, threw a handful of vegetables into my *ddukbaegi* along with some of my homemade vegetable broth, and before long, my own husband and I were slurping down some delicious *gamja guk*.

1. In a medium ddukbaegi or Dutch oven, heat the sesame oil over medium-high heat. Add the potatoes, leek, garlic, shallot, and squash and stir-fry until the shallot begins to turn translucent, 2 to 3 minutes. Season with the salt and pepper.

2. Add the vegetable broth and bring it to a boil. Reduce the heat and simmer until the potatoes are tender, about 15 minutes. Season with additional salt and pepper to taste.

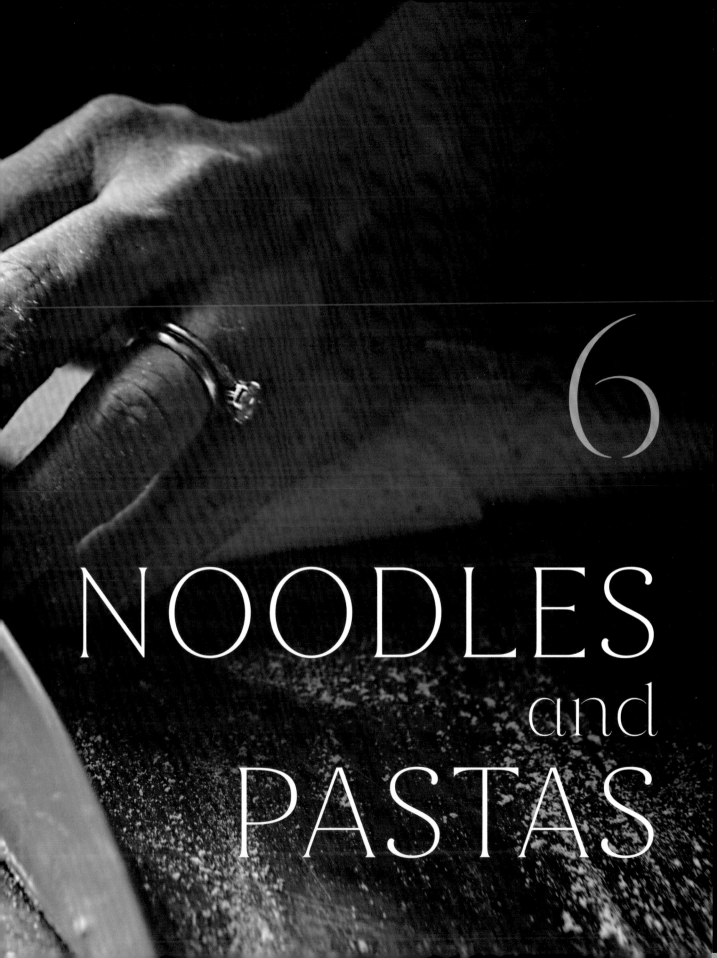

NOODLES and PASTAS

6

Guksoo or *myun* (sometimes spelled *myeon*) are both Korean words used to refer to noodles (e.g., *kimchi guksoo* and *jjajangmyun*). I wish I could tell you the difference between *guksoo* and *myun*, but there doesn't appear to be a consistent rule as to when to use *myun* and when to use *guksoo* (though most *guksoos* tend to be skinnier noodles). While the vast majority of Korean meals start with rice, if you are having a noodle-based meal instead, it will be served with few *banchan* (usually just kimchi). Some noodle dishes are sauce-based (like *jjajangmyun*), and others are broth-based (like *kimchi guksoo*). Most *guksoos* or *myuns* are made out of some amount of wheat flour, so they are not gluten-free. There *are* gluten-free noodle dishes in Korean cuisine, like *japchae*—made with sweet potato vermicelli, but they are considered *banchan* and not a main course. This chapter contains recipes for noodle dishes that you can eat without rice, as well as pastas—an homage to my late father-in-law, who inspired me to start cooking by introducing me to his own delicious recipes.

APPA AND K-POP NOODLES

My mother was a nurse and, sometimes, she had to work the night shift, which meant that she left before dinner and came home after all of us were asleep. After his first night waiting for my mother to return from a night shift at the hospital, instead of simply cooking for himself (which meant he didn't eat dinner at all), my father ventured into the kitchen and started "experimenting." Although it was, at times, painful for the rest of the family, my dad discovered he loved cooking his own food, and over time—a long time—he got pretty okay at it.

In fact, I now prefer my dad's rice cake soup (Tteokguk, page 149) over my mom's, or anyone else's for that matter. My dad also makes a tasty bean sprout soup (Kong Namul Guk, page 189) with thin slivers of jalapeño swimming lazily in a broth that's clear enough to see the bottom of the bowl, as well as a pretty good bowl of cold buckwheat noodles (Naengmyeon, page 177), with sliced Korean pears and julienned cucumbers and a smattering of toasted sesame seeds.

But, he didn't spend all his time in the kitchen. Every once in a while, my father took me and my little brother out into the city for lunch. Two kids in the backseat of the Honda hatchback with no mission but to eat my father's favorite noodles at the sleepy little Chinese-Korean eatery in K-town: a one-story square building squatting all alone in the middle of an empty parking lot, with a bright red roof held aloft by mint-green pillars.

At 11 a.m. (the minute they opened), we would be the restaurant's only patrons. Inside, Chinese lanterns dangle from the ceiling, their once-bright shades faded and dingy from the city sun flooding in through the windows. The cheerful hostess, dressed entirely in black with darting eyebrows, always greets us in Korean that sounds off

Daddy, Jaesun, and me

to even my Anglicized ears (most hostesses at these Chinese-Korean restaurants speak Chinese, Korean, and Japanese). She seats us at a table by the window, leaving only one menu for my father. Each of the place settings has a sheet of paper with a colorful rendition of the Chinese zodiac. Without touching the menu, my dad orders two *samsun jjajangmyuns*—one for himself and one to split between my brother and me.

Jjajangmyun is the stuff of K-pop legend. It's the noodle dish for which all the impossibly beautiful K-pop actresses have the caloric/carb count memorized, because it is their enshrined "cheat meal." It's the most frequently ordered item off Korea's version of Grubhub, the dish you eat when your boyfriend has just cheated on you, when your dog simply doesn't understand the concept of potty training, when you're feeling so gross the only rational thing to do is to eat something sinfully delicious. Made of fried *jjajang*—thick, black fermented soybean paste—and a deep, rich broth (usually from beef or pork), it's not the type of dish that you can burn off with an hour on the treadmill.

It was the dish my dad took us to eat when I lost my first tooth and on countless birthdays, and it was what he requested every single Father's Day. No other noodle dishes compared, no matter the restaurant, including the pasta at the Italian restaurant I took him to in the city when I got my first job at a large law firm.

My parents in Rome, Italy

During our *jjajangmyun* lunches, the waitress sets our table with fluorescent-yellow half-moon daikon pickles, a small dish of raw onions and *jjajang* paste, and some Chinese-style radish *kimchi*. The three of us break apart our wooden chopsticks in unison, picking our way through these starters without speaking. Shortly, the waitress returns with two bowls of naked noodles, two bowls of *jjajang* sauce, and one empty bowl. Using his chopsticks, my father expertly incorporates the sauce into the noodles before dividing one of the

bowls for me and my brother. Thick, black, and as shiny as molasses, the sauce clings to the pale, chewy noodles while healthy chunks of zucchini, onion, and potato promise something heartier then a mere gravy.

On our way home from lunch, Daddy rolls down the windows for me and my brother in the backseat. My brother stretches his hand out of the window while my father speeds down Peterson Avenue, back to our home in Skokie, Illinois. I can hear my brother, Jaesun, as he cups his hand in the air and beckons me to watch:

"Look, Noonah! I've caught an airball in my hand! Look!"

I remember, suddenly, something my father told me a long time ago.

I assume we all wore leotards for fun?

"When I was little, I loved catching fireflies, you know? By cupping my hands, just like this." Daddy cupped his dark brown hands to form a small cage.

"Why did you like fireflies so much, Daddy?"

He shrugs. "I dunno. Maybe, they made it less dark. I guess."

JJAJANGMYUN
(짜장면 · Black Soybean Noodles)

SERVES 4

DIFFICULTY: Easy

ALLERGENS: NF

3 large or 4 medium dried shiitake mushrooms

3 tablespoons extra-virgin olive oil

½ soy fillet, cut into ½-inch cubes (see Note)

2 to 3 cloves garlic, minced

½ cup chopped onion

1 Yukon Gold potato, diced

¾ cup diced Korean squash or regular zucchini

½ cup chopped cabbage

½ teaspoon salt

½ teaspoon cracked black pepper

¼ cup jjajang (see page 27)

1 tablespoon soup (light) soy sauce

½ cup Mushroom Dashi (page 39)

2 tablespoons brown rice syrup

2 tablespoons potato starch

4 servings cooked noodles (see Note)

1 cup julienned cucumber

Growing up, I called this dish "Korean spaghetti." It is probably one of the most popular noodle dishes in South Korea, made even more popular by the Oscar-winning movie *Parasite*. A rich, glossy, dark sauce of roasted fermented soybeans is paired with fresh julienned cucumbers. Interestingly, though, *jjajangmyun* is not a strictly Korean dish. It actually originated in a Chinese restaurant in Incheon's Chinatown, so most Koreans view it as Chinese. However, walk into the average Chinese restaurant and ask for *jjajangmyun* and they'll give you the "deer in headlights" look. *Jjajangmyun* can only be ordered at a Korean-Chinese restaurant (i.e., where they serve Chinese food but the owners speak Korean, too). It can all be a little tricky, which is why it's very convenient to be able to make your own!

1. Soak the shiitakes in cold water for 1 hour to reconstitute. Remove and discard the stems. Drain and thinly slice the mushrooms.

2. In a wok or very large pan, heat ½ tablespoon of the olive oil over medium-high heat. When the oil is hot, add the shiitakes and soy fillet and cook until the mushrooms and fillet are browned, about 5 minutes. Remove from the pan and set aside.

3. Add another ½ tablespoon of the olive oil to the pan over medium-high heat. Add the garlic, onion, potato, squash, and cabbage. Season with the salt and pepper. Cook until the onions turn translucent, 2 to 3 minutes. Remove the vegetables from the pan and set aside.

4. Add the remaining 2 tablespoons oil to the center of the pan and heat over medium-high heat. Once it gets hot, add the jjajang

recipe continues

directly to the oil. Using a wooden spoon, stir the paste into the oil constantly so that it doesn't burn, until it gets very shiny, 1 to 2 minutes.

5. Add the cooked mushrooms, soy fillet, and vegetables and coat them evenly with the fried black soybean paste.

6. Add the soy sauce to deglaze the pan. Add the dashi and brown rice syrup. Bring the sauce to a boil, then cover the pan and simmer until the potatoes are nearly cooked, about 5 minutes.

7. Add the potato starch to ¼ cup water (this is your slurry). Stir the slurry into the sauce and cook until the sauce is thick and shiny, an additional minute.

8. Serve with your favorite noodles and garnish each bowl with julienned cucumber. Use any leftover sauce over a bowl of rice.

NOTES

Did you know that the Chinese have been using meat alternatives in their cooking for hundreds of years? Take a cruise through the tofu section of your nearest Asian grocery store. I like soy fillets (a type of textured soy protein that is popular in Asia) for *jjajangmyun*, but you can also use tempeh or fried tofu!

This sauce is so delicious, you can use it with your favorite noodles. (I've even used it with gluten-free pasta when my husband was experimenting with a gluten-free diet.) However, for the more traditional approach, you can find fresh udon or "jjajangmyun" noodles in the frozen foods aisle of the Asian grocery store.

KAHL-GUKSOO
(칼국수 · Knife-Cut Noodles)

SERVES 4

DIFFICULTY: Medium
ALLERGENS: NF

FOR THE NOODLES

2½ cups (350g)
   all-purpose flour, plus
   more for dusting

2 tablespoons vegetable
   oil

1 teaspoon salt

FOR THE SOUP

1 tablespoon plus
   1 teaspoon sesame oil

2 tablespoons extra-virgin
   olive oil

3 tablespoons plus
   1 teaspoon gochugaru
   (see page 28)

3 cloves garlic, minced

1 teaspoon minced fresh
   ginger

3 to 4 dried shiitake
   mushrooms, rehydrated
   and julienned

4 scallions, cut into 2-inch
   lengths

¼ cup julienned leek

¼ cup chopped cabbage

¼ cup julienned Korean
   squash or regular
   zucchini

½ cup julienned onion

¼ cup julienned carrot

I dare anyone to tell me that making your own noodles is easy. Unless you are a seventy-five-year-old *hahlmuhnee* or *nonna*, or a trained chef, noodle-making can be a very intimidating process. I've watched hours and hours of videos and tutorials on making noodles, kneaded dough until my shoulders went numb, and scoured the Internet for the strangest ingredients to facilitate the lynchpin of successful noodle-making: elasticity. I have concluded that the Korean knife-cut noodles, or *kahl-guksoo*, are the easiest noodles out there, since they don't need to be kneaded until you injure yourself, placed through an expensive machine, or pulled into long ropes by what can only be described as sorcery. Here, I've paired the noodles with a seafood broth as an homage to *jjampong*, another of my father's favorite noodle dishes.

1. Make the noodles: In a stand mixer fitted with the dough hook (or in a large bowl), combine the flour, 1 cup water, the vegetable oil, and salt. With the mixer on low (or using a large spoon), begin mixing the ingredients together until a rough dough starts to form.

2. Knead with the dough hook on medium to high speed for 10 minutes. (Or remove the dough from the bowl and begin kneading the dough by hand, pressing the dough with the heel of your hand, folding the dough in half, rotating the dough by 30 degrees and repeating for 15 minutes.)

3. Once you have finished kneading the dough, roll it into a smooth ball. Place it in an airtight container and refrigerate for at least 4 hours and up to 24 hours.

recipe and ingredients continue

2 tablespoons kelp powder

1 teaspoon salt

1 tablespoon "Fishy" Sauce
(page 47)

2 tablespoons soup (light)
soy sauce

½ teaspoon maple syrup

6 cups Vegetable Broth
(page 43)

NOTES

Do not try adding
raw noodles directly
to the soup. Because
the noodles are coated
with flour, they will
thicken the soup
too much.

4. When the dough has rested, remove it from the refrigerator. Sprinkle your work surface with a little flour and divide the dough in half. Starting with one half, roll the dough out into a large oval or rectangle about 1/16 inch thick.

5. Dust your work surface with a little more flour and reposition the dough back onto the work surface. Dust the dough with a little flour as well to prevent the dough from sticking to itself. Carefully, starting from the bottom, fold 1½ inches of the dough up. Repeat until you have a long, layered stack of dough. Using a sharp knife, cut the folded dough into ¼-inch-wide pieces. Using your hands, gently shake the noodles, which, if they were adequately floured, should come apart easily. Repeat with the second half of the dough.

6. Make the soup: In a medium pot, heat 1 tablespoon of the sesame oil and the olive oil over medium-high heat. Add 3 tablespoons of the gochugaru to the oil and stir it constantly with a wooden spoon until it starts to froth.

7. Add the garlic, ginger, shiitakes, scallions, leek, cabbage, squash, onion, and carrot. Stir-fry the vegetables until the onions turn translucent, 2 to 3 minutes. Add the kelp powder and salt.

8. Add the "fishy" sauce, soy sauce, and maple syrup to deglaze the pot. Add the vegetable broth and bring it to a boil. Reduce the heat and allow the broth to simmer.

9. While the soup is simmering, bring a large pot of water to a boil. Add the noodles and cook for 2 minutes (the noodles will not be cooked yet). Drain and add the noodles to the broth and cook until the noodles are tender, 2 to 3 minutes.

10. During the last minute of cooking, add the remaining 1 teaspoon sesame oil and the remaining 1 teaspoon gochugaru.

NAENGMYEON
(냉면 · Cold Buckwheat Noodles)

SERVES 4

DIFFICULTY: Easy
ALLERGENS: NF

FOR THE SAUCE

1 Korean pear, peeled and cut into chunks

¼ red onion

4 scallions, cut into pieces

4 cloves garlic

2 teaspoons grated fresh ginger

½ cup gochugaru (see page 28)

¼ cup gochujang (see page 26)

½ cup brown rice syrup

6 tablespoons sesame oil

¼ cup rice vinegar

2 tablespoons soy sauce

2 teaspoons salt

2 teaspoons freshly ground black pepper

FOR THE NOODLES

25 ounces (720g) naengmyeon noodles (see Notes)

4 cups Vegetable Broth (page 43), at room temperature

¼ cup mirin

¼ cup rice vinegar

This dish always reminds me of my father because it is one of the first things he taught himself to make on his own. Therefore, my brother and I were subjected to countless watery, bland, and overcooked *naengmyeon* iterations before my dad finally perfected it. What does the perfect *naengmyeon* taste like? Well, there are two varieties—spicy *bibim* ("mixed") *naengmyeon* and *mool* ("water") *naengmyeon*. The first is a flavor bomb—fiery, tart, and savory all at the same time. The second, *mool naengmyeon*, is refreshing, because the broth is served ice cold. I never understood the reason why the two versions couldn't be combined to form a "more perfect" *naengmyeon*, and have discovered that no such reason exists! This *naengmyeon* combines the best of both *bibim* and *mool nangmyeon* for a complex but refreshing meal that you'll perfect a lot sooner than my dad!

1. Make the sauce: In a food processor, combine the Korean pear, onion, scallions, garlic, ginger, gochugaru, gochujang, brown rice syrup, sesame oil, vinegar, soy sauce, salt, and pepper and process until very smooth. Refrigerate the sauce. (The sauce will keep in the refrigerator for up to 1 week.)

2. Prepare the noodles: Bring a large pot of water to a boil. Add the noodles and cook until the noodles are chewy, about 3 minutes. Drain the noodles in a colander and run under cold water until they are cool to the touch.

3. In a medium bowl, mix together the vegetable broth, mirin, and vinegar. Ladle the broth into four deep bowls (for serving). Add three to four ice cubes to each bowl (see Notes).

recipe and ingredients continue

FOR THE GARNISH

1 Persian (mini) cucumber, sliced into ⅛-inch-thick rounds

1 Gyerranmari (page 97), sliced into small strips

½ cup Baechu Kimchi (page 117)

¼ Korean pear, julienned

2 tablespoons toasted sesame seeds

4 teaspoons sesame oil

4. Divide the noodles into four equal servings and place into each bowl of broth. Spoon 4 to 6 tablespoons of sauce (more or less, depending on one's spice tolerance) over the noodles.

5. Garnish the noodles with the cucumber, gyerranmari, kimchi, and Korean pear. Sprinkle with the toasted sesame seeds and drizzle the noodles with the sesame oil right before serving.

NOTES

Most Asian grocery stores sell *naengmyeon* noodles together with a packet for broth and sauce. There are two different varieties of *naengmyeon* noodles: *mool* ("water") *naengmyeon*, which usually has much more broth, and *bibim* ("mixed") *naengmyeon*. For this recipe, either variety will work, since you will not be using the broth or sauce packets.

In lieu of adding ice cubes, you can also place the broth in the freezer for about 30 minutes, until it turns into almost a slush. By the time you add the noodles, sauce, and garnish, the slush will have just started to melt into a refreshing broth for your noodles.

JAPCHAE
(잡채 • Korean Glass Noodles)

SERVES 4

DIFFICULTY: Easy
ALLERGENS: GFO, NF

7 ounces (200g) sweet
   potato vermicelli

4 cups adult raw spinach
   (do not use baby
   spinach)

2 tablespoons extra-virgin
   olive oil, plus more as
   needed

1 carrot, julienned

Salt and freshly ground
   black pepper

¼ cup julienned red bell
   pepper

¼ cup julienned yellow bell
   pepper

¼ cup julienned green bell
   pepper

½ cup julienned red
   cabbage

½ cup julienned onion

1 tablespoon minced garlic

4 to 5 mushrooms, thinly
   sliced

3 tablespoons soy sauce

2 tablespoons maple syrup

1 tablespoon sesame oil

1 tablespoon toasted
   sesame seeds

I am not ashamed to admit that I ask for this dish every single birthday, Thanksgiving, and Christmas. Why? Because it's so darn delicious. It's basically a Korean warm pasta salad, with naturally gluten-free pasta (sweet potato vermicelli) and a ton of vegetables. Because the vegetables have to be julienned and separately stir-fried, it can be time-consuming and labor-intensive, which is why I save my requests for only the most special of occasions.

1. Soak the sweet potato vermicelli in water for about 15 minutes.

2. In a pot of boiling water, cook the spinach until it turns bright green, about 2 minutes. Drain the spinach and run it under cold water to stop the cooking. Squeeze out as much excess liquid as possible and set it aside.

3. In a very large skillet, heat 1 tablespoon of the olive oil over medium-high heat. Add the carrots and sauté until they start to turn soft, about 2 minutes. Season with salt and pepper. Remove the carrots and place in a large bowl. Repeat with the red bell pepper, then the yellow bell pepper, and green bell pepper, followed by the red cabbage, seasoning each to taste with salt and pepper and adding to the bowl with the carrots. If necessary, add more oil to the pan as you go. The reason the vegetables are sautéed separately is to ensure that the flavors don't muddle together.

4. In the same pan, heat the remaining 1 tablespoon olive oil over medium-high heat. Add the onion, garlic, mushrooms, and salt and pepper to taste and sauté until the mushrooms are browned, about 5 minutes. Add 1 tablespoon of the soy sauce and 1 tablespoon of the maple syrup to deglaze the pan.

recipe continues

5. Transfer the onions, mushrooms, and garlic to the large bowl of vegetables. Add the cooked spinach.

6. Bring a large pot of water to a boil. Add the soaked vermicelli and cook them for 3 minutes. Add ½ cup cold water to the pot and when the water starts to boil again, add another ½ cup cold water. When the water comes to a boil, check the noodles to see if they are cooked (they should be tender and springy). If not, repeat.

7. Drain the cooked noodles and rinse them in very cold water. Shake off the excess water and add the noodles to the bowl of vegetables.

8. Add the remaining 2 tablespoons soy sauce and remaining 1 tablespoon maple syrup along with the sesame oil, a dash of black pepper, and the sesame seeds.

9. Mix using chopsticks or your hands. Taste and add additional soy sauce, maple syrup (I like mine sweet!), or black pepper, if desired.

KIMCHI GUKSOO
(김치국수 · Kimchi Noodles)

SERVES 4

DIFFICULTY: Easy

ALLERGENS: NF

2 tablespoons extra-virgin olive oil

2 cloves garlic, minced

2 cups sour Baechu Kimchi (page 117), roughly chopped

2 tablespoons gochujang (see page 26)

6 cups Mushroom Dashi (page 39)

16 ounces somyun (thin wheat noodles)

¼ cup kimchi liquid

2 tablespoons Spicy Soy Sauce Dressing (page 49)

1 teaspoon sesame oil

1 tablespoon toasted sesame seeds

This is another one of those dishes I like to make when I need something simple, hearty, and delicious, something that won't take a lot of time or require lots of ingredients but will still taste like I spent all day in the kitchen. If you go through the noodle aisle of your local Asian grocery store, you will no doubt see dozens of different colors, shapes, sizes, and brands. Most *guksoo* dishes are composed of thin noodles—kind of like angel hair pasta. Although I usually prefer thicker, chewier noodles (like ramen or *jjajanmyun*), after developing an appreciation for angel hair pasta, I decided to give a go at making my own spicy *kimchi guksoo*. It was so easy and delicious, I was done from start to slurp in 30 minutes!

1. In a medium pot, heat the olive oil over medium-high heat. Add the garlic and kimchi and sauté for 2 minutes.

2. Add the gochujang and stir until the kimchi is evenly coated. Add the mushroom dashi and deglaze the bottom of the pan. Bring to a boil, then reduce the heat and simmer for 15 minutes to make sure all the flavors are developed and the kimchi is slightly soft.

3. Meanwhile, bring a large pot of water to a boil. Cook the noodles according to the package directions (do not cook them too long—usually only 3 to 4 minutes). Drain the noodles and rinse under cold water to stop the cooking.

4. Divide the noodles among four serving bowls and portion the broth accordingly. Add 1 tablespoon of the kimchi liquid to each bowl. Spoon the spicy soy dressing over the top, drizzle with a little sesame oil, and sprinkle with sesame seeds.

ANGRY PENNE PASTA

SERVES 4

DIFFICULTY: Easy
ALLERGENS: GFO, NF

1 (12-ounce) box penne
   pasta

1 tablespoon extra-virgin
   olive oil

¼ cup chopped red onion

4 cloves garlic, minced

1 red bell pepper, chopped

1 Korean red chili or
   serrano chili, chopped

1 teaspoon salt

½ teaspoon freshly ground
   pepper

2 cups roughly chopped
   tomatoes

1 tablespoon gochugaru
   (see page 28)

1 tablespoon gochujang
   (see page 26)

When Anthony and I first started dating (neither of us was vegan), we used to frequent a small Italian cafe right by my apartment. During our very first meal there, I ordered the pasta arrabbiata— a glorious bowl of spaghetti coated in a fiery red sauce, topped with an ominous red chili pepper; the name *arrabbiata* literally translates into "angry pasta." When I started experimenting with incorporating the flavors of my childhood into the Italian dishes my husband grew up eating, I immediately thought of how well *gochujang* and *gochugaru* would work as a base for a different kind of "angry pasta."

1. Bring a large pot of water to a boil. Add the pasta and begin cooking according to the package directions.

2. Meanwhile, in a medium pot, heat the olive oil over medium-high heat. Add the red onion, garlic, bell pepper, Korean chili, salt, and black pepper and cook until the onions become translucent, about 3 minutes.

3. Add the tomatoes and more salt to the pot and continue stirring occasionally. Add the gochugaru and gochujang and stir until the vegetables are evenly coated. Add ¼ cup of the starchy pasta cooking water to the pot and stir.

4. Remove the vegetable mixture from the heat and blend the contents with an immersion blender (you can also transfer to a regular blender; be careful with the hot contents of the pot).

5. When the pasta has 1 more minute to go, drain the pasta and return it to the pot. Set the pot over medium heat and add the blended sauce. Cook until the pasta is al dente.

SUJEBI
(수제비 · Spicy Torn Noodles)

SERVES 4

DIFFICULTY: Practice
makes perfect

ALLERGENS: NF

FOR THE NOODLES

2½ cups all-purpose flour

¾ cup warm water

1 teaspoon salt

1 tablespoon vegetable oil

FOR THE SOUP

6 cups Vegetable Broth
(page 43)

Two 2-inch squares of
dashima (see page 29)

2 dried shiitake
mushrooms

1 shallot, diced

1 yellow potato, sliced into
⅛-inch-thick half moons

2 scallions, chopped

FOR THE SAUCE

1 tablespoon gochugaru
(see page 28)

1 tablespoon soup (light)
soy sauce

½ tablespoon gochujang
(see page 26)

½ tablespoon sesame oil

½ teaspoon maple syrup

"I hate torn noodle soup," my mother confesses over the phone. "Your grandmother made it for us with nothing but water. We were too poor for anything else." I will never tire of the revelations that occur during my daily phone calls with Omma. *Sujebi* is a favorite in the Korean food scene, and my mom was poo-pooing it like a bowl of mud. "So, it's literally called 'torn noodle soup,' not '*sujebi*'?" I asked. "In North Korea, it's called 'torn noodle soup,' but in South Korea, they may call it '*sujebi*,'" Omma replied. Yet another eye-popping morsel of information. Later, I showed her a photo of my *sujebi*, lamenting over how difficult it was to make the noodles as paper thin as her mother did. "Yes! The thinnest noodles are the best! I like the thin ones," she texted. I realized that maybe it wasn't really her mother's noodle soup she hated so much but the circumstances that required her mother to make it so often.

1. Make the noodles: In a food processor, combine the flour, warm water, salt, and vegetable oil. Process the ingredients for about 4 minutes, until a dough forms.

2. Remove the dough from the food processor and form it into a smooth ball. Wrap the dough and allow it to rest in the refrigerator for at least 1 hour and up to 24 hours.

3. Make the soup: In a large pot, combine the vegetable broth, dashima, and dried shiitakes and bring to a boil over high heat. Reduce the heat and cook for about 20 minutes.

4. Remove the dashima and mushrooms. Slice the dashima into ribbons. Discard the shiitake stems and slice the caps into thin

recipe continues

pieces. Return the dashima and mushrooms to the broth, along with the shallot, potato, and scallions. Cook over low heat until the potatoes are fork-tender, an additional 15 minutes.

5. Make the sauce: In a small bowl, mix together the gochugaru, soy sauce, gochujang, sesame oil, and maple syrup. Stir the sauce into the broth. Reduce the heat to a simmer.

6. Remove the dough from the refrigerator. Knead the dough for 2 to 3 minutes, then divide it into four equal portions, so that each portion easily fits within the palm of your hands. Take one piece of dough in your hands and knead it to make it pliable.

7. Over the rim of the soup pot, begin stretching the dough very slowly and gently, so that it becomes thin enough to see through and naturally tears apart. Drop a torn piece into the pot of soup. Once you've torn all the dough in your hand, use the remaining portions of dough until your pot is filled with the desired amount of torn noodles.

8. Note that the starch from the dough will thicken the soup. Keep an eye on the broth to make sure it does not thicken too much. If it does, simply add a little water or vegetable broth to thin it out.

9. Wrap up any remaining dough you may have and place it in the refrigerator or freezer for future use.

KONG NAMUL
(콩나물 라면 · Bean Sprout) CONSOMMÉ RAMEN

SERVES 4

DIFFICULTY: Practice
makes perfect

ALLERGENS: GFO, NF

1 cup bean sprouts,
  tails removed

2-inch square of dashima
  (see page 29)

4 teaspoons agar-agar
  (see Note)

2 (2-ounce) packages
  ramen noodles
  (or 5-ounce packages
  of gluten-free ramen
  noodles)

2 teaspoons salt

1 scallion, chopped

1 Korean green chili, thinly
  sliced

Kimchi, for serving

My father's go-to "I don't know what to make" dish for me and my brother while we were growing up was always *kong namul guk* (bean sprout soup). It was one of the soups my brother and I would eat with a bowl of rice and good kimchi. I always thought the loveliest thing about the soup was how clear the broth was, which was why I was determined to turn it into a consommé (a French technique that results in the clearest of broths). In honor of my father, the noodle king, I make this soup with ramen noodles.

1. In a large pot, combine the bean sprouts, dashima, and 8 cups water. Bring to a boil, then reduce the heat to medium and cook for about 1 hour.

2. Set a mesh sieve over a medium pot. Pour the liquid through a sieve into the pot. Discard the dashima, but reserve the bean sprouts.

3. Place the pot of broth over medium-high heat. Stir in the agar-agar and bring to a boil. Stir constantly, until the liquid starts to thicken, about 1 minute. Remove from the heat.

4. Place the pot of broth in the refrigerator until it sets like gelatin, about 1 hour.

5. Cut the jelled broth into large cubes and place the cubes into a freezer-safe container. Make sure that the cubes are not touching one another, as they will be difficult to separate when they are frozen. Allow the cubes to freeze for at least 12 hours.

recipe continues

6. When the cubes are completely frozen, take the container out of the freezer and allow the cubes to sit at room temperature in the containers until they have thawed enough to remove.

7. Line a large mesh sieve with cheesecloth (or use coffee filters if you don't have cheesecloth) and set over a small pot. Place as many cubes as you can into the sieve and allow them to melt right through the sieve and into the pot. This liquid is your consommé. Discard the dried-out "shells" of broth cubes and repeat until all the cubes have melted.

8. Bring the consommé to a boil and add the ramen noodles. Using your chopsticks or a fork, as the noodles cook, pull them up and out of the hot liquid for a few seconds every 30 or so seconds. Cook until the noodles are al dente, 4 to 5 minutes.

9. Add the cooked bean sprouts, salt, scallion, and green chili to the pot and cook for 1 more minute before serving with kimchi.

NOTES

Agar-agar is a gelatin made from seaweed. Because regular gelatin is often derived from animal products, agar-agar provides a great plant-based alternative. It's also a good source of nutrients like iron, fiber, and manganese. And don't worry—it's tasteless!

TTEOKBOKKI ARRABBIATA

SERVES 4

DIFFICULTY: Easy

ALLERGENS: GFO, NF

1 tablespoon extra-virgin olive oil

1 red bell pepper, chopped

1 Korean red chili or serrano chili, chopped

4 cloves garlic, minced

¼ cup chopped red onions

1 carrot, chopped

½ zucchini, diced

1 teaspoon salt

1 teaspoon freshly ground black pepper

2 cups roughly chopped tomatoes

21 ounces (600 g) tube-shaped garraetteok (see page 32), fresh or frozen

1 tablespoon gochugaru (see page 28)

1 tablespoon gochujang (see page 26)

½ cup Mushroom Dashi (page 39)

½ cup chopped cabbage

2 scallions, chopped

Tteokbokki, a popular Korean street food, is made with cylindrical tubes of *garraetteok* coated in a thick, fiery sauce that causes inconvenient amounts of perspiration in public settings. This is why I sometimes call them "firecakes." After creating my Angry Penne Pasta (page 185), I thought the sauce could easily be modified to make a sweeter and more complex base for *tteokbokki*, and I was right. While you won't ever find *tteokbokki* like these at any Korean food stall, they are every bit as heated as their namesake.

1. In a medium pot, combine the olive oil, bell pepper, Korean red chili, garlic, red onion, carrot, zucchini, salt, and black pepper. Cook over medium-high heat until the onions become translucent, about 2 minutes.

2. Add the tomatoes and a pinch more salt and continue cooking, stirring occasionally, until the tomatoes begin to break down, about 5 minutes.

3. Add the garraetteok, gochugaru, and gochujang and stir until the rice cakes are evenly coated in sauce. Add the mushroom dashi. Bring the sauce to a boil, then reduce the heat and simmer for about 3 minutes if fresh or 5 minutes if frozen, until the rice cakes are tender.

4. Stir in the chopped cabbage and scallions. Cook for 1 more minute. The sauce should be thick from the starch of the rice cakes.

BAR and STREET FOODS

My favorite Korean restaurant of all time is actually a bar in Niles, Illinois—a small suburb of Chicago. Not open until 7 p.m., its menu offers a variety of some of my favorite dishes—*tteokbokki*, *kimbap*, and tofu kimchi. The Korean bar and street food scene emerged to fill a need—the average midlevel professionals often finished their days long after the dinner hour, and after a grueling day of work, nothing says "You're gonna be okay" better than a bottle of soju (a Korean spirit) and salty comfort food. The recipes in this chapter are dishes you might find at a food stall amid the whirring lights of Gangnam or inside a low-key bar in Itaewon. Others are things you'd find at a bar here in the United States but with a bit of "Korean flair."

APPA'S DAUGHTER

My father and I haven't always had the easiest relationship. He is naturally aloof, and therefore affection—verbal or otherwise—is a bit like a foreign language to him. For most of my life, we got along by tacitly agreeing to stay out of each other's way. It got to the point that just the sound of my father's footsteps or his voice could cause me anxiety.

Being the first child of an immigrant also created a weird dynamic between us. As I began to speak English fluently, I quickly assumed the role of "translator." At nine years old, I was the one calling and asking to speak with customer service, interacting with the store clerk

at the cash register, or signing permission slips from school. At some point, before I was even a teenager, I witnessed how helpless my father seemed in the big American world, and as a result, *I* became the adult.

As my father grew older, I began to worry about how much time I had left to spend with him. I tried harder to find ways to hurdle the gap that had developed between us over the years. I never dreamed that running would be the thing that helped bring us together.

Despite a lifetime of hating running, in 2017, I signed up for my first marathon—the Chicago Marathon. My mother was in Korea, so she wasn't able to cheer me on from the sidelines. My father, though, insisted on taking the 5:30 a.m. bus with a group of people he didn't even know from a local Korean community organization, just so he could cheer for me at Mile 20. To be honest, I didn't want him there. Without my mom there to take care of him, it would be up to me to make

sure he was where he needed to be at the right time, and I already had twenty-six miles to worry about. I chatted with him on the phone the night before, hoping to dissuade him from coming.

"Daddy, are you sure you want to come? You really don't need to . . . I mean, it's so early in the morning and it might get cold . . ."

"Yah, I see you at Mile 20! Oh sure sure sure, I will be there! How long you think you going to take?"

I remember a lot of things from my first marathon: the fireflies stomping around my stomach while I waited for the starting pistol to pop off, my husband jogging with me through a bit of Chinatown before I waved him off in overheated delirium, and the handful of aspirins I downed at Mile 18 when the smooth Chicago pavement started to feel like shattered glass. But, my most memorable moment during the Chicago Marathon was at Mile 20. When I heard "Jo-ENNE!!" and saw my father's face split into a smile that struck my ribs open with a gong. My seventy-two-year-old father with prostate cancer and a bad back tried his best to jog next to me, handed me the water bottle he had been holding in his hands since the crack of dawn, for nearly six hours, so that he wouldn't miss this five-second window to pass it to me while asking, "Do you want me to run with you? Can I run with you?"

I left my father behind at Mile 20, wiping tears and sweat from my face, because in that moment, my dad, the one I'd spent my entire life protecting with my English-speaking shield, wanted to be and *was* stronger than his American daughter.

Three years later, I finally ceded to my father's yearly invitations to join him for a family trip to Korea. We spent ten days trying to cram in two decades' worth of visits I'd neglected to make. One day we decided to head to one of the nearby national parks, home to one of the most famous Buddhist temples and Buddhist monks.

2017 Chicago Marathon

Naejangsan National Park

We had driven hours to get to Naejangsan National Park and finally pulled into a large parking lot next to what appeared to be a sizable pond at the foot of a long and winding path that led up to the temple. We had packed some *kimbap* (Korean rolls) and *tteok* (rice cakes) left over from the feast we had had the night before, and we decided to refuel before climbing to the top of the sprawling hill.

Though my sister-in-law warned me that the *kimbap* we'd packed would no longer be tasty, they looked too inviting to pass up. I took one bite and instantly recalled that my sister-in-law is rarely wrong when it comes to food. Not wanting to waste it, though, I canvassed our little troupe to see who might eat my leftovers. Daddy stood at the edge of the pond, his left hand entwined in the strap of the camcorder I had bought him for this trip. A collar of happy trees, their boughs bright green and heavy with summer's promise, supplied a shaded spot from which he could consider the dark reflections that shimmered on the surface.

Clutching the half-eaten *kimbap*, I skipped over to him. Giggling, and before he could say anything, I fit the small *kimbap* in his empty hand and skipped away, leaving a ribbon of pink laughter in my wake. He called after me, "What? I don't want this!" But I just laughed harder, reveling in how perfectly the uneaten piece of food fit inside my father's curved fingers, how colorful it looked against his walnut skin and beneath the cool eaves of the shifting trees, how I was spending the entire day with my dad in a place that made me feel more like his little girl than any place on Earth.

KIMBAP
(김밥 · Seaweed Rice Roll)

MAKES 4 ROLLS
(8 TO 10 PIECES
EACH)

DIFFICULTY: Easy
ALLERGENS: GFO, NF

1 tablespoon plus
   ½ teaspoon sesame oil

2 carrots, julienned

1 teaspoon salt

2 cups cooked rice

½ tablespoon rice vinegar

4 sheets roasted seaweed

1 cup Kale Moochim
   (page 85)

1 cup Bulgogi (page 235)

4 strips danmuji (see Note)

1 Gyerranmari (page 97),
   cut into long ⅓-inch-
   wide strips

Growing up, we took lots of road trips and enjoyed the hospitality of Motel 6s across the Midwest.

Wherever we went, one thing we always had in the car with us was *kimbap*—a favorite Korean snack that's made by rolling rice with some roasted seaweed, together with some vegetables. My *hahlmuhnee* would spend hours filling each roll with bright yellow daikon, deep green spinach, carrots, and pieces of *gyerranmari*. Then she'd wrap them in foil to make sure they didn't get stale during the long ride in the backseat.

I hated them.

For me, *kimbap* was just an irritating reminder of my "Koreanness," when all I wanted to be was "American." I wanted to trade in my Korean long underwear for a pair of jeans from the Gap, and the *kimbap* my grandmother labored over for a Happy Meal.

There isn't a thing I wouldn't give, today, to have one more chance to peel back the foil on one of my *hahlmuhnee*'s *kimbap*s.

1. In a small skillet, heat 1 tablespoon of the sesame oil over medium-high heat. Add the carrots and ½ teaspoon of the salt and sauté until the carrots just begin to get soft, about 2 minutes. Set the carrots aside and let them cool.

2. In a large bowl, stir together the rice, vinegar, and remaining ½ teaspoon salt.

3. Set a sheet of seaweed shiny-side down. Spoon ½ cup of the rice onto the seaweed. Using wet fingers, spread the rice out evenly over three-quarters of the sheet of seaweed, leaving the top empty.

recipe continues

Danmuji is yellow or white pickled daikon radish. You can find it in the refrigerated food aisle of an Asian grocery store. Sometimes it will come in a thick log, which you will have to slice into thinner pieces. Most times, however, you can find them precut to be used in making *kimbap*.

4. Add the carrots, kale moochim, bulgogi, danmuji, and gyerranmari, one by one, to the center of the rice, just like filling a burrito (only, in this case, it's all right to have the ends sticking out). There should still be about ½ inch of rice on either side of your vegetables.

5. Lift the bottom part of the seaweed up and roll it over the vegetables in the center. Continue rolling until the roll is sealed. Set the roll aside sealed-side down. You can wet the seaweed if it has trouble sticking, but I've found that if you just allow the roll to sit for a minute on the seal, that does the trick. Repeat to make the remaining rolls.

6. Drop a few drops of sesame oil into your hands and coat the rolls with the remaining ½ teaspoon sesame oil. Slice the rolls into ½-inch-thick slices using a very sharp knife. If the knife gets sticky, dip it in water before continuing to cut the rolls.

OMMA'S EGG ROLLS

**MAKES 30 TO
40 EGG ROLLS**
(depending on
how much stuffing
you use for each one)

DIFFICULTY: Medium

ALLERGENS: NF

1 (16-ounce) block
    extra-firm tofu

1 tablespoon extra-virgin
    olive oil, plus more as
    needed

1 tablespoon sesame oil

2 cloves garlic, roughly
    chopped

¼ red onion, roughly
    chopped

2 scallions, roughly
    chopped

1 portobello mushroom,
    roughly chopped

1 cup Baechu Kimchi
    (page 117)

1 tablespoon soy sauce

1 carrot, roughly chopped

1 stalk celery, roughly
    chopped

1 Yukon Gold potato,
    roughly chopped

1 teaspoon salt

½ teaspoon freshly ground
    black pepper

1 cup roughly chopped
    cabbage

2½ ounces (70g) sweet
    potato vermicelli
    (about 1 handful),
    cooked according to
    package directions

I will never forget how my father waited patiently on the living room sofa as my mother frantically fried dozens and dozens of egg rolls for his work holiday party. It was around midnight, because my dad worked the night shift. It was the one time of the year that my father, who was probably the most introverted and socially awkward employee at the United States Postal Service, became the most popular man at the office. The holiday party wasn't complete without my mom's egg rolls. I've used my mother's egg rolls to win over grumpy teachers and colleagues alike, and even my own mother-in-law declared them to be worthy of attempted bribery.

1. Press the tofu for about 10 minutes to remove excess liquid (see Note, page 101).

2. In a large skillet, heat the olive oil and sesame oil over medium-high heat. Add the garlic, onion, scallions, mushroom, and kimchi. Season with salt and pepper and cook until the onions turn translucent, 2 to 3 minutes.

3. Add the soy sauce to deglaze the pan and stir the vegetables so they are evenly coated with sauce. Remove the onion/mushroom mixture from the pan and place in a large bowl.

4. Add a little more olive oil to the pan and then add the carrots, celery, and potatoes. Season with the salt and pepper and cook until the carrots soften, about 3 minutes. Transfer the carrot/celery/potato mixture to the large bowl with the onion/mushroom mixture.

5. Add a little more olive oil to the pan and cook the cabbage until it begins to soften, about 2 minutes. Transfer the cabbage to the bowl of vegetables.

recipe and ingredients continue

1 (16-ounce) package egg roll wrappers

About 4 cups vegetable oil, for frying

Sweet and sour sauce, for serving

6. In a large food processor (or in batches if necessary), combine all the sautéed vegetables and the cooked vermicelli. Pulse 7 to 10 times, until the vegetables are chopped (but not ground into a paste). Return the vegetables to the large bowl.

7. Pat dry the pressed tofu and crumble it into the large bowl of vegetables, using a fork. Place the bowl in the refrigerator until you are ready to wrap the egg rolls. Season with salt.

8. Place an egg roll wrapper on a work surface so that it is positioned as a diamond (not a square) with a point facing you. Using the back of a small spoon or your fingers, wet the edges with a little water. Place two healthy spoonfuls of filling onto the wrapper. Lift the bottom corner up and over the filling and press the corner down to seal. Then, bring both the left and right corners into the center and, while holding them in place, roll upward until the top is sealed, just like an envelope. Repeat to make more rolls until the filling is used up.

9. Pour 4 inches of vegetable oil into a deep fryer or large cast-iron pan. Heat the oil to about 350°F (use a thermometer or test by throwing a little bit of leftover filling into the oil—if it immediately sizzles, you are ready to fry). Line a plate with paper towels and have nearby.

10. Working in batches of two to three at a time (do not crowd the pan), add the egg rolls to the hot oil and cook both sides until they are a light golden brown, about 3 minutes on each side. Drain them on the paper towel–lined plate.

11. When all egg rolls have been fried, fry them again for about 30 seconds on each side. This time, you don't need to worry about overcrowding.

12. Serve plain or with sweet and sour sauce.

DOOBOO KIMCHI
(두부김치 · Tofu and Kimchi)

SERVES 4

DIFFICULTY: Medium

ALLERGENS: GFO, NF

1 (16-ounce) block medium-firm tofu

1½ tablespoons extra-virgin olive oil

2 large trumpet mushrooms, sliced into ⅛-inch-thick pieces (see Note)

Salt

½ tablespoon plus 1 teaspoon sesame oil

½ large onion, julienned

3 cloves garlic, minced

1 teaspoon salt

1 teaspoon freshly ground black pepper

2 cups Baechu Kimchi (page 117), roughly chopped

¼ cup plus 1 tablespoon Spicy Gochujang Dressing (page 51)

1 scallion, chopped

1 Korean green chili, thinly sliced

1 tablespoon toasted sesame seeds

This is one of my favorite ways to eat kimchi—stir-fried in a sweet and spicy sauce, with a little tofu to sop it up. I used to order *dooboo kimchi* at the local Korean bar I went to all the time before going vegan. It's one of those dishes that you order when you're feeling pretty salty with your boss or you're about to throw down with your significant other for failing to empty the dishwasher for the thirty-seventh time in a row, because it's spicy and sweet and savory and leaves a good kinda burning in the pit of your stomach.

1. In a small pot, bring 4 cups water to a boil over high heat. Add the whole block of tofu gently to the pot. Cook the tofu for 8 to 9 minutes.

2. Meanwhile, in a large nonstick skillet, heat 1 tablespoon of the olive oil over medium-high heat. Add the sliced mushrooms in a single layer and cook until both sides are evenly browned, 7 to 8 minutes. Add a pinch of salt and then remove the mushrooms from the pan and set aside. Do not cover the mushrooms. Hold on to the pan.

3. Remove the tofu from the boiling water and gently slice the block in half. If the center is still cool to the touch, place both halves back into the boiling water and cook until the centers are warm, about 2 more minutes. When the tofu is completely cooked, pat the block(s) dry with a clean kitchen towel or paper towel. Slice the block into ⅓-inch-thick pieces. You should have 8 to 9 pieces of tofu. Set them aside.

4. Set the reserved large nonstick skillet over medium heat. Add ½ tablespoon of sesame oil and the remaining ½ tablespoon olive oil

recipe continues

The trumpet mushrooms should be sliced lengthwise into the same thickness as you would thickly slice pork belly—which is what they are replacing. Trust me, it works.

to the pan. When the oil is hot, add the onion and garlic and cook until the onions turn translucent and the garlic starts to brown, about 2 minutes.

5. Add the baechu kimchi to the pan and continue to sauté all the vegetables until the kimchi starts to brown, 2 to 3 minutes. Add ¼ cup of the gochujang dressing to the pan and stir all the ingredients until they are evenly coated with the sauce. Cook for an additional 2 minutes.

6. Add the scallion and chili, sprinkle with the toasted sesame seeds, and drizzle with the remaining 1 teaspoon sesame oil.

7. To serve, place the sautéed kimchi mixture in the center of a round platter and arrange the tofu slices in a circle along the edge of your platter. Drizzle with the remaining 1 tablespoon gochujang dressing.

KOREAN-STYLE SUPPLI
(Rice Balls)

**MAKES 7 OR
8 SUPPLI**

DIFFICULTY: Medium
ALLERGENS: GFO, NF

Vegetable oil

3 cups cooked rice

2 cloves garlic, minced

¼ red onion, finely diced

1 carrot, diced

½ cup corn kernels, cooked

½ cup peas, cooked

Gyerranmari (page 97)
(optional), chopped

3 teaspoons salt

1 teaspoon freshly ground
black pepper

1 teaspoon sesame oil

2 tablespoons potato
starch

½ cup plant milk

1 cup panko bread crumbs
or gluten-free bread
crumbs

1 slice vegan cheese
(optional), torn into
7 to 8 pieces

When people ask me why I started cooking, I'll usually say that it was to be able to eat vegan. But the truth is, I started cooking a lot for a slightly embarrassing reason: to impress a man. I know. Totally lame. When I started dating my husband, Anthony, I learned how to make different pasta dishes and also got serious about baking to satisfy his sweet tooth.

When I met Anthony's father, Roberto, it became clear rather quickly that Roberto, originally from Rome, was the chef of the Molinaro family. Though he spent most of his life on a race course, tennis court, or soccer field, cooking was also second nature to Roberto. One of his favorite dishes was *suppli*.

Many people think of arancini when I describe how risotto is shaped into a ball, breaded, and deep-fried. To be sure, *suppli* is very similar to arancini. But the Roman version of this deep-fried deliciousness is smaller and shaped like a large egg, not a softball. The classic *suppli* is made with a marinara-based risotto, but one day I had some leftover Korean fried rice and thought how fun it would be to "*suppli*" it.

They turned out so perfectly, I daresay Roberto would be pleased. I know his son was.

1. In a large skillet, heat 1 tablespoon of the vegetable oil over high heat until very hot. Add the rice and fry until the rice starts to brown, 4 to 5 minutes. Remove the rice from the pan.

2. Add a little more vegetable oil to the pan if needed, then add the garlic, red onion, carrot, corn, peas, gyerranmari (if using), 1 teaspoon of the salt, and the pepper and cook until the onions

recipe continues

start to become translucent, 2 to 3 minutes. Return the rice to the pan, mix everything together, and cook for an additional 1 to 2 minutes. Add the sesame oil and stir.

3. Set the rice aside and let it cool before refrigerating it for at least 4 hours and up to 24 hours.

4. When ready to make the rice balls, set up a dredging station: Place three shallow bowls on your work surface. In one, mix together the potato starch and 1 teaspoon of the salt. In the second, add the plant milk. In the third, add the panko plus the remaining 1 teaspoon salt.

5. Spoon 2 to 3 tablespoons of rice into the palm of one hand and, using both hands, shape the rice into an oval, about the size and shape of a large egg. If desired, before shaping the rice, add a bit of vegan cheese to the center and finish shaping.

6. Once shaped, coat the rice ball first in the potato starch. Tap off any excess starch before dipping it in the plant milk. Next, coat the rice ball with panko by rolling it gently in the panko bowl. Set the rice ball aside on a baking sheet. Repeat with remainder of the rice.

7. Pour 4 inches of vegetable oil into a medium pot. Heat the oil to about 350°F (I like to use a thermometer to be sure, but you can also check to see whether the oil is ready by flicking a bread crumb into it. If it sizzles immediately, you know you're good).

8. Working in batches (don't crowd the pot), gently drop the rice balls into the oil. Cook for about 2 minutes and then flip the rice ball and cook for an additional 2 minutes to make sure it is evenly cooked. Remove the rice ball from the oil with a slotted spoon and set it on a wire rack to drain any excess oil.

BULGOGI WASABI MELT

**MAKES
2 SANDWICHES**

DIFFICULTY: Easy

ALLERGENS: GFO, NF

2 tablespoons hummus

1½ teaspoons wasabi powder

2 tablespoons vegan butter

4 slices of your favorite sandwich bread (the Milk Bread on page 73 is perfect for this; use gluten-free bread to keep this recipe gluten-free)

1 tablespoon extra-virgin olive oil

2 slices vegan cheese

¼ cup julienned red onion

½ cucumber, sliced lengthwise into ¼-inch-thick slices

1 cup cooked Bulgogi (page 235)

Before I went vegan, I had ONE go-to sandwich that was ALWAYS a crowd pleaser—even with my parents, who generally are not fans of non-Korean cuisine. It was my roast beef wasabi melt. This sandwich returns my claim to sandwich glory. If you have leftover Bulgogi (page 235), you have no choice but to make this sandwich. Actually, this sandwich is so good, just go ahead and make some bulgogi now!

1. In a small bowl, mix together the hummus and wasabi powder.

2. Spread the vegan butter onto one side of each slice of bread. Spread the wasabi hummus on the other side of each slice of bread.

3. In a large nonstick skillet, heat the olive oil over medium-low heat. Place two slices of bread, butter-side down, into the pan. To each slice, quickly add 1 slice of vegan cheese, a few slivers of red onion, two slices of cucumber, and ½ cup of bulgogi.

4. Top the sandwiches with the other slices of bread, butter-side up. Press down on the sandwiches with a spatula. Cover the pan with a lid and let the sandwiches cook until the bottoms are golden brown, 3 to 4 minutes. Gently flip the sandwiches and repeat, until both sides are golden brown.

KOREAN BBQ BLACK BEAN BURGERS

MAKES 4 BURGERS

DIFFICULTY: Medium

ALLERGENS: GFO, NFO

FOR THE SIMPLE RED CABBAGE SLAW

1 cup julienned red cabbage

1 carrot, julienned

¼ cup julienned red onion

1 tablespoon white wine vinegar

1 tablespoon yellow mustard

1 tablespoon maple syrup

1 teaspoon salt

1 teaspoon freshly ground black pepper

FOR THE BURGERS

1 (15-ounce) can black beans, undrained

1 tablespoon extra-virgin olive oil

3 cloves garlic, chopped

1 large onion, sliced into rings

2 teaspoons salt

1 teaspoon freshly ground black pepper

5 tablespoons Omma's Korean BBQ Sauce (page 45)

½ cup day-old cooked rice

¼ cup chopped walnuts (see Note)

One of the questions I get asked a lot when people find out my diet is plant based is whether I miss meat. The truth is that during the first year I did miss chowing down on a fried chicken sandwich or a juicy burger. In fact, before I went vegan, I used to have this rule for myself: If I had to travel for work, I was allowed to order a burger and fries through room service the first night. Going vegan meant eliminating that little "treat." There were other days throughout that first year when I looked longingly at the grill—Memorial Day, Labor Day, Independence Day—for the sight of a delicious cheeseburger.

So, one of the first things I aimed to perfect was a black bean burger that could be my new "delicious burger" on days when my cravings were strong. Some black bean burgers can be super mushy, crumbly, dry, and flavorless. After a few years of experimentation, I came up with a recipe (borrowing a few tips from the fabulous website Serious Eats) that guarantees a moist and flavorful black bean burger that won't fall into your lap after the first bite.

1. Preheat the oven to 475°F.

2. Make the simple red cabbage slaw: In a large bowl, mix together the cabbage, carrot, onion, vinegar, mustard, maple syrup, salt, and pepper. Set the slaw in the refrigerator until you are ready to assemble your burgers.

3. Make the burgers: Reserving ¼ cup of the liquid, drain the beans and spread them onto a baking sheet in a single layer. Place them in the oven and roast until the beans are dried out and cracked, 11 to 13 minutes. Let the beans cool for about 10 minutes.

recipe and ingredients continue

1 tablespoon plus ½ cup
    potato starch

½ cup panko bread
    crumbs

2 tablespoons
    vegetable oil

4 slices vegan cheese

4 hamburger buns (use
    gluten free buns to keep
    this recipe gluten-free)

NOTES

You can substitute
sunflower seeds for the
walnuts to keep this
recipe nut-free.

4. Meanwhile, in a small skillet, heat the olive oil over medium-high heat. When the oil is hot, add the garlic, onion, salt, and pepper. Cook until the onions are translucent and charred around the edges, about 4 minutes. Add 2 tablespoons of the barbecue sauce. Reduce the heat and allow the onions to cook down and caramelize for about 10 minutes.

5. Once the black beans are cool, transfer them to a food processor and pulse until they reach a pebble-like consistency. Dump the beans into a large bowl, along with the rice.

6. Add the walnuts to the food processor, along with half the caramelized onions and the remaining 3 tablespoons barbecue sauce. Pulse until the nuts reach a small pebble-like consistency.

7. Add the mixture to the bowl with the beans and rice and mix, packing firmly together, until a "dough" forms. Divide the dough into 4 portions. Shape each into a patty about the circumference of your burger buns and about ½ inch thick—the thinner they are, the less mushy they will be.

8. Coat each of the patties with a little potato starch (do not overcoat, as this will dry them out). Spoon a little bit of the reserved black bean liquid over both sides of the patties to make them sticky. Coat the patties with an even layer of panko.

9. In a large skillet (or on a griddle), heat the vegetable oil over medium-high heat. Add the burgers and cook each side until golden brown, about 2 minutes on each side. Add a slice of vegan cheese to the top of each burger and cover the pan. Continue to cook the patties until the cheese begins to melt, about 1 minute.

10. Assemble the burgers on the buns. Top with the remaining caramelized onions and slaw. Add more barbecue sauce for extra sauciness.

KOREAN-STYLE TOAST

SERVES 2

DIFFICULTY:
Practice makes
perfect

ALLERGENS: GFO, NF

**FOR THE CHEESY
GYERRANMARI**

1 cup egg replacer
(preferably JUST Egg)

½ teaspoon salt

Pinch of black salt
(optional)

½ teaspoon freshly ground
black pepper

1 scallion, chopped

⅛ red bell pepper, finely
diced

1 tablespoon extra-virgin
olive oil

1 slice vegan cheese,
halved

**FOR THE CARROT
AND CABBAGE SLAW**

1 carrot, julienned

½ cup julienned red
cabbage

½ English cucumber,
julienned

1 tablespoon yellow
mustard

1 tablespoon maple syrup

1 teaspoon white wine
vinegar

Pinch of salt

½ teaspoon freshly ground
black pepper

If you visit Korea anytime soon, you'll notice adorable little "toast cafes" popping up like dandelions throughout the country's more urban areas. They remind me a lot of the cafes in Italy, with their flashy displays of panini neatly stacked together like a column of small books. "Toast" in Korea, however, does not refer to what we typically view as toast in the United States—that is, pieces of bread placed into a toaster, slathered with some type of spread. Rather, "toast" in Korea often refers to a slice of bread that's been fried on a griddle, like a grilled cheese sandwich. It usually contains egg, cheese, and some kind of sweetness (like jam). Here, I use my basic *gyerranmari* recipe with a pinch of black salt (which gives the egg replacer a more sulfur-forward "eggy" flavor), along with some vegan cheese and jam. I made this for my husband, and he proclaimed it the best sandwich he's ever eaten.

1. Make the gyerranmari: In a small bowl or measuring cup, mix together the egg replacer, salt, black salt (if using), black pepper, scallion, and red bell pepper.

2. In an 8-inch nonstick skillet, heat ½ tablespoon of the olive oil over medium heat. Add half of the "egg" mixture to the pan until the mixture reaches the edges of the pan (if it does not, your pan is too large).

3. Cook until the edges start to bubble, about 2 minutes. Using a silicone spatula, gently pull the edges away from the pan and tilt the pan so the uncooked egg mixture reaches the edges of the pan.

4. Add ½ slice vegan cheese to the middle of the egg "crepe." Cook for another 2 minutes, then use your spatula to lift the right edge of the crepe and begin rolling it to the left (just like you would roll a sheet of wrapping paper), until the entire crepe has been rolled.

recipe and ingredients continue

8 slices sandwich bread
(use gluten-free bread
to keep this recipe
gluten-free)

2 tablespoons vegan
butter

2 tablespoons maple syrup

2 tablespoons jam or fruit
preserves

2 slices vegan cheese

5. Add half of the remaining amount of egg mixture to the pan, so that the uncooked mixture touches the very end of the "rolled" portion. Repeat steps 3 and 4 (adding the second piece of cheese).

6. Add the remaining uncooked egg mixture to the pan and repeat steps 3 and 4 (without cheese). When you are finished, you should have what looks like a well-done omelet, about 8 inches long by 3 inches wide. Set it aside and let it cool. When cooled, cut the gyerranmari in half so that you have two portions, roughly the size of the palm of your hand.

7. Make the carrot and cabbage slaw: In a medium bowl, mix together the carrot, red cabbage, cucumber, mustard, maple syrup, vinegar, salt, and pepper until all of the vegetables are evenly coated.

8. Assemble the sandwiches: Spread one side of each of 4 slices of bread with the butter. Spoon ½ tablespoon of maple syrup onto each buttered side of bread and spread it out evenly with the back of your spoon.

9. Spread the jam or fruit preserves onto one side of the other 4 slices of bread.

10. Set a large nonstick skillet over medium-high heat. Place 2 slices of the buttered bread, butter-side down, in the pan. To each slice add 1 slice of vegan cheese and one piece of the gyerranmari. Top the gyerranmari with 1 slice of jammed bread, jam-side up. Add another jammed slice, this time jam-side down, and top with the slaw. Top the slaw with the 2 final slices of buttered bread, butter-side up.

11. Press the entire sandwich down with a spatula and cook until the bottom of the sandwich is golden brown, about 3 minutes. Carefully flip the sandwich, using two spatulas or one spatula and your hand to keep the sandwich together (if it falls apart, you can always reassemble it in the pan while the bottom is cooking). Cook until the bottom of the sandwich is golden brown, an additional 3 minutes.

CHEESY HOTTEOK
(치즈 호떡 · Fried Stuffed Pancakes)

While my father has an undeniable sweet tooth, I like salty foods. Here's the classic *hotteok*, turned on its head, stuffed with a creamy, cheesy filling. Pair this with a traditional *hottoek* and you've got yourself a full meal plus dessert!

2¼ teaspoons active dry yeast

1 teaspoon sugar

¼ cup warm water (warmed to between 100°F to 110°F)

2 cups all-purpose flour

½ cup sweet white rice flour

1 teaspoon salt

1 tablespoon vegetable oil

1¼ cups plant milk, warmed to between 100°F to 110°F

1 Yukon Gold potato, boiled

1 carrot, roasted or boiled

3 slices vegan cheese

Pinch of salt

Vegetable oil or other neutral oil, for frying

1 onion, sliced into ¼-inch-thick rings

1. In a small bowl, combine the yeast, sugar, and warm water. Set the mixture aside until it begins to foam, about 10 minutes.

2. In a large bowl, combine the flour, rice flour, salt, and oil. Add the yeast mixture and then slowly add the plant milk. Stir with a wooden spoon or chopsticks until a dough begins to form.

3. Lightly oil your hands and knead the dough for about 5 minutes. Add flour if the dough becomes impossible to work with, but expect it to be tacky. Shape the dough into a very sticky ugly ball with your hands.

4. Place the dough ball into a greased bowl. Cover the bowl with plastic wrap or the lid of a pot and set it aside in a warm place until it doubles in size, about 1 hour. Then punch down the dough gently to release the gas and set it aside in a covered bowl once more until it again doubles in size, an additional 20 to 30 minutes.

5. In a small bowl, mash the cooked potato and carrot with the vegan cheese and salt until the potato filling becomes creamy.

6. Once the second proof is complete, divide the dough into 10 equal portions. Take one piece to work with and keep the remaining pieces in the bowl covered with the plastic wrap or lid.

7. Shape the portion of dough into a small ball, then flatten the ball into a disc by using the heels of your hands or a rolling pin. Once the disc is a little larger than the palm of your hand, place the dough on one hand and place 1 generous tablespoon of potato filling right in the center of the disc. Pull the edges of the disc up and over the mound of filling and seal them at the top, pinching together to form a pouch. Roll the pouch between your hands to form a ball. Set aside and cover with a kitchen towel. Repeat with the remaining portions of dough and potato filling.

8. Pour ½ inch of vegetable oil into a large nonstick skillet. Heat the oil over medium-high heat until it is nice and hot (throw a tiny piece of dough into the oil, and if it sizzles, it's ready).

9. Place a couple of slices of onion into the pan and then place a dough ball over them. Using a spatula, press gently down and flatten the dough ball into a thick pancake (making sure not to tear the dough). Cook until golden brown on the bottom and the onions are caramelized, about 3 minutes. Flip, press down gently, and cook until the second side is golden brown, an additional 3 minutes.

SWEET HOTTEOK
(호떡 · Fried Stuffed Pancakes)

MAKES
10 PANCAKES

DIFFICULTY: Medium

2¼ teaspoons active
  dry yeast

1 teaspoon sugar

¼ cup warm water
  (between 100°F to
  110°F)

2 cups all-purpose flour

½ cup sweet white rice
  flour

1 teaspoon salt

1 tablespoon vegetable oil,
  plus more for frying

1¼ cups plant milk,
  warmed to between
  100°F to 110°F

¼ cup pistachios

¼ cup pine nuts

¼ cup pecans

2 tablespoons light brown
  sugar

1 tablespoon sesame seeds

2 teaspoons ground
  cinnamon

1 teaspoon cornstarch

Some of my father's fondest memories are of eating street food. Back when he was little, he often had to survive on beans and whatever plants his family was able to grow in the small plot of land they were allowed to farm. So, you can only imagine what a treat it was for him when he got to close his hands around a piping hot piece of fried dough, still glistening with oil. He told me once that *hottoek* was his favorite thing to eat. Naturally, I had to make them with my own little twist! For this recipe, you can use any plant milk, but soy and oat milk work best because they have a higher protein content.

1. In a small bowl, combine the yeast, sugar, and warm water. Set the mixture aside until it begins to foam, about 10 minutes.

2. In a large bowl, combine the flour, rice flour, salt, and oil. Add the yeast mixture and then slowly add the plant milk. Stir with a wooden spoon or chopsticks until a dough begins to form.

3. Lightly oil your hands and knead the dough for about 5 minutes. Add flour if the dough becomes impossible to work with, but expect it to be tacky. Shape the dough into a very sticky ugly ball with your hands.

4. Place the dough ball into a large greased bowl. Cover the bowl with plastic wrap or the lid of a pot and set it aside in a warm place until it doubles in size, about 1 hour. Then punch down the dough gently to release the gas and set it aside in a covered bowl once more until it again doubles in size, an additional 20 to 30 minutes.

recipe continues

5. Chop the pistachios, pine nuts, and pecans (you can also pulse them in a food processor a few times) and place them in a small bowl. Add the brown sugar, sesame seeds, cinnamon, cornstarch, and 2 tablespoons water, and combine. Set the nut filling aside.

6. Once the second proof is complete, divide the dough into 10 equal portions. Take one piece to work with and keep the remaining pieces in the bowl covered with the plastic wrap or lid.

7. Shape the portion of dough into a small ball, then flatten the ball into a disc by using the heels of your hands or a rolling pin. Once the disc is a little larger than the palm of your hand, place the dough on one hand and place 1 generous tablespoon of nut filling right in the center of the disc. Pull the edges of the disc up and over the mound of filling and seal them at the top, pinching together to form a pouch. Roll the pouch between your hands to form a ball. Set aside and cover with a kitchen towel. Repeat with the remaining portions of dough and nut filling.

8. Pour ½ inch of vegetable oil into a large nonstick skillet. Heat the oil over medium-high heat until it is nice and hot (throw a tiny piece of dough into the oil, and if it sizzles, it's ready).

9. Working in batches, add one or two dough balls to the hot oil. Using a spatula, press gently down and flatten the dough balls into thick pancakes (making sure not to tear the dough). Cook until the first side is golden brown, about 3 minutes. Flip, press down gently, and cook until the second side is golden brown, an additional 3 minutes.

CURRIED TTEOKBOKKI
(카레떡꼬치 · Rice Cake) SKEWERS

MAKES 12 TO 14 SKEWERS

DIFFICULTY: Medium

ALLERGENS: GFO

FOR THE CURRY PASTE

2 tablespoons extra-virgin olive oil

½ cup chopped onion

¼ cup chopped red bell pepper

3 cloves garlic, minced

¼ cup roasted cashews, soaked for 1 hour, drained

2 teaspoons ground cumin

1½ teaspoons garam masala

¼ teaspoon ground turmeric

1 teaspoon salt

½ teaspoon freshly ground black pepper

1 tablespoon gochujang (see page 26)

1 tablespoon soup (light) soy sauce

A friend of mine whose family is from India gifted me with a small vial of his father's homemade garam masala blend. It smelled fragrant and spicy and chocolaty and I could not wait to go home and do something with it. I rummaged through my fridge and noticed a bag of leftover rice cakes and decided I would try making some *tteokbokki* with a creamy curry sauce. It was absolutely divine. Instead of eating the rice cakes right out of the pan (though sorely tempted), I stuck them on a skewer, just like you would see on the streets of Seoul, and put them on a grill for a little extra "soul."

1. Make the curry paste: In a large skillet, heat the olive oil over medium-high heat until hot and shimmering. Add the chopped onion, bell pepper, garlic, cashews, cumin, garam masala, turmeric, salt, and black pepper. Sauté the vegetables until the onions begin to soften, 2 to 3 minutes.

2. Add the gochujang and stir until the vegetables are evenly coated. Add the soy sauce to deglaze the pan.

3. Scrape the mixture out of the skillet into a high-powered blender and blend until it turns into a smooth paste. Add 1 to 2 tablespoons water, if necessary, to get the blade turning.

4. Prepare the skewers: In the same skillet used for the curry paste, heat the olive oil over medium-high heat. Add the chopped onion, julienned bell peppers, and green chili and sauté until the onions begin to brown, about 5 minutes.

recipe and ingredients continue

1 tablespoon extra-virgin
   olive oil

½ cup chopped red onion

2 tablespoons julienned
   red bell pepper

1 Korean green chili or
   jalapeño, thinly sliced

17 ounces (482g)
   tube-shaped fresh or
   frozen garraetteok
   (see page 32)

1 teaspoon maple syrup

1 cup Vegetable Broth
   (page 43)

5. Add the rice cakes to the pan, along with the curry paste and maple syrup, and stir until all the rice cakes and vegetables are evenly coated with the paste.

6. Add the vegetable broth and bring to a boil. Reduce the heat to a simmer and cook until the rice cakes are completely tender and the liquid has reduced and thickened, 7 to 10 minutes. Let cool enough to handle.

7. Heat a grill pan or grill. When the rice cakes are cool enough to handle, thread 5 rice cakes onto each skewer.

8. Place the skewers on a very hot grill pan or grill topper to achieve a nice char, about 2 minutes on each side. Serve with curry sauce and vegetables from the pan ladled over the skewers.

8

MAIN DISHES

Dooboo is a word I grew up with. It means "tofu." While many view tofu as a substitute for meat, to me, tofu has its own unique role in cuisine and should not be treated as a mere "understudy" to other proteins. Thus, a plate of braised or fried *dooboo* was often on our dining table, and you'll also see multiple dishes featuring *dooboo* on any Korean menu. Indeed, there are whole Korean restaurant concepts that are based entirely on tofu. *Dooboo* comes in multiple different textures, usually categorized by firmness. "Firm" or "extra-firm" tofu comes in a block and has a texture similar to chicken or sausage. "Medium" tofu has more liquid and is therefore softer, having a texture similar to soft cheeses. "Silken" or "soft" tofu is barely firm enough to hold its own shape (sometimes coming in squeezable tubes instead of boxes) and has a texture similar to sour cream or yogurt. The great thing about *dooboo* is that it has almost no discernible taste and therefore easily takes up the flavors surrounding it.

This chapter includes what I like to refer to as "main dishes." Even though, as I've described elsewhere, there are no real "main" dishes on the Korean *bapsang*—everything is a *banchan* satelliting a bowl of rice—the dishes in this chapter are those that you would bring out last, perhaps on your most beautiful platter, with the hope of invoking "oohs" and "aaahs."

APPA

When I was ten years old, my father lugged a massive dinosaur of a typewriter into my bedroom. He showed me how to load a sheet of paper into the worn rubber platen by turning the roller knob on the side. He flipped the "on" switch and the metal strikers locked in abruptly, reminding me of the underbite that revealed itself when he grew frustrated or angry. He showed me how to replace the ribbon when the letters became too faded to read. Then he handed me a small bottle of Wite-Out, together with a handwritten note addressed to his boss.

"You type this up," he said.

I must have typed up hundreds of letters for my dad. The overwhelming majority of these letters consisted of my father's "grievances" over workplace injuries or run-ins with his colleagues. I was intimately familiar with my father's little quirks, the types of things that might make him a social oddity— the way he closed his eyes when he chewed his food, the prevailing scent of kimchi on his breath, the accent that might make him difficult to understand to some or down-

My father (middle) and his two brothers

right unintelligent to others. From his letters, I was able to catch a glimmer of the wide non-Korean world that waited just outside the screen door of our Skokie house, and learned that, sometimes, that world was hostile to those who might appear to be "too different."

The only thing that stood between that world and my father was me and his typewriter.

My parents and their grandson (my nephew)

And I hated it. At first, it was because I'd rather be watching TV or playing with my friends or doing nothing. But over time, as the stack of my father's handwritten letters grew taller, what I really hated was being coerced into documenting my father's humiliation at work, a humiliation sharpened by the fact that my dad had to rely on his ten-year-old daughter to type up his stupid letters.

Of course, it was a small favor to ask, compared with all the little things my father did for us without complaint, from driving to and from friends' houses, picking me up after orchestra rehearsal, dropping off a bag of McDonald's when I had to stay late at school, doling out a $20 bill when I wanted to hang out at the mall, making me and my brother his watery version of *naeng-myun* when Omma was working late and Hahlmuhnee no longer lived with us. But it wasn't so much the imposition on my time; I just didn't want to see my dad being hurt or weak or ashamed, and I resented him for making me a witness to even the vaguest shape of those things.

A few years ago, after some tests came back positive for a potential diagnosis of prostate cancer, my father went in for a biopsy. Two weeks before my father got his biopsy done (unbeknownst to me), I had read a study on prostate cancer in East Asian men. At the time, I had no idea my own father was being tested for cancer. According to the study, the sharp jump in prostate cancer among East Asian men was linked to their increased consumption of red meat. It made no impression on me at the time, as I considered my father to be relatively healthy for a man his age. Within twenty-four hours of his biopsy, he was burning up with a fever and my mother found him unconscious in their bedroom. He was rushed to the emergency room and admitted to the ICU. The doctors confirmed he was in septic shock, and for a few hours he was in a coma.

By the time I made it over to the hospital myself, I was shaking and terrified, thinking of all the different times I'd blown him off when he needed me to help type up a letter, review some document

he'd received from the insurance company, make a phone call to his bank, figure out how to connect his Wi-Fi. I walked into his room in the ICU to see him lying inside a cage of tubes and wires and pulsing machines. My mother left his side, pressed her cool hands against my face as if to coax some life back into my cheeks. I went to him, assuming the spot my mother had just vacated, and took his hand in mine.

"Hi, Daddy," I whispered.

"Joanne," he croaked, "you didn't have to come."

My mother's care shifted from clinical, on the one hand, to nurturing, on the other, as she fielded physicians and nurses and technicians while placing her hands on my father's brow. My parents have always had a thorny marriage—there were many years throughout my childhood during which I felt I was responsible for pulling them both back off the brink of divorce. But there, amid all the tubes and the beeping machines and the sterile white lab coats, my mother gently called "Keun-hyung"—a nickname she'd had for him since I could remember, meaning "Big Big Brother"—and

she pressed her palm against his cheek, as if to collect him from darkness. Later, she confided in me how she'd found Daddy, knocked out on the floor of their bedroom, and her voice was still so jagged and raw, it sliced me open.

Two days later, while my father was still recovering in the ICU from sepsis, his biopsy came back positive for prostate cancer.

I stopped eating meat that same day.

BULGOGI
(불고기 · Grilled Steak)

SERVES 4

DIFFICULTY: Easy

ALLERGENS: GFO, NF

1 cup Soy Curls

3 to 4 dried shiitake
  mushrooms

½ cup Omma's Korean
  BBQ Sauce (page 45)

1 scallion, cut into
  2- to 3-inch lengths

¼ red onion, julienned

¼ cup chopped green bell
  pepper

Oil for grilling

½ tablespoon sesame oil

1 teaspoon toasted
  sesame seeds

Many people believe that Korean food = Korean BBQ and bibimbap. My hope is that with the recipes in this book, you will realize that like all other cuisines, Korean food is more than its most known dishes, in this case, grilled meat and rice bowls. That said, a Korean cookbook—even a vegan one—wouldn't be worth its salt if it did not include some grilled deliciousness. *Bulgogi* translates into "fire meat." It's usually made with flank steak, rib eye, or other cuts of beef. In order to re-create that texture, I use Soy Curls, which are just soybeans that have been cooked and then dehydrated. Soy Curls hold up exceptionally well against the rich and intense flavors of the marinade and the heat of the grill.

1. Soak the Soy Curls in water for at least 1 hour. Drain and squeeze out any excess liquid. At the same time, soak the shiitake mushrooms to rehydrate, then chop.

2. In a large zip-top plastic bag or reusable silicone bag, place the Soy Curls, shiitakes, barbecue sauce, scallions, red onion, and bell pepper. Make sure all the Soy Curls are submerged in the sauce. Place the bag in the refrigerator and marinate for at least 4 hours or up to 24 hours.

3. Preheat a grill or a grill pan (or a cast-iron skillet). Slightly oil the grates or pan. When the grill is hot, place the marinated Soy Curls, mushrooms, scallions, onions, and bell pepper on the grill pan or grill topper, basting with the remaining marinade. Cook until the Soy Curls are slightly charred, about 3 to 4 minutes.

4. Drizzle with the sesame oil and garnish with the sesame seeds before serving.

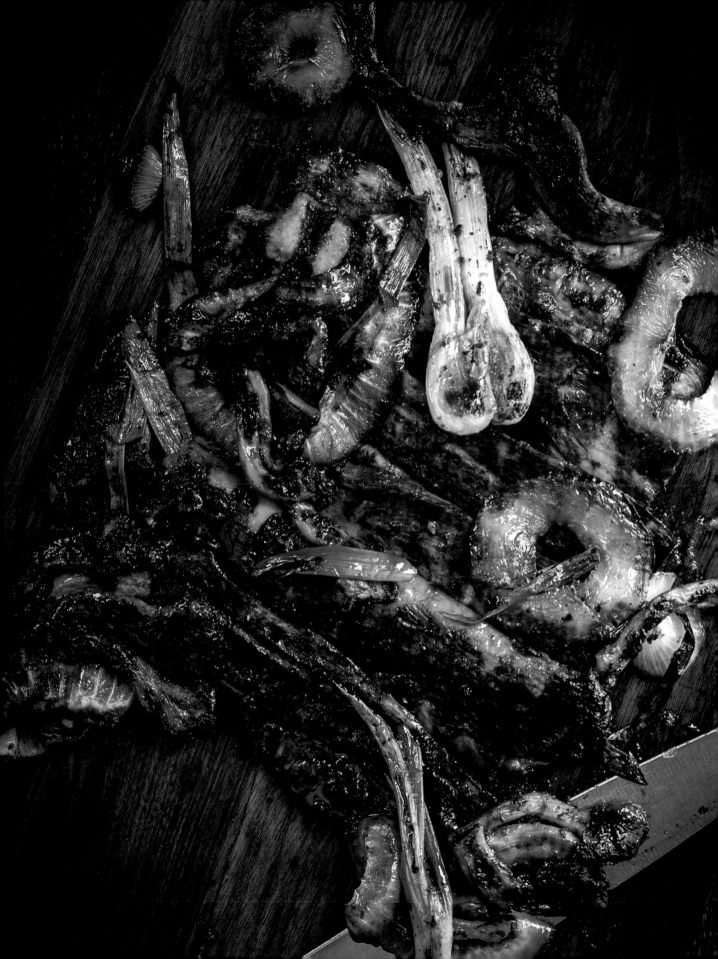

MUSHROOM GALBI
(갈비 · BBQ Short Ribs)

MAKES 8 "RIBS"

DIFFICULTY: Easy

ALLERGENS: GFO, NF

2 large trumpet
   mushrooms

1 cup Omma's Korean
   BBQ Sauce (page 45),
   plus more for basting

Up to 2 tablespoons
   extra-virgin olive oil

¼ white onion, sliced into
   ¼-inch-thick rings

2 scallions, cut into
   1- to 2-inch lengths

I have many memories as a child of watching my father pound short ribs with a tenderizer while my mother prepared the marinade. My uncle would man the grill while my aunts prepared all the *banchan*. In some ways, I was afraid that by losing *galbi*, I would be losing all those memories with it.

Luckily, my *omma*'s Korean barbecue sauce packs so much flavor, I soon learned that all my favorite family BBQ memories can remain intact, even if I am grilling up vegetables instead of meat. As I have discovered over and over again, it isn't so much about the ingredients you're eating, it's about how the food makes you feel. For *galbi*, I use massive trumpet mushrooms, which are a member of the oyster mushroom family. They sear and char beautifully and soak up all the umami goodness of my mother's sauce.

1. Cut the mushrooms lengthwise into four slices about ½ inch thick. Score one side of each mushroom slice by running a small sharp knife down the length of the mushroom (do not cut all the way through the mushroom), then repeat along the width of the mushroom to create hatch marks. Brush both sides of the mushroom slices generously with the barbecue sauce. Place the mushrooms in the refrigerator for at least 1 hour before grilling.

2. Preheat a grill or grill pan (I use a stovetop grill, but you can use a traditional grill as well). When the grill is hot, add a little of the oil and the onions. Move the onions over the surface of the grill—believe it or not, this will impart a lovely flavor to the galbi. Working in batches if needed, add the mushroom "ribs" to the grill and cook them until they are slightly charred, about 2 minutes, basting with additional BBQ sauce as necessary. Flip the ribs and cook until slightly charred, basting with additional BBQ sauce. Add the scallions to the grill toward the end.

KKANPOONGI
(깐풍기 · Spicy Crunchy Garlic Wings)

MAKES 10 WINGS

DIFFICULTY: Practice
makes perfect

ALLERGENS: GFO, NF

FOR THE "WINGS"

1 (16-ounce) container
extra-firm tofu

2 (20-ounce) cans
jackfruit in brine

1 tablespoon vegan
chicken-flavored base
(see Note)

About ½ cup potato starch

¼ cup plant milk

2 burdock roots, well
scrubbed and cut into
2-inch lengths
(see Note)

Vegetable oil, for frying

FOR THE SAUCE

¼ cup brown rice syrup

2 tablespoons Vegetable
Broth (page 43) or
water

1 tablespoon soy sauce

½ tablespoon soup (light)
soy sauce

1 teaspoon rice vinegar

1 tablespoon potato starch

1 tablespoon gochugaru
(see page 28)

1 teaspoon cracked black
pepper

My grandmother on my mother's side loved the concept of all-you-can-eat buffets. When we were little, our family's favorite restaurant on earth was Ponderosa, for its endless refills on not just drinks but plates. For someone who spent the majority of her life outrunning starvation, the sight of her grandchildren bringing back their eighth plate of chicken wings and chocolate cake brought my grandmother incalculable joy. Chicken wings were one of my grandmother's favorite buffet plate fillers.

One evening at Ponderosa, she pounded down so many plates of wings, I laughed and said, "Look at how many chicken wings Hahlmuhnee ate!" Later my mother said to me, "You embarrassed her."

Even then, at ten years old, I knew what a truly horrible thing it was to embarrass your grandmother. And I wished then what I wish even now—that I could go back in time and shut myself up. But, I can't. What I can do, though, is cook up a version of "wings" that may not contain any chicken, but will still have you coming back for more. Here, I freeze the tofu, which creates a ton of emptied air pockets, allowing for a chewier texture as well as maximum flavor absorption. I also add some jackfruit, which mimics the tenderness of meat. Finally, for the "bones," I love using burdock root—they are sturdy but also quite delicious when covered in the sauce. So, keep coming back for more. As often as you like.

No judgment here.

1. Make the "wings": Freeze the tofu, thaw it completely, then press out as much liquid as possible. Freeze, thaw, and press a second

recipe and ingredients continue

1 teaspoon grated fresh
   ginger

1 tablespoon extra-virgin
   olive oil

½ cup diced red onion

7 cloves garlic, minced

1 leek, julienned

1 carrot, finely diced

¼ cup finely diced red bell
   pepper

1 cup dried Szechuan red
   chilies

2 scallions, chopped

time. The tofu will become quite spongy and brittle. Break the tofu
into 2- to 3-inch chunks and place them in a very large bowl.

2. Drain the jackfruit. Remove the hard seeds and trim off the hard
core of any pieces, so that all you're left with are the softer parts.
Add the jackfruit to the bowl with the tofu. Add the bouillon base
and 2 tablespoons of potato starch and mix everything together
gently so that the tofu doesn't break apart too much.

3. In a small bowl, mix together 1 tablespoon of potato starch
with the plant milk. This will serve as your "glue" for adhering the
burdock "bones." Scoop a handful of tofu/jackfruit mixture and
shape it into an oval (like an egg), packing it tightly. Take one end
of a length of burdock root, dip it in your glue, and pierce the tofu/
jackfruit ball gently. Continue to pack the tofu/jackfruit ball tightly
around the burdock root, dusting with additional potato starch
as necessary to make it "stick." Set the "wing" aside on a baking
sheet lined with parchment paper. Repeat with the remaining tofu/
jackfruit mixture and burdock root pieces and place the "wings" in
the refrigerator for 1 hour.

4. Remove the wings from the refrigerator. Rub your hands with
potato starch and gently coat the wings with additional potato starch.

5. Pour 4 inches of oil into a deep skillet or medium pot. Heat the
oil to 350°F (use a thermometer).

6. Working in batches (do not let the wings touch), fry the wings
until golden brown, about 2 minutes on each side. Set them aside
on a wire rack to drain any excess oil. Fry them a second time if you
want them to be extra crispy.

7. Make the sauce: In a small bowl, stir together the brown rice
syrup, broth, regular soy sauce, soup soy sauce, vinegar, potato
starch, gochugaru, black pepper, and ginger.

8. In a large wok or skillet, heat the olive oil over medium-high heat. When the oil is hot, add the red onion, garlic, leek, carrot, red bell pepper, and dried chilies. Sauté until the onion begins to soften, about 2 minutes. Add the soy sauce mixture to the sautéed vegetables and stir until the sauce begins to thicken, about 1 minute.

9. Remove from the heat, add the fried wings to the sauce, and gently stir so each is coated with sauce. Garnish with the scallions. Do not continue to cook, as the heat will cause the wings to get soggy.

NOTES

The vegan chicken-flavored base that I like to use is called Better Than Bouillon Vegetarian No Chicken Base. You can also use a non-chicken-flavored vegetable base. Unlike bouillon, these broth bases are wet (think of a very thick gel of concentrated broth flavors). If you can't find a base, you can substitute your favorite vegan chicken seasoning mix. I love using burdock roots as the "bones." However, they can be difficult to find. If you have trouble finding burdock root, you can substitute parsnip.

KKANPOONG TOFU
(깐풍두부 · Spicy Crunchy Garlic Tofu)

SERVES 4

DIFFICULTY: Easy

ALLERGENS: GFO, NF

½ cup potato starch

1 teaspoon salt

1 teaspoon fresh cracked black pepper

1 teaspoon onion powder

1 teaspoon garlic powder

1 (16-ounce) container extra-firm tofu, pressed (see Note, page 101) and sliced into bite-size cubes

Vegetable oil, for frying

FOR THE SAUCE

¼ cup brown rice syrup

2 tablespoons water

1½ tablespoons soy sauce

1 teaspoon rice vinegar

1 tablespoon potato starch

1 tablespoon gochugaru (see page 28)

1 teaspoon fresh cracked black pepper

1 tablespoon extra-virgin olive oil

½ cup diced red onion

7 cloves garlic, minced

This is the "kid sister" or *dongseng* recipe to Kkanpoongi (page 239). It's what you put together when you're cooking for no one but yourself and your similarly "I'm just hungry and don't care if it looks impressive" friend or spouse or kids. This is also the perfect recipe for those of you who are new to tofu and worried it may live up to its reputation as being bland, mushy, and generally unpalatable. Not only is this recipe easy to make, it is uniformly praised by tofu veterans and noobs alike as being the exact opposite of bland and mushy. The potato starch provides for a delightfully crispy texture, and the sauce hits all the right notes—tangy, sweet, and packed with garlic. In other words, you simply cannot go wrong with this recipe, whether you're proving to your skeptical self or your teenagers that tofu can be a complete star in and of itself.

1. Mix together the potato starch, salt, black pepper, onion powder, and garlic powder. In a large bowl, combine the potato starch mixture with the tofu. Make sure that all the tofu is evenly coated.

2. Add enough vegetable oil over medium-high heat to generously coat the surface of your largest nonstick skillet. When the oil begins to shimmer, add one layer of the coated tofu, making sure the pieces do not touch one another (they will stick). You may have to work in batches. Cook the tofu cubes on one side until they brown, about 3 minutes. Carefully flip the tofu and cook until the bottoms brown, about 3 more minutes. As each batch finishes, place the tofu on a wire rack to drain any excess oil. For extra crispiness, fry all the tofu a second time for about 30 seconds on each side.

recipe and ingredients continue

1 carrot, finely diced

1 cup dried Szechuan red
 chilies

2 scallions, chopped

3. Make the sauce: In a small bowl, stir together the brown rice syrup, water, soy sauce, vinegar, potato starch, gochugaru, and black pepper.

4. In a large wok or skillet, heat the olive oil over medium-high heat. When the oil is hot, add the red onion, garlic, carrot, and dried chilies. Sauté until the onion begins to soften, about 3 minutes. Add the soy sauce mixture to the sautéed vegetables and stir until the sauce begins to thicken, about 1 minute.

5. Remove from the heat, add the fried tofu to the sauce, and gently stir so each piece is coated with sauce. Garnish with the scallions. Do not continue to cook, as the heat will cause the tofu to get soggy.

TANGSUYUK
(탕수육 · Sweet and Sour Mushrooms)

SERVES 4

DIFFICULTY: Medium

ALLERGENS: GFO, NF

1 cup plus 2 tablespoons potato starch

1 teaspoon salt

½ teaspoon freshly ground black pepper

¼ cup unsweetened plain plant milk

18 to 20 dried shiitake mushrooms, rehydrated and stems removed

Vegetable oil, for frying

FOR THE SAUCE

1 tablespoon extra-virgin olive oil

½ cup chopped red onion

2 cloves garlic, minced

1 teaspoon salt

4 to 5 woodear mushrooms

1 carrot, sliced into thin discs

¼ cup chopped red bell pepper

¼ cup chopped green bell pepper

¼ cup chopped apple

1 tablespoon rice vinegar

Tangsuyuk is a dish for special SPECIAL occasions. It consists of deep-fried hunks of meat covered in a delicate sweet and slightly tart sauce. In Korea, there are a few dishes so popular, so necessary, that an entire segment of the food industry is devoted to delivering them wherever, whenever. The first of these is Jjajangmyun (page 171). And what goes perfectly with black bean noodles? *Tangsuyuk.*

My brother and I visited Korea when we were seven and ten years old, respectively. We stayed with my aunt, one of my mother's younger sisters. In response to our relentless whining, my aunt picked up the phone, said a handful of words to the stranger on the line, and within minutes, a man on a bike with a yellow vest knocked on her door. He unloaded from his portable warmer two ceramic bowls (not plastic, not paper, not disposable) filled with perfect noodles with julienned cucumber, together with two separate bowls of mouthwatering *jjajang* sauce, a large platter of deep-fried glory, and yet another bowl of sweet and sour sauce on the side. I discovered that the deep umami of the *jjajangmyun* paired perfectly with the tart sweetness of the *tangsuyuk.* After we were finished eating everything in sight, she left the dirty dishes on her doorstep, called the same magical *jjajangmyun* man, and he biked over to grab them before I was done licking my lips clean.

1. In a medium bowl, combine 1 cup of the potato starch, the salt, black pepper, and 3 cups water and set the mixture aside in the refrigerator for 1 hour 30 minutes, until all the starch has sunk to the bottom of the bowl.

recipe and ingredients continue

1 cup Vegetable Broth (page 43) or water

¼ cup brown rice syrup

¼ cup pineapple juice

1 tablespoon soy sauce

2 tablespoons potato starch

⅓ cucumber, sliced into thin discs

½ cup chopped (not crushed) pineapple

2. Pour out the water at the top of the bowl. The potato starch at the bottom will seem rock hard. Add the plant milk and stir with a spoon until a thick paste forms.

3. Coat the shiitakes with the remaining 2 tablespoons dry potato starch. Then add the shiitakes to the bowl of the potato starch paste and make sure they are fully coated with the paste.

4. Pour 2 inches of oil into a deep fryer or large pot. Heat the oil to 350°F and then reduce the heat to medium-low.

5. Working in batches (to not crowd the pot), add the shiitakes and cook until the batter starts to turn light yellow, 3 to 4 minutes. Drain the shiitakes on a wire rack. Keep the oil hot while you make the sauce (the mushrooms get fried a second time).

6. Make the sauce: In a large skillet, heat the olive oil over medium-high heat. Add the onion, garlic, salt, and woodear mushrooms and sauté for 3 to 4 minutes. Add the carrots, bell peppers, and apple and sauté for an additional minute or so. Add the vinegar to deglaze the pan. Add the broth, brown rice syrup, pineapple juice, and soy sauce and bring everything to a boil before reducing the heat to a simmer.

7. While sauce is simmering, fry the shiitakes for a second time for about 30 seconds.

8. In a small bowl, stir together the potato starch and ½ cup water to make a slurry. Add the cucumbers, pineapple, and the slurry to the sauce and increase the heat to medium-high. Cook while stirring until the sauce is nice and thick, 1 to 2 minutes.

9. Place the shiitakes on a large serving platter or bowl. Just before serving, pour the sauce over the top. (Do not do this until just before serving or the mushrooms will lose their delightful crunchiness.)

POWER BOWL

SERVES 1

DIFFICULTY: Easy
ALLERGENS: GFO, NF

½ tablespoon sesame oil

1 carrot, julienned

½ teaspoon salt

1 cup cooked rice

2 to 3 pieces braised tofu
(Dooboo Jorim,
page 267)

1 sweet potato, baked,
peeled, and cut into
bite-size pieces

4 or 5 Pickled Perilla
Leaves (page 133)

¼ cup Bulgogi (page 235)

2 tablespoons Spicy Soy
Sauce Dressing
(page 49) or Spicy
Gochujang Dressing
(page 51)

Bibimbap—which literally translates as "mixed rice"—was a staple of our *bapsang* (dinner table). While many people may believe that bibimbap has a specific recipe, the truth is bibimbap is really just rice, leftover *banchan*, and a sauce to bind it all together. As we saw in the *banchan* chapter, *banchan* is designed to last for several days, sometimes even weeks. So, at any given time, a Korean fridge—like my mom's—will have anywhere from 8 to 10 *banchan* ready to go. Add to that any leftovers from last night's BBQ . . . and you've got yourself a very robust rice bowl! This power bowl is a combination of rice, protein, and healthy carbs. It's one I make for myself almost on a weekly basis, usually the night before a long run or in the days leading up to a race. It's delicious, packed with tons of flavor, and full of nutrients.

1. In a medium skillet, heat the sesame oil over medium heat. Add the carrot pieces and cook until they start to get soft (not mushy), about 2 minutes. Sprinkle on the salt.

2. Add the rice to a bowl and top with the sautéed carrot, tofu, sweet potato, perilla leaves, and bulgogi. Drizzle with the dressing.

MANDOO
(만두 · Dumplings)

**MAKES 40 TO 50
SMALL DUMPLINGS**

DIFFICULTY: Easy

ALLERGENS: NF

1 tablespoon extra-virgin
olive oil

1 tablespoon sesame oil

1 potato, roughly chopped

2 carrots, roughly chopped

4 scallions, roughly
chopped

10 cremini mushrooms,
roughly chopped

1 cup Baechu Kimchi
(page 117), roughly
chopped

2 to 3 cloves garlic, roughly
chopped

2 teaspoons salt

1 teaspoon freshly ground
black pepper

1 tablespoon regular soy
sauce

2 ounces sweet potato
vermicelli, cooked
according to package
directions

1 (16-ounce) block extra-
firm tofu, pressed
(see Note, page 101)

1 tablespoon soup (light)
soy sauce

1 (14-ounce) package
dumpling wrappers

Spicy Soy Sauce Dresssing
(page 49), for serving

Growing up, my mother would spend hours chopping up all the
vegetables for her famous dumplings. She would then hunker over
the kitchen counter or sit on the floor to wrap row after quiet row
of pillowy little pockets of deliciousness. While wrapping dumplings
with my mother, aunts, and cousin, my *eemo* (my mother's sister)
recalled, laughing, "Your grandmother would trick us into wrapping
these all day long by telling us how extra talented we were at it! And
how beautifully we made our dumplings!" My dumplings are not
nearly as lovely as my mother's (yours don't need to be either), but
there are few recipes in this book that make me feel more like her
daughter, and my *hahlmuhnee*'s granddaughter.

1. In a large skillet, heat the olive oil and sesame oil over medium-
high heat. Add the potato, carrots, scallions, mushrooms, kimchi,
garlic, salt, and pepper and cook until the vegetables are soft, about
5 minutes. Add the regular soy sauce to deglaze the pan and cook
for 1 more minute.

2. Scrape all the cooked vegetables into a food processor. Add the
sweet potato noodles and pulse 16 to 20 times, until the vegetables
are at almost a paste-like consistency. Transfer the mixture to a large
bowl. Add the tofu and use a fork to mash up the tofu and mix it
into the processed vegetables. Add the soup soy sauce. *This is your last
opportunity to season the filling.* Use the filling to stuff the dumplings
right away or place it in the refrigerator until you are ready to wrap.
(The process is easier if the filling has been in the refrigerator for
about 1 hour.)

3. To make the dumplings, wet the rim of a dumpling wrapper
with a little water, then place the wrapper in the palm of your hand.
Place about 2 teaspoons of the filling in the center and fold the

recipe continues

wrapper in half over the filling. Pinch the two edges of the wrapper firmly together with your fingers. Set these aside on parchment paper or another nonstick surface and make sure the dumplings do not touch each other (as they will stick together). You can freeze these for up to 3 months for future use.

4. The dumplings can be boiled, steamed, pan-fried, deep-fried, or air-fried. Serve with spicy soy dressing for dipping.

TOFU HOT POT

SERVES 4

DIFFICULTY: Easy
ALLERGENS: GFO, NF

1 tablespoon extra-virgin olive oil

1 (16-ounce) block extra-firm tofu, sliced into ½-inch-thick pieces

10 large to 12 small or medium Brussels sprouts, trimmed and halved

3 Yukon Gold potatoes, halved

¼ cup red bell pepper slices

¼ cup Spicy Soy Sauce Dressing (page 49)

1 cup Vegetable Broth (page 43)

5 kale leaves, roughly chopped (see Note, page 85)

Tofu has gotten a bad rap. In addition to all the misinformation about soy, many people view tofu merely as a rather uninspired alternative to meat. Not so! Many Asian cultures embrace tofu as a delicious and nutritious source of protein. I grew up loving it, especially in *chigae* (stew). This tofu hot pot is kind of like a quick *chigae*, or a fast stew, and something I cook on the regular because it is so sinfully easy to make—particularly if you have my spicy soy dressing sitting in your refrigerator. This is not a traditional Korean recipe, but it reminds me of the hot pots packed with tasty ingredients all boiling together in an enticing broth that my family would order to share at many Korean restaurants. Here, I like to add a bunch of healthy greens and my favorite food of all time—the potato—for a go-to recipe when I am, quite frankly, too tired to really cook but too hungry to settle for toast!

1. In a very large skillet (I use a very large cast-iron pan), heat the olive oil over medium-high heat. When the pan is hot, add one layer of tofu (you may have to cook it in batches) and let the tofu cook until one side is golden brown, 7 to 10 minutes. Flip and cook the second side until golden brown.

2. Add the Brussels sprouts, potatoes, bell peppers, spicy soy dressing, and vegetable broth. Bring to a boil, then reduce the heat to low, cover, and simmer until the potatoes are fork-tender, about 15 minutes.

3. Add the kale, cover, and cook until the kale is wilted and bright green, about another minute. Using a wooden spoon, gently stir the kale into the sauce (which should be almost a glaze) just before serving.

KIMCHI BOKKEUM BAP
(김치볶음밥 · Fried Rice)

SERVES 2

DIFFICULTY: Easy

ALLERGENS: GFO, NF

2 tablespoons vegetable oil, plus more if needed

1½ cups day-old cooked rice

1 carrot, diced

½ green bell pepper, diced

¼ red onion, diced

½ zucchini, diced

1 scallion, chopped

3 cloves garlic, minced

1 cup Baechu Kimchi (page 117), roughly chopped

1 teaspoon salt

½ teaspoon freshly ground black pepper

½ cup Bulgogi (page 235)

½ Gyerranmari (page 97)

2 tablespoons Spicy Gochujang Dressing (page 51)

Like the cuisine of many cultures, Korean dishes are designed to make use of every scrap of food before it goes bad. Kimchi fried rice is, like bibimbap, a "recipe" that was born of need, when grocery stores weren't around every corner and folks had to make do with whatever they had in the refrigerator. Well, I have never seen a Korean kitchen without kimchi or rice! Like *kimchi chigae*, kimchi fried rice is best made when the kimchi is on the older side. Same thing with the rice—this recipe is best with day-old rice. For the rest of the ingredients, use the proportions listed here, but just ransack your refrigerator for whatever odds and ends you've got, because just about any veggie is fair game!

1. In a large wok or skillet, heat 1 tablespoon of the oil over high heat until it is very hot. Add half of the rice and fry until the rice starts to brown slightly around the edges. Remove the rice from the pan and set it aside. Fry the remaining half of the rice, adding more oil if necessary.

2. Return all the rice to the pan, pushing it to the edges of the pan, creating a small well in the middle. Add the remaining 1 tablespoon oil to the center of pan. Add the diced vegetables, garlic, kimchi, salt, and pepper to the center of the pan and stir-fry in the well until the kimchi starts to soften, 1 to 2 minutes. Then incorporate the rice and continue to stir-fry everything for 1 more minute.

3. Add the bulgogi, gyerranmari, and the gochujang dressing. Continue stirring everything over medium heat until the rice takes on a lovely orange color, about 1 minute.

MUSHROOM JUUK
(버섯죽 · Rice Porridge)

SERVES 4

DIFFICULTY: Medium

ALLERGENS: GFO, NF

1 tablespoon extra-virgin
  olive oil

3 large or 4 small to
  medium dried shiitake
  mushrooms, rehydrated
  and sliced

Salt

2 cups day-old cooked rice

4 cups Mushroom Dashi
  (page 39)

2 tablespoons Spicy Soy
  Sauce Dressing
  (page 49)

1 teaspoon sesame oil

For Korean children, there are few things more predictable than
your mother sending you into school with a piping-hot thermos
of *juuk* (Korean rice porridge) when you are feeling under the
weather. Likewise, as confirmed for decades by the authority of all
things Korean (that is, Korean dramas), the single best way to show
anyone you REALLY love them is to stay up into the wee hours of
the night hand-churning this comforting dish. Like risotto, you must
stir the rice often to release the starch that provides for the dish's
trademark creaminess. However, *juuk* is cooked for a bit longer
than risotto, until the rice has no more bite left to it and all that
remains is the warm residue of your tender love and care.

1. In a dolsot, Dutch oven, or other medium pot, heat the olive oil
over medium-high heat. When the oil is hot, add the shiitakes and
cook for about 1 minute. Add 1 teaspoon salt and cook until the
mushrooms are browned, an additional 4 to 5 minutes.

2. Add the rice and break it up with a wooden spoon, then stir
it together with the sautéed mushrooms. Add one ladleful of
mushroom dashi and stir it into the rice over medium-low heat until
the liquid has evaporated. Continue to add dashi, one ladleful at a
time, while stirring, until only 1 cup of dashi remains. This process
can take up to 45 minutes, which is why juuk is considered to be a
labor of love.

3. Add the final cup of dashi to the rice, cover the pot, and let it
simmer until the liquid has evaporated and the rice has turned into
a porridge consistency, 5 to 7 minutes. Add more salt to taste.

4. Right before serving, spoon the spicy soy dressing over the top
and drizzle with the sesame oil.

LASAGNA WITH GOCHUJANG RED SAUCE

SERVES 6

DIFFICULTY: Medium

ALLERGENS: GFO

FOR THE OVEN-ROASTED TOMATOES

2 tablespoons extra-virgin olive oil

1 teaspoon gochujang (see page 26)

3 Roma (plum) tomatoes, sliced into ⅓-inch-thick rounds

2 teaspoons salt

1 teaspoon freshly ground black pepper

FOR THE ROASTED ZUCCHINI

2 zucchini, sliced into ⅓-inch-thick rounds

Salt

2 tablespoons extra-virgin olive oil

1 teaspoon doenjang (see page 25)

1 teaspoon freshly ground black pepper

Lasagna can often be an intimidating dish to tackle. There are a lot of different components that have to come together just right in order to elevate this Italian fare beyond the average casserole. But once you've mastered a combination of flavors that you really enjoy, your lasagna recipe will be your most loyal. Speaking of a combination of flavors, the key to this lasagna is the red sauce. I consulted a lot with my late father-in-law (who was from Rome) about creating a red sauce that is full of depth with a hint of sweetness, and in particular, whether using tomato paste is necessary. His take? "You don't really need it." And he was right—I've never used tomato paste in my red sauce. However, in order to add a little extra oomph and heat, I add some *gochujang*. I also use a little of my *omma*'s Korean barbecue sauce when preparing the mushroom filling for this lasagna. These little "twists" add just a hint of the flavors I grew up with.

You can prepare this lasagna in advance, the leftovers will reheat beautifully, and it will always be delicious.

THE DAY BEFORE:

1. Make the oven-roasted tomatoes: Preheat the oven to 250°F. Mist a large baking sheet with cooking spray.

2. In a small bowl, mix together the olive oil and gochujang. Coat all the tomato slices with the gochujang/olive oil mixture (I like to brush it on with a pastry brush, but you can also dress the tomatoes in a large bowl).

3. Arrange the tomatoes in a single layer on the baking sheet. Season them with half the salt and pepper. Flip and repeat.

recipe and ingredients continue

FOR THE RED SAUCE

2 tablespoons extra-virgin olive oil

2 small shallots, chopped

4 cloves garlic, chopped

1 carrot, diced

2 teaspoons salt

1 teaspoon freshly ground black pepper

1 tablespoon dried oregano

2 tablespoons gochujang (see page 26)

1 tablespoon balsamic vinegar

¼ cup white wine

18 large or 24 small to medium Campari tomatoes (or 8 to 10 large heirloom tomatoes, if they are in season), roughly chopped

3 bay leaves

FOR THE AVOCADO BÉCHAMEL

1 avocado, halved and pitted

1 teaspoon salt

1 cup fresh basil leaves

1 tablespoon fresh lemon juice

1 clove garlic, peeled

½ cup cashews

¼ cup plant milk

1 tablespoon nutritional yeast

4. Transfer the baking sheet to the oven and bake until the tomatoes look dried out and slightly caramelized, 1 hour to 1 hour 30 minutes. Let cool, then store overnight in the refrigerator.

5. Make the roasted zucchini: Position a rack in the lowest position and preheat the oven to 475°F. Line a baking sheet with parchment paper. On a large kitchen towel or paper towel, arrange the zucchini slices in one layer. Salt each one. Flip them over and repeat. Set them aside for 15 to 20 minutes. Remove the excess liquid from the zucchini slices by patting them dry.

6. In a small bowl, mix together the olive oil and doenjang. Using a brush or a spoon, coat the zucchini. Arrange the zucchini slices in a single layer on the lined baking sheet, making sure not to crowd the sheet (use two baking sheets if necessary). Transfer to the oven and roast until the bottoms of the zucchini are nice and brown, about 12 minutes. Flip and bake until the bottoms are brown, an additional 1 to 2 minutes. Store overnight in the refrigerator.

7. Make the red sauce: In a large Dutch oven, heat the olive oil over medium-high heat. Add the shallots, garlic, carrot, salt, pepper, and oregano and cook until the shallots are translucent, about 3 minutes. Add the gochujang and stir the vegetables with a wooden spoon until all the vegetables are evenly coated. Add the balsamic vinegar and white wine to deglaze the pot, scraping the bottom of the pot with the spoon to pick up all the browned bits.

8. When the liquid has reduced to a thick glaze, add the tomatoes and bay leaves. Bring to a boil, then reduce the heat to low and let the tomatoes stew, stirring occasionally, until the liquids are reduced by one-third, about 45 minutes. Depending on your tomatoes, your sauce may be very wet (if the tomatoes give off a lot of water). If so, continue to cook your sauce until reduced by one-third.

9. Remove the bay leaves. Using an immersion blender, blend the sauce to your desired consistency (I prefer a chunkier sauce).

FOR THE TOFU RICOTTA

5 large or 6 small to medium dried shiitake mushrooms, rehydrated and sliced

1 tablespoon balsamic vinegar

1 teaspoon salt

1 teaspoon freshly ground black pepper

1 (16-ounce) block extra-firm tofu, pressed (see Note, page 101)

FOR THE MUSHROOM FILLING

1 tablespoon extra-virgin olive oil

3 portobello mushroom caps, cleaned, gills scraped out, and caps diced

¼ cup diced onion

1 teaspoon salt

½ cup finely diced carrot

2 tablespoons Omma's Korean BBQ Sauce (page 45)

FOR ASSEMBLY

12 to 15 lasagna noodles or gluten-free lasagna noodles, depending on their size

Roasted Doenjang-Glazed Onions (page 87)

Extra-virgin olive oil, for drizzling

THE DAY OF:

1. Make the avocado béchamel: Scoop the avocado flesh into a high-powered blender and add the salt, basil, lemon juice, garlic, cashews, plant milk, and nutritional yeast and blend until smooth.

2. Make the tofu ricotta: In a food processor, combine the shiitakes, balsamic vinegar, salt, pepper, and tofu and process for about 20 seconds.

3. Make the mushroom filling: In a small skillet, heat the olive oil over medium-high heat. Add the portobellos, onion, and salt and cook until the onions begin to caramelize, 3 to 4 minutes. Add the carrot and sauté for an additional 2 minutes. Stir in the BBQ sauce. Remove the vegetables from the heat and set them aside for assembly.

4. Assemble the lasagna: In a large pot of boiling water, cook the lasagna noodles for half the cook time listed on the package. Drain and place them back in the pot with cold water (to keep them from sticking).

5. Preheat the oven to 425°F.

6. Ladle enough red sauce to completely cover the bottom of a 7 × 11-inch baking dish. On top of the sauce, assemble the lasagna layers in the following order: (a) pasta, (b) tofu ricotta, (c) avocado béchamel, (d) mushroom filling, (e) roasted zucchini and glazed onions, (f) red sauce. Repeat until you have used up all the red sauce.

7. Top the lasagna with the oven-roasted tomatoes and drizzle with a little olive oil.

8. Transfer the lasagna to the oven and bake until the sides begin to bubble, 45 to 55 minutes. Allow the lasagna to rest for 15 minutes before serving.

OMURICE
(오므라이스 · Omelet Rice)

SERVES 2

DIFFICULTY: Medium

ALLERGENS: GFO, NF

FOR THE FRIED RICE

2 tablespoons vegetable oil or any high smoke-point oil

2 cups day-old cooked rice

¼ cup diced carrots

¼ cup diced red onion

¼ cup diced button mushrooms

¼ cup chopped scallions

¼ cup diced red bell pepper

¼ cup frozen green peas

2 cloves garlic, minced

2 teaspoons salt

1 teaspoon freshly ground black pepper

1 teaspoon Omma's Korean BBQ Sauce (page 45)

FOR THE OMELET

1 cup egg replacer (preferably JUST Egg)

1 teaspoon salt

½ teaspoon freshly ground black pepper

1 slice vegan cheese, cut into ½-inch squares

Omurice, a dish that originated in Japan and was then adapted by Koreans, is the marriage of the two English words: *omelet* and *rice*. As the name suggests, it is composed of rice (usually fried rice), topped with an omelet, and slathered in ketchup. I never liked omelets and I reserve ketchup for my French fries and that's about it. That said, after watching my seventeenth Korean drama wherein *omurice* is featured as one of the go-to dishes of all lovelorn romantic leads, I decided to give it another whirl—vegan style. I discovered that the trick to making *omurice* really special is to replace the boring old ketchup with a sauce you actually like. CUE OMMA'S KOREAN BBQ SAUCE. The garlicky sweet richness of the BBQ sauce pairs so well with the salty/savory flavors of the omelet and rice. Don't believe me? Give it a try yourself!

1. Make the fried rice: In a very large skillet or wok, heat 1 tablespoon of the vegetable oil over high heat until the oil is very, very hot. Add 1 cup of the rice to the pan (to avoid overcrowding the pan) and cook until it begins to brown around the edges, 4 to 5 minutes. Remove from the pan. Add the remaining 1 cup rice to the pan and repeat.

2. Reduce the heat to medium-high. Return the rice to the skillet and create a small well in the center. Add the remaining 1 tablespoon vegetable oil to the center. When it gets hot, add the carrots, onion, mushrooms, scallions, bell pepper, green peas, garlic, salt, and black pepper. Cook the vegetables in the center of the pan until they start to soften, about 2 minutes. Then, mix them together with the rice. Stir in the BBQ sauce. Cover to keep the rice warm while you prepare the omelet.

recipe and ingredients continue

2 tablespoons diced red
  bell pepper

2 tablespoons chopped
  scallion

1 tablespoon extra-virgin
  olive oil

Omma's Korean BBQ
  Sauce (page 45),
  for serving

3. Make the omelet: In a bowl, mix together the egg replacer, salt, black pepper, vegan cheese, bell pepper, and scallion. In a small nonstick skillet, heat ½ tablespoon of the olive oil over medium heat. When the oil is hot, add half of the "egg" mixture to the pan. Cook until the bottom is completely cooked, about 2 minutes. Flip the omelet with a spatula and cook for an additional minute. Remove the omelet from the pan and set it aside. Repeat with the remaining ½ tablespoon olive oil and the remaining half of the egg mixture.

4. Gently place each omelet into its own bowl, so that it lines the bowl completely. Divide the fried rice into two portions. Pack each serving into the bowl lined with the omelet. Cover the bowl with a plate and flip the bowl over so that the rice lands on the plate in a dome shape.

5. Drizzle with BBQ sauce before serving.

DOOBOO JORIM
(두부조림 · Braised Tofu)

SERVES 4

DIFFICULTY: Easy

ALLERGENS: GFO, NF

1 (16-ounce) block medium-firm tofu

1 tablespoon extra-virgin olive oil

3 tablespoons Spicy Soy Sauce Dressing (page 49), plus more for serving

½ cup Vegetable Broth (page 43)

1 onion, julienned

1 carrot, finely diced

3 large or 4 small to medium mushrooms, thinly sliced

2 scallions, chopped

1 tablespoon toasted sesame seeds

Have I mentioned how much I love recipes that are absolutely "stupid proof"? You can call it "noobie proof" or "I'm exhausted from work proof" or "I barely know how to boil water proof," too. We've all been there: For whatever reason, your brain is on autopilot, and therefore, the recipe better be damn near automated lest you burn your house to the ground. This is one of those rare recipes that practically makes itself but looks and tastes like you slaved over it all day long. I keep it in my arsenal for quick meals and dinner parties alike—it never fails to satisfy. And I'll bet this may be the first vegan recipe you've seen that doesn't call for extra-firm tofu. This dish celebrates how soft and velvety tofu can be, so play around with medium or firm tofu!

1. Slice the block of tofu crosswise into ⅓-inch-thick pieces (I usually end up with 8 to 9 pieces).

2. In a very large skillet, heat the olive oil over medium-high heat. When the oil is hot, place the tofu in the pan in a single layer (you may have to cook in batches if your pan is not large enough) and cook the tofu until the bottom is browned, 7 to 10 minutes. Flip the tofu and repeat until both sides are evenly cooked.

3. Add the spicy soy dressing and vegetable broth to the pan. Bring to a boil and then reduce the heat to very low. Sprinkle the onion, carrot, and mushrooms over the tofu. Cover the pan and cook until most of the braising liquid has evaporated, 15 to 20 minutes, popping the lid open occasionally and spooning a little bit of the braising liquid over the top of the tofu and vegetables as they cook.

4. Garnish with the scallions and toasted sesame seeds. Serve with additional dressing over the top or on the side.

MAPO DOOBOO
(마파두부 · Mapo Tofu)

SERVES 4

DIFFICULTY: Medium
ALLERGENS: NF

5 large or 6 small to medium fresh shiitake mushrooms, stems discarded, caps finely chopped

1 teaspoon sesame oil

1 teaspoon plus 1 tablespoon soy sauce

½ teaspoon freshly ground black pepper

1 tablespoon potato starch

Salt

1 (16-ounce) block silken tofu, cut into ½-inch cubes

3 tablespoons vegetable oil

1½ tablespoons doubanjiang (see Notes)

½ tablespoon gochugaru (see page 28)

4 cloves garlic, minced

2 scallions, chopped, white and green parts kept separate

1 teaspoon thinly sliced fresh ginger

½ tablespoon fermented black soybeans (see Notes)

1 teaspoon maple syrup

½ tablespoon ground pink peppercorns

This was one of my favorite dishes to order at a Chinese restaurant. However, I have not been able to find a vegan one at any of the Chinese restaurants I used to haunt during my pre-vegan days, which is why I decided I needed to veganize it. Working on this recipe was pretty daunting—I am entirely unfamiliar with some of its components. For example, it was my first time using *doubanjiang*, or fava bean paste (similar to but more pungent than soybean paste) and pink peppercorns. *Doubanjiang* is what injects the intense savory flavor that I love about *mapo tofu* and the pink peppercorns add a light zip to the sauce. Although it was intimidating, I'm glad I tried working with ingredients I'm so unfamiliar with, as it taught me not only to appreciate a completely new flavor but also that the single most important ingredient in any good dish is a dash of humility.

1. In a small bowl, toss the mushrooms with the sesame oil, 1 teaspoon of the soy sauce, and the pepper. Set aside.

2. In a separate small bowl, stir the potato starch into 3 tablespoons water. Set the slurry aside.

3. Bring a large pot of water to a boil. Add a pinch of salt to the water before gently adding the tofu. Cook for 1 minute. Remove the tofu and pat dry with a kitchen towel.

4. In a wok or a very large skillet, heat 2 tablespoons of the vegetable oil over high heat. When the oil begins to shimmer, add the mushrooms and cook until they start to crisp around the edges, about 5 minutes. Remove the mushrooms and set aside.

recipe continues

5. Add the remaining 1 tablespoon oil, the doubanjiang, and gochugaru to the pan and cook for about 1 minute, making sure to stir constantly so that it does not burn. Add the garlic, scallion whites, ginger, and fermented black beans. Stir-fry for an additional 30 seconds.

6. Add 1 cup water to pan and bring to a boil. Carefully add the silken tofu to the pan along with the remaining 1 tablespoon soy sauce, the maple syrup, and the cooked mushrooms. Reduce the heat and allow the contents to simmer, stirring occasionally, until the liquid reduces by half, about 7 minutes.

7. Stir the slurry to recombine and add half of it to the pan along with the scallion greens, stirring as you add. If the sauce has not thickened to the desired consistency, add the remaining slurry and stir.

8. Sprinkle with the pink peppercorns and more salt to taste.

NOTES

Doubanjiang is a chili paste made out of Erjingtiao chilies from Pixian and broad beans (fava beans) instead of soybeans (like many Korean pastes). *Doubanjiang* is used in many Szechuan recipes. It is spicy and salty, so do not go overboard on the salt in this recipe and be sure to use lower-sodium soy sauce.

Fermented black soybeans, referred to as *douchi* in Chinese, should not be confused with fermented black soybean *paste* or *sauce*, which is often sold in Korean grocery stores for making *jjajangmyun*.

OMMA'S CASSEROLE

SERVES 6

DIFFICULTY: Easy

ALLERGENS: GFO

FOR THE "CREAM OF MUSHROOM" SAUCE

3 tablespoons extra-virgin olive oil

1 cup roughly chopped mushrooms (see Notes)

3 cloves garlic, minced

1 large shallot, chopped

½ cup thinly sliced russet potato

1 cup unsalted roasted cashews

1 tablespoon garlic powder

1 tablespoon onion powder

Salt

½ teaspoon freshly ground black pepper

1 tablespoon doenjang (see page 25)

¼ cup white wine

¾ cup Mushroom Dashi (page 39)

2 tablespoons nutritional yeast

1 cup plant milk

This casserole is my *omma*'s attempt to address our endless petitions for more "American" food at the dinner table. At the time, my mom used all the advantages she could find at the grocery store: canned soup, frozen vegetables, and ground meat. I decided not only to veganize my *omma*'s casserole but also to "healthify" it, by using cashews and fresh mushrooms for my "cream of mushroom" sauce and adding kale (kale, in my mind, immediately elevates a dish on the healthy spectrum!). This casserole is packed with nutritious ingredients and is as delicious as the one Omma used to make.

1. Preheat the oven to 350°F.

2. Make the "cream of mushroom" sauce: In a small pot, heat the olive oil over medium-high heat. Add the mushrooms, garlic, and shallot and sauté until the shallots become translucent, about 3 minutes.

3. Add the potato, cashews, garlic powder, onion powder, 1 teaspoon salt, the pepper, and doenjang. Stir the contents of the pot so that they are all coated in the spices and doenjang.

4. Add the wine to deglaze the pot, using a wooden spoon to scrape up any browned bits on the bottom. Allow the wine to reduce until it thickens. Add the mushroom dashi, bring the mixture to a boil, then reduce to a simmer and cook until the potatoes are falling-apart tender, about 10 minutes (if you sliced them really thinly).

5. Transfer the mixture to a high-powered blender. Add the nutritional yeast and plant milk and blend on the highest setting for about 1 minute, until the sauce is creamy and smooth. Season the cream of mushroom sauce with more salt to taste.

recipe and ingredients continue

NOTE

The casserole often tastes better the next day. Reheat at 425°F for about 35 minutes (when you stick a knife down the center, if it comes out warm, you're good to go!).

FOR THE CASSEROLE

12 ounces ziti or gluten-free pasta

2 links vegan sausage

1 tablespoon extra-virgin olive oil, plus more for drizzling

3 portobello mushrooms, gills scraped, and finely diced

3 cloves garlic, minced

¼ cup diced onion

Salt

½ teaspoon freshly ground black pepper

2 tablespoons chopped walnuts

1 cup julienned lacinato kale

½ tablespoon balsamic vinegar

1 tablespoon soy sauce

3 large or 4 medium Yukon Gold potatoes, cut into ⅛-inch-thick rounds

2 cups frozen French-cut green beans

6. Make the casserole: Cook the pasta for half the cook time listed on the package.

7. Meanwhile, in a food processor, grind the vegan sausage until it has the consistency of very small pebbles.

8. In a large skillet, heat the olive oil over medium-high heat. Add the ground vegan sausage, the portobellos, garlic, and onion and sauté until the mushrooms start to crisp around the edges, about 4 minutes. Season with a pinch of salt and the pepper.

9. Add the walnuts and kale and continue to cook until the kale starts to wilt, about 1 minute. Add the vinegar and soy sauce to deglaze the pan and cook until the liquid has reduced to a near glaze.

10. Mist a 9 × 9-inch baking pan with cooking spray. Make layers in this order: potatoes sprinkled with a pinch of salt, pasta, a generous amount of cream of mushroom sauce, vegan sausage mixture, and a sprinkling of frozen green beans. Repeat the layering until all of the ingredients have been used. End with the sausage mixture and top with a handful of potato slices and a sprinkle of salt. Drizzle the top of the casserole with extra-virgin olive oil.

11. Transfer the baking pan to the oven and bake until you see the sauce bubbling on the sides, about 45 minutes.

12. Allow the casserole to cool for a few minutes before cutting and serving. You can also store it in the refrigerator and serve the next day (see Notes).

NOTES

For the sauce, you can use almost any kind of mushroom you like: shiitake, cremini, portobello, button, enoki, oyster, etc.

The "cream of mushroom" sauce is a stand-alone recipe that you can use for any number of dishes—pasta, risotto, or over a roasted cauliflower. The possibilities are endless!

9 SWEETS

The word *gam*, which means "persimmon," always makes my mouth water. It is perhaps the sweetest, most succulent fruit I've ever eaten. My father would bring home a box from the Korean grocery store in winter, and they would sit on the counter like a crate of bright rubies until my grandmother told me they were ready to eat. Most of the persimmons you see in the markets these days come in two varieties: Fuyu and Hachiya. Fuyu persimmons look like squat miniature pumpkins and can be eaten while still firm. Hachiya persimmons resemble red bell peppers and need to be soft and fully ripe before being consumed. Both types of persimmons have tannins, a bitter compound that can make persimmons downright inedible if the fruit has not had adequate time to ripen. When it comes to desserts, most Korean meals conclude with fresh fruit, and when persimmons are in season, they are usually in high demand. This chapter, however, will include far more than fresh fruit! Here, you'll see all the usual suspects you'd find in a pastry shop, but many of them will have a little "Korean" twist.

The persimmon blossoms fell and covered the ground like snow.
I picked them off the floor and I ate them. They tasted sweet and pretty.
I thought I was getting pretty. Like the flowers, after eating them.

—OMMA

Omma nearly died when she was less than one year old while being carried on her mother's back, toward the Yellow Sea. Her home, Ongjin, was under fire—one of the earliest skirmishes of the Korean War—and the only route to safety was on a US Navy ship that waited for them just offshore. In the movies, it seems wartime refugees are able to walk endlessly, for miles and miles, with babies on their backs and minimal food and water. It took my grandparents nearly two weeks to arrive at the curling lips of the Yellow Sea, and by that time my one-year-old mother was, quite literally, starving to death.

My grandparents and their two daughters were herded on board. But, while they had secured passage to South Korea, there was no food. By that time, Omma's crying had grown agonizing. Without knowing how long they would be at sea, my grandparents' eyes eventually turned from my mother's swollen face to the churning gray water beneath them.

They decided to drown her.

I've shared this story many times and as often as not, those I've shared it with flinch in horror. Some have gone so far as to call my grandparents attempted murderers. And to be honest, I also struggle, sometimes, to understand what sort of desperation

Article from
the New York Times

could have possibly driven them to this conclusion. They climbed up to the uppermost deck of the ship, hoping to deposit my mother into the water with no one but themselves to bear witness to their crime.

But, just as they were preparing themselves to do the unthinkable, two American GIs approached, with their muddy green uniforms and English words. Even had my grandparents known or understood what they were saying, they wouldn't have had any idea how to explain their situation or what they were planning to do.

As the soldiers continued their attempt to communicate with my grandparents, Omma's angry fists thrashed at the air between them.

One of the American GIs placed a Hershey's bar in Omma's hands.

"They saved my life," Omma recounts, sixty-eight years later, to her American daughter.

———

Seoul Hahlmuhnee slipped in and out of a coma during her last few weeks. End-stage renal failure, liver cancer, and the biting knock of pneumonia conspired to bear her out of the present and into a place where her body was stronger, even if the world around her was perhaps more demanding.

Seoul Hahlmuhnee and me

She pawed at the bedsheets, as if she were digging a groove in the soil to plant seeds, something I'd seen her do countless times. In her dreams, her body no longer ached from bones stiff with age but from the pleasant pain that attends a day's work on a farm. Her own farm. A small piece of land that would never span past the horizon, but land that was her own nonetheless. Not too far,

Seoul Hahlmuhnee and Grandpa

Seoul Hahlmuhnee and me
at law school graduation

a persimmon tree, heavy with autumn, would tell her: "Your daughter will one day take me all the way across the sea to America, where her own daughter will swallow my heart."

"Sunbee, the persimmons are so large! They are so large and look so sweet!" Hahlmuhnee would murmur in her sleep. My mother would try to hold her hands, but they were too agitated. Hahlmuhnee would smack her lips like a child, the sweet orange flesh of a ripe persimmon dribbling down the sides of her chin, as she dove back into dreams.

That night, I went home and thought about my *hahlmuhnee*, the *gam* in her dreams, the fruit she bore in Korea, my mother—the seeds she carried all the way to America, the persimmons she brought home from the market, the chambers of the persimmon heart singing through my teeth in fall, the gilded branches that inveigled their way through my ribs and into my lungs until I was breathing the sweet fermented breath of my grandmother as she climbed up to a place I couldn't yet reach.

My final memories of Seoul Hahlmuhnee are of how she held my fingers—like an infant, clutching at whatever warmth could fit within her small hands. She wouldn't let go, even as the smell of fresh white snow hid behind the trees to draw her away from us.

CHOCOLATE SWEET POTATO CAKE

SERVES 16

DIFFICULTY: Medium
ALLERGENS: NF

FOR THE CAKE

2⅔ cups (370g) all-purpose flour, sifted

2 cups (400g) organic sugar

1 tablespoon baking powder

1½ teaspoons baking soda

1 teaspoon salt

1½ cups (120g) unsweetened cocoa powder or cacao

¾ cup (125g) cubed, cooked Garnet yams

¼ cup (57g) vegetable oil or vegan butter

1 tablespoon white wine or apple cider vinegar

2 shots espresso

2 tablespoons vanilla extract

When I think of my mother, two foods immediately spring to mind: chocolate and sweet potatoes. Both of these foods were instrumental in saving her life. I could think of no better way to celebrate my mother than a chocolate sweet potato cake. Here, I use the American Garnet yam as well as Korean sweet potatoes—which have less water and carry a nuttier flavor (kinda like chestnuts)—to marry both the Korean and the American in her. This cake is moist, full of intense chocolaty flavors, with a fluffy sweet potato frosting.

1. Make the cake: Preheat the oven to 350°F. Mist two 7-inch springform pans with cooking spray and line the bottoms with rounds of parchment paper.

2. In a large bowl, combine the flour, sugar, baking powder, baking soda, and salt. Stir with a whisk to break up any clumps.

3. In a medium pot, combine the cocoa, yams, oil, vinegar, espresso, vanilla, and 2 cups water and heat over medium-low heat. When the mixture begins to boil, stir until it comes together in a sauce. Set aside and let cool for about 5 minutes.

4. Pour the cocoa/yam mixture into the bowl with the dry ingredients and continue stirring with a whisk until all the ingredients are just incorporated. Do not overmix the batter.

5. Divide the cake batter evenly into the two springform cake pans, or use three pans if you want thinner layers. Use a scale if you want to be precise.

recipe and ingredients continue

1 cup (90g) powdered
   sugar

¼ cup (25g) unsweetened
   cocoa powder or cacao

2 cups (300g) cubed and
   roasted Korean sweet
   potatoes (see Note)

¼ cup (57g) vegan butter

1 teaspoon vanilla extract

1 tablespoon soy or
   oat milk

6. Transfer the pans to the oven and bake until a toothpick inserted into the center of the cakes comes out clean, 25 to 28 minutes.

7. Let the cakes cool in the pans on a wire rack for about 10 minutes. Run a sharp knife along the edges and then gently release the latches of the springform pans. Carefully remove the cakes and set them on the rack to cool completely. (You can also wrap them in plastic wrap after they've cooled and place them in the refrigerator if you are in a rush.)

8. Make the sweet potato frosting: Bring all of the frosting ingredients to room temperature. In a stand mixer fitted with the whisk attachment, combine the powdered sugar and cocoa. Add the sweet potatoes, butter, vanilla, and milk and mix until a smooth and creamy frosting is achieved.

9. Use an offset spatula or the back of a spoon to frost both cakes for two cakes, or place them on top of each other to make a layer cake.

NOTES

Korean and/or Japanese sweet potatoes are much denser and drier than their Western counterparts. So if you were to substitute regular sweet potatoes or yams in the frosting, it would be too wet. To compensate, add up to another ½ cup powdered sugar to achieve the right consistency.

CHOCOLATE PERSIMMON CUPCAKES

MAKES
12 CUPCAKES

DIFFICULTY: Medium
ALLERGENS: NF

FOR THE CUPCAKES

1 cup soy or oat milk

1 tablespoon white wine
vinegar

1 cup (240g) self-rising
flour

½ cup plus 2 tablespoons
(60g) unsweetened
cocoa powder

2 cups (225g) powdered
sugar, sifted

½ teaspoon baking
powder

½ teaspoon baking soda

Pinch of salt

2 tablespoons vegan
butter, slightly melted

¼ cup (80g) Persimmon
Puree (recipe follows)

**FOR THE PERSIMMON
BUTTERCREAM
FROSTING**

2 cups (225g) powdered
sugar, sifted

2 teaspoons cream of
tartar

¼ cup (80g) Persimmon
Puree (recipe follows),
at room temperature

Up to 1 cup (225g)
vegan butter, at room
temperature

I remember the first time I handed my husband a persimmon. He bit into it, made a face, spit it out into the palm of his hand, and declared, "That's the worst thing I've ever tasted!" I burst out laughing and explained, "It's not ripe yet!" A few weeks later, I handed him another persimmon, he took a bite, and said, "My god, that's the most delicious thing I've ever eaten. Why is this my first time eating this?" A ripe persimmon is, indeed, a gift from the gods.

1. Make the cupcakes: Preheat the oven to 350°F. Line 12 cups of a muffin tin with paper liners.

2. In a small bowl, mix together the soy milk and vinegar. Set aside.

3. In a large bowl, whisk together the flour, cocoa powder, powdered sugar, baking powder, baking soda, and salt. Add the butter, soy/vinegar mixture, and persimmon puree. Whisk all the ingredients together until they are well combined.

4. Using two spoons or an ice cream scoop, scoop even portions of the batter into each muffin cup.

5. Transfer the pan to the oven and bake until a toothpick inserted into the center of one of the cupcakes comes out clean, 18 to 20 minutes. Gently remove the cupcakes and let them cool completely on a wire rack. If you try to frost them too early, the frosting will melt.

6. Make the frosting: In a stand mixer fitted with the whisk attachment, combine the powdered sugar, cream of tartar, and persimmon puree. Mix at medium speed, then increase the speed

recipe continues

to high while gradually adding the vegan butter (see Notes), 1 to 2 tablespoons at a time, until the desired consistency of frosting is reached.

7. Frost the fully cooled cupcakes with a pastry bag or with the back of your spoon (either way tastes amazing).

PERSIMMON PUREE

Makes 1½ cups

1 cup dried pitted persimmons, roughly chopped (see Notes)

In a blender, combine the dried persimmons with ¼ cup water. If the blender gets stuck, keep adding water by the teaspoon until it blends.

NOTES

Depending on the ambient temperature, the frosting may be more prone to "break" or "curdle" if too much fat is added too quickly. To help make the frosting creamy, add only a little bit of vegan butter at a time, while continuing to mix at high speed.

While most puree recipes call for fresh persimmon, this recipe calls for dried persimmon to ensure you can make it year-round. You can purchase dried persimmon—called *gotgam*—at the Asian grocery store. Dried persimmon can have no seeds or multiple seeds. Make sure to check for seeds before adding them to your blender.

NOTES

This recipe works very well
with gluten-free flour!

PECAN PAHT PIE

SERVES 8 TO 10

DIFFICULTY: Medium

ALLERGENS: GFO

FOR THE PIE CRUST

1½ cups (210g) all-purpose flour (see Note)

1 tablespoon sugar

1 teaspoon salt

⅔ cup (152g) cold vegan butter, cut into ½-inch cubes

3 to 4 tablespoons ice water

FOR THE PIE FILLING AND TOPPING

¾ cup (300g) brown rice syrup

6 tablespoons soy or oat milk

1 cup (320g) paht (see page 32)

¼ cup (50g) light brown sugar

4 tablespoons (57g) vegan butter, melted and cooled

½ teaspoon salt

1 teaspoon vanilla extract

2 cups (220g) chopped pecans

3½ tablespoons (35g) potato starch

1 cup (110g) pecan halves

One Thanksgiving I decided I wanted to make pecan pie that my family would actually eat. We're not fans of overly sweet desserts, but my father absolutely loves pecans. The answer to creating a less cloyingly sweet filling was simple—*paht*! Not only is the red bean paste far less sugary than the typical custard-like filling of a traditional pecan pie, I knew my family would instantly appreciate the familiar flavor. I presented my little pie that Thanksgiving, and since then, I have been asked to make it every year.

1. Make the pie crust: In a food processor, combine the flour, sugar, and salt and pulse while adding the butter, a few pieces at a time. Add the ice water, 1 tablespoon at a time, until a dough starts to form.

2. Shape the dough into a ball. Do not handle more than necessary. Wrap with plastic and refrigerate for at least 4 hours, but best if overnight.

3. Preheat the oven to 350°F.

4. Make the pie filling and topping: In a medium bowl, combine the brown rice syrup, soy milk, paht, brown sugar, melted butter, salt, vanilla, chopped pecans, and potato starch.

5. Place the pie dough between two sheets of parchment paper. Using a rolling pin, roll out the pie dough gently until it is large enough to line a 9-inch pie pan. Ease the crust into the pan and trim any excess dough at the edges with kitchen shears or a sharp paring knife. Pour in the filling. Top the filling with the pecan halves.

6. Transfer the pie to the oven and bake until the pie filling sets (i.e., doesn't jiggle too much), 1 hour to 1 hour 15 minutes. Cool the pie on a wire rack for 2 hours before serving.

DATE AND GINGER TEA

SERVES 10

DIFFICULTY: Easy

ALLERGENS: GF

30 to 40 dried jujubes (Korean dates)

5 teaspoons minced fresh ginger

About ¾ cup sugar

Pine nuts, for garnish

Nothing pleases me more than when my husband proclaims that a Korean dish or specialty is the best thing he's ever tasted. He's gone on record saying that bibimbap is his favorite food, and he's also claimed on numerous occasions that date tea is his favorite drink. Last summer, in Korea, my sister-in-law's mother made him a cup of home-brewed date tea, and it was the perfect top-off to what he later described as one of the best meals he'd ever eaten. Traditional date tea is made with fresh jujubes, which are hard to find here in Chicago. But dried jujubes are available at most Asian markets. This version may not be as magical as the one my husband had in Korea, but as he says, it is "still delicious."

1. Soak the dried jujubes in water for 24 hours. Once softened, seed the jujubes. Chop the jujubes and keep them in separate groups of 3 or 4 jujubes.

2. In a pint-size mason jar, layer the ingredients in the following order: 3 or 4 chopped jujubes, ½ teaspoon ginger, and 3 to 4 teaspoons sugar (1 teaspoon for each jujube). Press the ingredients down with the back of a small spoon or your fingers. Repeat until all the jujubes, ginger, and sugar are packed into the mason jar.

3. Refrigerate the mason jar for at least 1 month, at which point much of the sugar will have turned into a glaze.

4. For each serving, steep 2 tablespoons of the date mixture in 1 cup of hot water for about 5 minutes. Pour the tea through a strainer over 1 teaspoon of pine nuts.

KKWABAEGI
(꽈배기 · Twisty Sugar Donuts)

MAKES 16 DONUTS

DIFFICULTY: Practice makes perfect

ALLERGENS: NF

2¼ teaspoons active dry yeast

2 tablespoons plus ¼ cup sugar

1 cup (240g) soy or oat milk, warmed to between 100°F to 110°F

3 cups (420g) bread flour

Pinch of salt

2 tablespoons vegan butter, melted

3 tablespoons aquafaba (canned chickpea liquid) or more plant milk

Vegetable oil, for frying

2 tablespoons ground cinnamon

My father is a donut fiend. In college, I would bring home a baker's dozen to share with my entire family, and Daddy would claim at least eight of them for himself. In a day. Now that he has successfully fought off cancer, my mom and I like to keep his donut intake to a minimum, but I must confess, I was inspired to veganize these Korean donuts for my dad. My mother-in-law has also become a huge fan. I daresay your family will love them, too!

1. In a small bowl, combine the yeast, 2 tablespoons of the sugar, and the plant milk. Set aside until the mixture foams, about 10 minutes.

2. In a stand mixer fitted with the dough hook (or in a large bowl using a wooden spoon), combine the flour and salt. Add the yeast mixture, melted butter, and aquafaba (or more milk). Mix on low (or by hand with the spoon) until a sticky dough forms. Continue kneading the dough at medium speed for an additional 8 minutes (or by hand for an additional 15 minutes).

3. Shape the dough into a ball and place it in a clean (preferably warm) bowl. Cover the bowl and set it in a warm location until the dough has doubled in size, at least 1 hour.

4. Punch down the dough to release the gas and reshape it into a ball. Cover the bowl and let the dough rise until it has once more doubled in size, an additional 40 to 45 minutes.

5. Divide the dough into 16 equal portions. Working with one portion at a time (leaving the rest covered in the bowl so they don't dry out), create a small ball between your hands. Then roll the ball

recipe continues

into a 12- to 14-inch-long rope, adding flour to your work surface if the dough keeps sticking. The rope should be thinner in the middle than at the ends.

6. Place your right palm over the right end of the rope and the left palm over the left end of the rope. Gently roll your right hand up and your left hand down, so that you create tension in the rope. Be careful not to break the rope by rolling too much. Bring the ends up and join them—the tension in the rope will naturally cause the dough to twist into a braid. Seal the ends and set the donut aside. Repeat with the remaining pieces of dough.

7. Cover the twisted dough pieces for about 10 minutes with a light kitchen towel until they get slightly puffy. Flip them over and let sit covered for another 10 minutes.

8. Meanwhile, pour 4 inches of vegetable oil into a large pot and heat over medium-high heat to about 350°F.

9. Working in batches (add only one at a time if your pot is small), gently add the shaped pieces of dough to the oil and cook until golden brown, about 2 minutes per side. Remove them from the oil and let them cool on a wire rack.

10. In a paper bag (not a plastic bag), combine the remaining ¼ cup sugar and the cinnamon. While the donut is still warm (not hot), add it to the brown bag and shake it gently. Remove and enjoy your kkwabaegi. Try not to eat them all at once.

STEAMED CHALTTEOK
(떡 · Sweet Rice Cakes)

SERVES 8 TO 10

DIFFICULTY: Medium

ALLERGENS: GF

5 cups (800g) frozen wet sweet white rice flour (see Note)

3 tablespoons sugar

½ teaspoon salt

1 cup (186g) dried black soybeans, soaked for 4 hours

12 dried jujubes, pitted and sliced

4 to 5 dried persimmons, pitted and sliced

¼ cup (30g) pistachios, chopped

¼ cup (35g) cooked chestnuts, chopped

Chaltteok or *chapsal tteok* is a variety of steamed rice cake made from glutinous rice that is ground into a fine powder. The rice flour is then steamed into a cake. Yes, you will need a steamer for this recipe! A 12-inch bamboo steamer works best. *Chaltteok* is often called a "healthy *ttoek*" because it's packed with beans and fruits, with very little sugar added. While we were in Korea last summer, my sister-in-law took me to a fancy Korean bakery located inside one of Seoul's largest department stores. The rice cakes were on display beneath a glass case, like jewelry. We bought some *chaltteok* with some pretty rose petals, embossed with little flecks of gold leaf. I can't re-create something quite that fancy in my own kitchen, but I add some dried persimmons and pistachio for a little flair.

1. In a large bowl, whisk together the rice flour, sugar, and salt. Add 1½ tablespoons water and mix together with your hands. The flour should feel evenly moistened, and the large clumps should be broken up.

2. Add the soybeans, jujubes, persimmons, pistachios, and chestnuts to the flour and stir everything together, preferably by hand.

3. Bring water to a boil in a steamer. Meanwhile, line the steamer insert with cheesecloth. Spoon the rice flour mixture into the lined steamer insert. If you're using a smaller steamer than the typical 12-inch bamboo steamer, you can still pack the entire amount of the rice flour mixture into the steamer—you will just have a thicker (still delicious) rice cake. Smooth out the top with the back of a spoon. Fold the ends of the cheesecloth over the top or, if your cheesecloth is not large enough, cover the top with a second cheesecloth or cotton cloth.

recipe continues

This recipe will only work with frozen wet sweet white rice flour. You can find this ingredient in the frozen food aisle of your local Asian grocery store.

4. When the water in the steamer is boiling, set the steamer insert in the pot, cover, and steam until the rice cake is gooey on the inside, 30 to 45 minutes, depending on the size of your steamer and the thickness of your rice cake.

5. Remove the insert from the steamer and uncover. When the rice cake is cool enough to handle, using the cheesecloth, lift out the rice cake and flip it over onto a smooth surface. Shape the rice cake into a large rectangle, about 8 by 6 inches. Slice into 1-inch-wide slices for serving.

6. Store in an airtight container or freeze for future use. Reheat in the microwave before serving.

LEMON AND CORIANDER BLUEBERRY MUFFINS

MAKES 6 JUMBO
MUFFINS

DIFFICULTY: Easy

ALLERGENS: NF

1 tablespoon fresh lemon
juice

½ cup (120g) soy or
oat milk

2⅓ cups (327g)
all-purpose flour

2 teaspoons baking
powder

½ teaspoon baking soda

¼ teaspoon salt

½ teaspoon ground
coriander

2 teaspoons grated
lemon zest

⅔ cup (152g) vegan butter
or coconut oil

¾ cup (150g) sugar

¼ cup aquafaba (canned
chickpea liquid)

1 tablespoon vanilla
extract

1½ cups (150g) blueberries

This blueberry muffin recipe is one of the oldest in my recipe box. That's right—I actually have a box of handwritten recipes that I've been keeping ever since I went vegan. I've made this recipe so many times, I could probably do it in my sleep, and there's a reason for that—it's so freaking good. I almost didn't include it in this book because there's nothing "Korean" about it and no ties to my family (other than they go gaga whenever I bake these). But, these muffins are truly the best I've ever had in my life—vegan or not—and I thought it would be a SIN not to include them here.

1. Preheat the oven to 425°F. Line 6 cups of a jumbo muffin tin with paper liners or mist with cooking spray.

2. In a small bowl or measuring cup, mix together the lemon juice and soy milk and set aside until the milk curdles, about 10 minutes.

3. In a large bowl, sift together the flour, baking powder, baking soda, and salt. Add the coriander and lemon zest.

4. In a separate bowl, using an electric mixer, cream together the butter and sugar. Add the milk/lemon juice mixture, aquafaba, and vanilla and mix until well combined.

5. Add the flour mixture in three parts to the wet ingredients, beating until just barely combined (there might still be some flour on the sides of the bowl, but that's okay).

6. Fold in the blueberries with a spatula so they don't burst and catch any of the flour still sticking to the sides of the bowl. The batter will be pretty thick.

recipe continues

7. Using two spoons or an ice cream scoop, scoop the batter into each liner so it's nearly full.

8. Transfer the muffin tin to the oven and bake for 8 minutes. Reduce the oven temperature to 350°F and bake until a toothpick inserted into the center of a muffin comes out clean, another 19 to 21 minutes. Cool the muffins in the pan for 10 minutes before serving.

SWEET MAPLE-ROASTED CORN TEA

SERVES 4 TO 6

DIFFICULTY: Easy
ALLERGENS: GF, NF

4 ears corn, unshucked

2 tablespoons maple syrup

1 lemon, thinly sliced, for garnish

1 jalapeño, seeded and sliced, for garnish

NOTES

In lieu of drying out the corn pieces in the oven, you can leave them outdoors in the sun for 1 to 2 days.

You can also purchase preroasted corn kernels and skip to step 4.

If we were running low on *boricha* (barley tea) in the house, my grandmother always had a backup: corn tea. It got to the point where it became difficult for me to notice any difference between barley or corn tea. When my grandmother moved out, my brother and I said goodbye to both *boricha* and corn tea. Plain water (*meng mool*) would be good enough for us, according to my parents! Here, I decided to add a sweet twist to my beloved corn tea, along with a little zip for summer.

1. Preheat the oven to 175°F. Shuck the corn but reserve the silk. Remove the corn kernels from the ears by using your fingers or a spoon. This will take the bulk of your time. Place the corn kernels, corn silk, and the cobs onto a large baking sheet in a single layer.

2. Transfer the baking sheet to the oven and bake for 1½ hours (see Notes). Remove the corn silk and set aside. Return the baking sheet to the oven and bake until the corn kernels and cobs are completely dried out, another 2½ hours.

3. Transfer the corn kernels to a large cast-iron pan or Dutch oven. Add the maple syrup and stir over medium heat until the kernels are evenly coated. Cook the corn kernels until they turn dark brown, about 10 minutes. Make sure they do not burn.

4. Add the corn cobs and corn silk to the pan along with 8 cups water. Bring the water to a boil, then reduce the heat and simmer until the water turns a rich brown color, about 15 minutes.

5. Set a sieve over a pitcher and pour the contents of the pan through the sieve (discard the solids). Store the tea in the refrigerator and serve over ice with lemon slices and fresh jalapeño as garnish.

CHOCOLATE CHIP PAHT
(Sweet Red Bean) COOKIES

MAKES 12 COOKIES

DIFFICULTY: Easy

ALLERGENS: NF

4 tablespoons (57g) vegan butter (see Note)

¼ cup (50g) light brown sugar

½ cup (100g) granulated sugar

½ cup (160g) paht (see page 32)

2 tablespoons plant milk

1 tablespoon vanilla extract

1¼ cups (315g) all-purpose flour

1 teaspoon baking soda

½ teaspoon salt

1 bar (17 oz/90g) dark chocolate, chopped into chunks

NOTES

You can use coconut oil instead of vegan butter, though it will make the cookies much harder.

My husband, Anthony, loves chocolate. There is no easier way to elevate a sweet recipe, in his mind, than to add chocolate chips. I don't have as developed a sweet tooth as my husband, but I do love a good chocolate chip cookie. Adding sweet red bean paste gives this recipe a lightness, while also imparting chewiness. Add to that the flavor of red beans, and you'll soon understand why Anthony calls these the best chocolate chip cookies he's ever had!

1. Preheat the oven to 375°F. Line a baking sheet with parchment paper.

2. In a stand mixer fitted with the paddle attachment, beat together the vegan butter, brown sugar, granulated sugar, red bean paste, plant milk, and vanilla on low speed until the ingredients are combined.

3. In a separate bowl, whisk together the flour, baking soda, salt, and chocolate chunks. Slowly incorporate the dry ingredients into the wet ingredients, using the stand mixer or a wooden spoon, until a dough forms.

4. Using a large spoon or ice cream scoop, scoop out balls of dough (roughly the size of golf balls) and place on the prepared baking sheet. Using the back of a spoon, press down on them a little, as they will not spread the way normal cookies do.

5. Transfer the baking sheet to the oven and bake for 11 minutes. The cookies will seem undercooked, but trust me. Cool the cookies on a wire rack for about 2 minutes before diving in.

CHOCOLATE-COVERED SHORTBREAD STICKS

MAKES 40 TO 50 STICKS

DIFFICULTY: Medium

¼ cup (57g) vegan butter

2 tablespoons powdered sugar

1 teaspoon vanilla extract

2 tablespoons (28g) coconut milk

1 cup (240g) self-rising flour

½ teaspoon baking powder

Pinch of salt

FOR DIPPING

12 ounces dark chocolate, chopped

1 teaspoon coconut oil

Sea salt

A visit to a Korean grocery store is not complete without shrimp chips and Pocky sticks. I'm still working on a vegan recipe for the former, but here's a fun recipe for the latter! You can coat the ends of the shortbread sticks with whatever you want, but here I went with the classic chocolate and a little sea salt.

1. Preheat the oven to 350°F.

2. In a stand mixer fitted with the paddle attachment, cream the butter and sugar at medium speed for about 1 minute. Beat in the vanilla and coconut milk at low speed until all the wet ingredients are well combined.

3. In a separate bowl, whisk together the self-rising flour, baking powder, and salt. Add the dry ingredients to the wet ingredients and stir until combined and a dough forms. The dough will be sticky and soft. Place the dough in the refrigerator for at least 1 hour and up to 2 days.

4. Line a baking sheet with a silicone baking mat or parchment paper. Divide the dough in half. Leave half the dough in the refrigerator while you work with the first half. Pinch off a small piece of the dough, roughly the size of a small gumball. Using the palms of your hands, roll the piece on a lightly floured surface into a rope 6 to 8 inches long and about ¼ inch thick. Carefully transfer the rope to the lined baking sheet. Repeat with the remaining dough. If the dough starts to get too soft to work with, place it in the freezer for 10 minutes.

recipe continues

5. Transfer the baking sheet to the oven and bake until the edges of the shortbread begin to turn golden brown, about 15 minutes.

6. Let the shortbread sticks cool completely on the pan before attempting to move them (they are quite fragile).

7. Meanwhile, make the dip: Melt the chocolate in the microwave. Stir in the coconut oil until the chocolate turns shiny.

8. While the sticks are still on the pan, using a spoon, pour the chocolate over the shortbread to coat as you desire. Sprinkle with a little sea salt. Allow the chocolate to set before removing and serving, about 5 minutes.

MOTHER-IN-LAW'S ÉCLAIR CAKE

SERVES 9

DIFFICULTY: Easy
ALLERGENS: NF

FOR THE CHOCOLATE CAKE

⅓ cup (76g) vegan butter

½ cup (113g) soy or oat milk

½ cup (118g) coffee

1 tablespoon white wine vinegar

1 tablespoon vanilla extract

¼ cup (20g) unsweetened cocoa powder

1½ cups (187g) all-purpose flour

1½ teaspoons baking powder

¾ teaspoon baking soda

Pinch of salt

¾ cup plus 2 tablespoons (175g) sugar

My mother-in-law makes one of my favorite cakes in all the world: éclair cake. After doing a little research, I discovered that "éclair cake" has very little do with its glorious namesake. Rather, it's just a casserole, if you will, of whipped cream, instant pudding, graham crackers, and melted chocolate. Whether you think it in any way resembles an actual éclair, it tastes delicious. I add a rich chocolate cake layer, and it is the stuff of legends, you all. Legends.

1. Preheat the oven to 350°F. Mist a 9 × 9-inch baking pan with cooking spray.

2. In a small pot, combine the vegan butter, milk, coffee, vinegar, vanilla, and cocoa. Stir over medium heat with a whisk until the butter is completely melted.

3. In a large bowl, whisk together the flour, baking powder, baking soda, salt, and sugar. Pour in the chocolate mixture while it is still warm. Whisk until well combined. Pour the cake batter into the baking pan.

4. Transfer the pan to the oven and bake until a toothpick inserted into the center of the cake comes out clean, 18 to 22 minutes. Let the cake cool in the pan for at least 20 minutes before assembling the rest of the cake.

5. Meanwhile, make the "éclair" filling: Prepare the pudding according to the package instructions, using the soy milk (this should be only half the amount in the package instructions).

recipe and ingredients continue

One 1-ounce (145g)
    package instant vanilla
    pudding mix

1½ cups (350g) soy or oat
    milk

One 9-ounce (255g)
    container vegan
    whipped cream

5 ounces (141g) dark
    chocolate, melted

2⅔ cups (8 ounces) vegan
    graham crackers or
    vanilla wafers

Melted chocolate,
    for drizzling (optional)

Incorporate the vegan whipped cream into the thick instant pudding.

6. In a separate bowl, stir one-quarter of the pudding mixture into the melted chocolate and whisk together until smooth. This will be for the final chocolate layer of the cake.

7. To assemble, spread a layer of the vanilla filling over the top of the chocolate cake (it should still be in the pan it was baked in). Top the filling with a layer of graham crackers. Repeat for one more layer of filling and cookies.

8. Spread the chocolate pudding mixture over the top of the second layer of graham crackers/cookies. If desired, drizzle the top of the cake with a little extra melted chocolate.

9. Place the cake in the refrigerator for at least 4 hours before serving. It is best served after being allowed to set in the refrigerator for 24 hours (to allow the graham crackers to soften).

PAHT (Sweet Red Bean) MARBLE CAKE

MAKES 12 SLICES

DIFFICULTY: Medium

ALLERGENS: NF

1 cup (240g) soy or oat milk

1 tablespoon white wine vinegar

2½ cups (312g) all-purpose flour

4½ tablespoons potato starch

1 tablespoon baking powder

½ teaspoon baking soda

Pinch of salt

⅔ cup (151g) vegan butter

¾ cup plus 2 tablespoons (175g) sugar

1 tablespoon vanilla extract

¼ cup (78g) paht (see page 32)

Red food coloring (optional)

One day, I was messing around in my kitchen with some leftover *paht* and wondered what would happen if I simply mixed some into my regular cake batter. It turns out it creates a lovely cake with a moist crumb and just a hint of the red bean flavor. This delicious marble cake makes you wonder, "What exactly is in this?" It's a total showstopper that combines American (vanilla) and Korean (*paht*) flavors.

1. Preheat the oven to 350°F. Mist a 10-cup Bundt pan with a generous amount of cooking spray.

2. In a measuring cup, stir together the soy milk and vinegar and set it aside until the milk curdles, about 10 minutes. This is vegan buttermilk.

3. In a bowl, whisk together the flour, potato starch, baking powder, baking soda, and salt.

4. In a stand mixer fitted with the paddle attachment (or with a hand mixer), cream the butter and sugar on high speed for about 1 minute.

5. Add the vanilla and the vegan buttermilk and mix on low speed. Sift the flour mixture into the wet ingredients. Continue mixing on low speed until the flour mixture is mostly incorporated. Use a rubber spatula to scrape down the sides and stir until all ingredients are well combined into a batter.

6. In a separate bowl, place one-third of the batter. Add the paht and a couple of drops of food coloring (if using) and mix the

recipe continues

ingredients together with a hand mixer or whisk (the red bean paste is thick, so it will be a workout without an electric mixer!). The batter will be slightly lumpy (kind of like blueberry muffin batter).

7. Scoop 6 large spoonfuls of the plain batter into the Bundt pan. Then, scoop 2 large spoonfuls of the paht batter over the plain batter. Repeat this process until both batters are completely used. Place a chopstick into the batter and swirl it around throughout the cake.

8. Transfer the pan to the oven and bake until a toothpick inserted halfway between the edge and the center of the cake comes out clean, 50 to 55 minutes.

9. Allow the cake to cool for 10 minutes in the pan before inverting, slicing, and serving.

CARDAMOM AND LEMON MADELEINES— THE SEXY COOKIE

MAKES
12 MADELEINES

DIFFICULTY: Medium

ALLERGENS: NF

1 cup (130g) cake flour

2 teaspoons baking powder

¼ teaspoon salt

2 teaspoons grated lemon zest

1 teaspoon ground cardamom

¾ cup (150g) aquafaba (canned chickpea liquid)

1 teaspoon cream of tartar

½ cup (50g) powdered sugar

½ cup (113g) vegan butter, melted

1 tablespoon light brown sugar

Melted butter and cake flour, for the pan

"Sexy cookie!" I will forever associate madeleines with my all-time favorite Korean drama, *My Lovely Sam Soon*. There's a scene in which the goddess of K-dramas, Sam Soon, explains that this delicate French dessert is, according to Marcel Proust, a "sexy cookie!" French food and, in particular, French pastries, occupy a hallowed place in the Korean culinary scene. Once, my mother called me in a panic when her dream of baking her own perfect little seashell cookies was dashed by two dozen burnt blobs that looked about as unsexy as you can imagine. I decided it was high time that I veganize these cookies!

1. In a medium bowl, whisk together the flour, baking powder, salt, lemon zest, and cardamom.

2. In a stand mixer fitted with the whisk attachment (or in a bowl using a hand mixer), combine the aquafaba, cream of tartar, and powdered sugar and whip on high speed into soft and glossy (not stiff) peaks, 5 to 10 minutes.

3. Sift in the dry ingredients and gently fold them into the whipped aquafaba using a rubber spatula (not a whisk).

4. In a separate small bowl, stir together the melted butter and brown sugar until it dissolves. Scoop ¼ cup of the batter and add it to the melted butter, using a spatula to incorporate it fully.

5. Slowly dribble the butter-batter mixture back down the side of the bowl containing the rest of the batter. Fat is heavy, and

recipe continues

the idea is to add it back gradually, so that it doesn't deflate the batter completely (it will inevitably deflate a little). Fold in the vegan butter–batter using a spatula. Then place the bowl in the refrigerator for at least 1 hour.

6. Preheat the oven to 425°F. Using your fingers, grease a madeleine pan generously with melted butter. Sprinkle a pinch of flour into each shell-shaped mold. Shake the pan around until the flour coats the entire mold. Flip the pan over your sink or garbage can to remove any excess flour.

7. Using two large spoons or an ice cream scoop, scoop the batter into the center of each mold. You do not need to spread the batter to fill the entire mold, as it will spread in the oven.

8. Transfer the pan to the oven and bake until the cookies are a beautiful golden color, 10 to 12 minutes. Allow them to cool in the pan for about 10 minutes before you try removing them (as they are prone to stick otherwise).

OMMA'S COFFEE CAKE

SERVES 9

DIFFICULTY: Easy

ALLERGENS: NF

FOR THE CRUMBLE TOPPING

¾ cup (105g) all-purpose flour

¾ cup (150g) light brown sugar

1½ tablespoons granulated sugar

2 tablespoons ground cinnamon

Pinch of salt

⅓ cup (70g) vegan butter, cut into ½-inch pieces

FOR THE CAKE

½ cup (115g) soy or oat milk

1 tablespoon white wine vinegar

2⅔ cups (335g) cake flour

4 teaspoons baking powder

1 teaspoon baking soda

¼ teaspoon salt

1 teaspoon potato starch

1 cup shaved dark chocolate (about 6 ounces)

½ cup (113g) vegan butter

1 cup (8 ounces) vegan cream cheese or vegan sour cream

My mother's culinary pièce de résistance was her ricotta cheesecake. She baked a pan for every major event in our lives, and to this day neighbors and family members alike flock to her front door for a slice. TBH, though, I never really liked the ricotta part! I much preferred the fluffy yellow cake layer (which she made from a box mix). I decided to create a version of my mother's coffee cake without the parts I don't like—this is, after all, one of the main benefits of adulthood, isn't it?

1. Preheat the oven to 350°F. Mist a 9 × 9-inch baking pan generously with cooking spray.

2. Make the crumble topping: In a medium bowl, combine the flour, brown sugar, granulated sugar, cinnamon, and salt. Using your fingers, incorporate the butter into the dry ingredients until the texture is crumbly. Place this in the refrigerator while you prepare the cake batter.

3. Make the cake batter: In a small bowl or measuring cup, stir together the soy milk and vinegar and set it aside to curdle, about 10 minutes. This is vegan buttermilk.

4. In a bowl, whisk together the cake flour, baking powder, baking soda, salt, and potato starch. Add the shaved chocolate.

5. In a stand mixer fitted with the paddle attachment (or in a bowl with a hand mixer), combine the vegan butter, vegan cream cheese, brown sugar, and granulated sugar and mix together on medium-high speed. Add the vanilla, aquafaba, and the vegan buttermilk and mix together on low speed.

recipe and ingredients continue

½ cup (100g) light brown sugar

½ cup (100g) granulated sugar

1 tablespoon vanilla extract

6 tablespoons aquafaba (canned chickpea liquid; see Note)

6. Add the dry ingredients to the wet ingredients and stir until they are just combined. Pour the cake batter into the baking pan and sprinkle the crumble over the top.

7. Transfer the pan to the oven and bake until a toothpick inserted into the center comes out clean, 38 to 40 minutes. Allow the cake to cool for about 15 minutes in the pan before serving.

NOTES

Instead of aquafaba, you can substitute 2 "flax eggs": 2 tablespoons ground flaxseed mixed together with 5 tablespoons of warm water.

GOCHUJANG-GLAZED PERSIMMON UPSIDE-DOWN CAKE

SERVES 12

DIFFICULTY: Easy

ALLERGENS: NF

¾ cup (180g) soy or oat milk

1 tablespoon white wine vinegar

3 tablespoons ground flaxseeds

3 cups (400g) all-purpose flour

2 teaspoons baking powder

½ teaspoon baking soda

1 teaspoon ground cinnamon

½ teaspoon ground nutmeg

¼ teaspoon ground cloves

Pinch of salt

2 sticks (226g) vegan butter, plus 2 tablespoons melted vegan butter

2 cups (400g) sugar

1 teaspoon vanilla extract

2 tablespoons maple syrup

1 tablespoon gochujang (see page 26)

1 to 2 Fuyu persimmons, sliced into ¼-inch-thick discs

Since *gochujang* has been taking the culinary world by storm over the past couple of years, I thought it might be fun to try using it in a dessert. Glazing persimmons with *gochujang* actually enhances their natural flavor while also providing an interesting kick. This is a rich and indulgent cake that packs a massive flavor punch— I suggest you pair it with a glass of your favorite red wine and some excellent conversation.

1. Preheat the oven to 350°F. In a small bowl or measuring cup, mix together the soy milk, vinegar, and ground flaxseeds. Set it aside until the milk curdles, about 10 minutes. This is vegan buttermilk.

2. In a medium bowl, sift together the flour, baking powder, baking soda, cinnamon, nutmeg, cloves, and salt.

3. In a separate bowl, with an electric mixer, cream the 2 sticks vegan butter and the sugar. Add the vegan buttermilk and vanilla and slowly stir all the wet ingredients together. Add the dry ingredients to the wet ingredients and stir until well combined.

4. In a small bowl or measuring cup, stir together the 2 tablespoons melted vegan butter, maple syrup, and gochujang.

5. Add the butter/maple/gochujang mixture to a 9-inch cast iron pan. Place the persimmons in the pan. Pour the batter into the pan.

6. Transfer the pan to the oven and bake until a toothpick inserted into the center comes out clean, 30 to 32 minutes.

THE LEES IN KOREA

MY FATHER IS A CINEPHILE. HE LOVES MOVIES—ROM-COMS,
a good action flick, even horror films. When I was about seven years
old, we watched the old musical *South Pacific* together and for weeks,
I sang "I'm gonna wash that man right outta my hair" in the bath. I
promised my dad one afternoon while pumping my legs on the swing
set at the playground a couple of blocks from our Skokie house,
"Daddy, when I grow up, I'm going to take you to paradise, the land
in the clouds, like in *South Pacific*. Bali Hai."

At Yonsei

More than two decades later, I took my
father (and the rest of my family) to Hawaii.
I booked a suite of rooms at a luxury beach-
front resort, made reservations at the best
sushi house in Maui, and booked the back
nine of the most outrageously beautiful golf
course on the island. My father spent most
of the ten-day trip sitting on the patio of our
hotel suite, reading the dictionary.

In 2019, I finally agreed to visit South
Korea with my parents. Partly in preparation
for the trip, I asked both my mom and my
dad to share with me their stories—many of which I've now shared
with you in this book. Some of these stories I'd heard before, some I
hadn't. But retracing their footsteps through Korea, armed with their
words, allowed me to see a side to them I'd never bothered to look
for: their humanity. I'd only ever seen them as parents; but watching

My dad at his elementary school

my father spread his arms out in front of the sleepy squat building with a faded blue sign as he exclaimed, "This is my elementary school!!" made me realize that a trip to paradise, for Daddy, would never be something I could pay for with an American Express card.

After hearing about how a Hershey's bar quite literally saved my mother's life, I was quite anxious to visit my mother's village—the one that took her family in as refugees after they'd narrowly escaped North Korea. Omma always talked about the village that "took her in," that adopted them and gave them a home and food and clothing. It was located a couple of hours from where we were staying, and one afternoon, we finally drove up to a small hamlet tucked between quiet swatches of rolling green hills. We drove around a warren of dirt roads darting through sparkling rice paddies like dark arteries pulsing through the chambers of a silver heart.

Omma didn't recognize anything, though, and the GPS was largely unhelpful. It had been decades since Omma had been back to the village. Eventually, we decided to take a tiny road that seemed to traverse the rice paddies to a small, official-looking, red-roofed building on the other side. We figured we could find someone there to ask for directions.

There were three old ladies standing around the tiny parking lot in front of the building, which appeared to be a meeting hall. They peered into the car as we drove up. Each of them wore brightly colored bonnets designed to protect their skin from the sun, though it was clear that all three of them spent quite a bit of time outdoors. They all had faces that looked like walnuts, black eyes glittering beneath hooded lids, curious and a little apprehensive. Each of them was shod in high platform slippers, the kind you can wear comfortably with socks so that your feet slip right into them for a quick jaunt to a neighbor's house for a bit of gossip.

We unloaded ourselves from the car and only then did I realize that my mom was also wearing a bright pink wide-brimmed sun hat—one that she'd picked up at a

street vendor earlier that morning when we stopped for a coffee. But that's where the similarities ended. My mom, at sixty-nine years old, still had a smooth face, wrinkle free. Prescription sunglasses protected her eyes, and she wore a pair of floral canvas sneakers I picked up for her at Nordstrom for watching my dog. Wrapped loosely around her shoulders was a white linen scarf I'd bought her from a small shop by the Pantheon in Rome the summer before. No dirt beneath her fingernails, which had been meticulously mani- cured the week before we left for Korea. I understood why she took such pains with her appearance—she wanted to "show off," but not in the mean-spirited way some might think. She wanted to show the village that had invested in her how much that investment had paid off.

Omma approached the three ladies and explained to them that she'd lived there many, many years ago, in the basement of one of the families who owned a large home. Within minutes, one of the ladies was nodding her head up and down, pulling on my mother's elbow and telling her to follow her. She flip-flopped up the road impres- sively in her platform slippers without waiting for my mom before turning around to wave us along.

My father whipped out his camcorder and I took out my camera as we made our way up the road, giving my mother and her guide a wide berth. At the top of the short incline perched a modest but sprawling home, with a red-tiled roof—similar to the one atop the meeting hall we'd parked in front of. High- heeled platform slipper lady rapped smartly on the door, and soon an older gentleman appeared behind the screen. A few words were exchanged between the three (I was too far away to hear), and our village guide, her job successfully completed, scampered back down the short road in her impossible heels.

The older gentleman was clad in a gray long-sleeved shirt and gray slacks. He looked to be about my father's age, perhaps older.

Omma's village

He stepped out of the house and onto the front stoop. My mother made a small bow, her right hand pressing down on the top of her sun hat. She began to talk and he nodded his head, his eyes shifting from curious to kind. Omma never turned around to invite me into their conversation, so Daddy and I stood back, unable to hear what was said. Still, I figured if we were not in the right place, Omma would've told us by now.

After about five minutes, she turned around with a bright smile and waved me over.

"This is the house! This is the house we were refugees in!" she called out, her voice animated in a way I was not used to hearing. And she immediately turned back to the man on the doorstep.

"This is my daughter. She is here all the way from America." I bowed my head and smiled.

"And that is my husband, back there, with the camera," she gestured vaguely behind us.

Eventually, the gray-clad man joined us as we slowly made our way down the sloping road, back to the parking lot. Shortly, they made their goodbyes, and the old man shuffled back up the road to his home, his hands clasped behind his back.

"So?" I asked Omma. "Who's that man?"

"He's the son!" Omma gushed. "He is the son of the family that let us live in their basement, when we were refugees!"

"So, we're in the right place? This is your village?"

"Yes! But, my goodness, it's changed so much. That's why I couldn't recognize! And his house—it's very modernized, it looks nothing like when I lived there. And that poor man!"

"Which poor man? The son? The man you were just talking to? I thought you said he was rich."

"No, no. He lost his wife *and* his son. They both died. So, he's all alone now." She grew quiet and lifted her hand to her hat as a stray finger of wind riffled through her hair.

I looked around at the small but neatly built homes across the rolling hills, with the bright red tiles lining their roofs stacked together like decks of Hwatoo* cards. About one hundred yards in front of me, nestled at the very bottom of the hill, I could see through the gaping rents of an abandoned shed holding rusted farming equipment. Somewhere, a dog barked urgently as the tiled apses of the village exhaled pale puffs of smoke into the sky like silent prayers. To my left, the rice paddies seemed to murmur, as if to lure me in with their secret stories of the abandoned shed, the man who returned my mother's smile with a pair of kind but unspeakably sad gray eyes, the tiled rooftops and stones that guarded the huddled mysteries of the people who lived beneath them.

Somewhere, beneath it all, was the soil my mother used to comb through with her bare hands until she unearthed a yam as red as the rooftops, as red as the flowers dotting her shoes, as red as the lips that stretched around the words:

"This is my daughter. From America."

* Cards used for a popular Korean card game, sometimes referenced as "Go Stop." The cards are often marked by their bright red backs.

ACKNOWLEDGMENTS

A couple of years ago, while sitting on the el taking me home from work, my phone buzzed. I looked down and saw an email from my father. The subject read, "My dear Jason and Joanne." Attached to the email was a Word document, which started: "Here is my family background in which I try to seek the truth as much as possible." By the time I got to my stop, I had tears streaming down my nose, as I read about my great-grandmother's suicide, my grandfather's encounter with a tiger, and my father's stint in Vietnam. A few months later, with some arm twisting, my mother also sent me a Word document with her story. And once again, her words blurred together as I wept over my grandfather's final words to his beloved daughter, my mother's triumphs as a student without enough money for books or shoes, and Omma's encounter with a psychic on Lake Shore Drive. This book would not exist without their stories and courage. I am so proud to be their daughter, and I hope this book honors them.

I would also like to thank my Eemo (Cheemin Omma), my Wehsoongmoh (Hyungsung Omma), my Samchoon (Hyungsung Appa), and my cousin Yemin. Thank you for all those hours testing recipes with me; giving me advice on how to make things taste *just* right; showing me how to wrap kimchi; carting around heavy photography equipment and props; wrapping hundreds of dumplings; and being willing to let me take a million photographs of your faces, hands, and hearts. Thank you to Judy, the best mother-in-law on the planet, who recipe-tested and made kimchi with me, proofread the entire book back and forth, and was always so supportive!

Thank you to my sister-in-law, Youngjung, for scouting out all the best vegan places to eat in Korea and for being so brutally honest about my food.

Thank you to my brother, Jaesun; my brother-in-law, David; and to all my cousins—Cheemin, Hyungsung, Yoonsung, Yemin—for being my biggest cheerleaders.

Thank you to my dearest friend, Kim-Julie, who believed in me long before I had the gumption to believe in myself. This book would not exist without you.

Thank you to Deborah, for always cooking the most delicious meals and providing me a safe space in which to write down my stories, recipes, and thoughts.

A million thank-yous to Betty. You are not only the most talented food photographer I know, you are the Unni I never knew I needed. Thank you so much for showing me how much difference a little perspective can make. Thank you for being brave enough to find your own way in life and art, and for inspiring me to do the same.

Thank you to Nisha, for your cheerful and practical advice on writing a cookbook, for inspiring me to take the road less traveled.

Thank you to the Original New York Vegan House Party crew (Kim-Julie, Nisha, Berto, Rebecca, Haile, and Charmaine). You ate my food and gave me the confidence to share my food with everyone.

Thank you to Timothy, for teaching me that details matter and that I deserve beautiful things (like a silent book spine!).

Thank you to Charlie, aka The Brit Who Makes My Dreams Come True. I am so lucky to have an agent who not only understands my vision but fights for it.

Thank you, Lucia, and the full Penguin team. Every Zoom call always left me feeling like I could conquer the world! Your patience with this full-time lawyer/first-time author was incredible and never went unnoticed. To everyone—from the best and kindest editor ever; to the sales team, who got excited at my Twitter followers; to the PR team, who huddled with me a year out from publication; to the art director, who whittled down the options for my cover; to the copy-editors, who painstakingly noted every error—thank you so much for helping me create something I am so proud of.

Thank you to Teri, not just for the beautiful bowls but for being my friend when I had ten thousand followers and no one else thought I was important enough to notice. Your loyalty means the world to me.

Thank you to Aron, the best and most talented ceramicist on the planet. My book would not look as beautiful as it does without you. I hope I do your work justice here.

Thank you to Yashar. It's amazing how my entire life changed from just one tweet. I am so, so grateful that you chose to extend your generosity to me!

Thank you to all the amazing Korean chefs, amateur cooks, and food bloggers (Maangchi, Korean Bapsang, Serious Eats) who taught me so much about Korean cooking when my mom was too busy.

I'd also like to thank my Foley family. I am so grateful to all my colleagues who have not only supported me throughout the creation of this book but have nurtured me as I grew up at the Firm. Specifically, I'd like to thank Geoff, my work BFF, and Bill, my work dad, for being my biggest cheerleaders as I wrote this book.

And finally, thank you to my husband, Anthony, without whom there'd be no "The Korean Vegan." Thank you for believing I am extraordinary. I endeavor, every day, to live up to your belief in me.

INDEX

Note: Page numbers in *italics* refer to illustrations.

A

Acorn Jelly, 95–96
agar-agar, 191
aioli sauce, 139
allergen information, 23
Angry Penne Pasta, 185
Appa (father)
  author's relationship with, 38,
    197–99
cooking skills of, 163, 167, 177,
    189, 237
  death of mother, 13–15
  and donuts, 291
  escape from North Korea,
    11–12
  family photos, *11*, *13*, *38*, *168*,
    169, *197*, *198*, *231*, *232*, *233*,
    320
  health concerns of, 232–33
  and *jjajangmyun* lunches,
    167–69
  and mealtimes in author's
    youth, 9–10, 13–15
  and rice market, 37
  rice rage of, 38
  and street food, 223
  trips to Korea, 198–99, 320–24,
    321
  and typed letters, 231–32
  in Vietnam, *14*
aquafaba, 33

B

Baechu Kimchi (Napa Cabbage
    Kimchi), 117–20
  and *Kimchi Chigae* (Kimchi
    Stew), 155
  and *Kimchi Guksoo* (Kimchi
    Noodles), 183
bagels: Seaweed Sesame Bagels,
    69–71
bakeries, Korean, 56, 73, 295
banchan, 249. *See also* side dishes
Bap. See rice

bar and street foods, 194–227
  about, 196
  and author's family history,
    223
  Bulgogi Wasabi Melt, 213
  Cheesy *Hotteok* (Fried Stuffed
    Pancakes), 220–21
  Curried *Tteokbokki* (Rice Cake)
    Skewers, 225–27
  Dooboo Kimchi (Tofu and
    Kimchi), 207–8
  Kimbap (Seaweed Rice Roll),
    201–2
  Korean BBQ Black Bean
    Burgers, 215–16
  Korean-Style *Suppli* (Rice Balls),
    209–11
  Korean-Style Toast, 217–19
  Omma's Egg Rolls, 203–5
  Sweet *Hotteok* (Fried Stuffed
    Pancakes), 223–24
Barely Pickled Kimchi (*Geotjuri
    Kimchi*), 121–23
barley: *Boricha* (Cold Barley
    Tea), 53
Battered Squash (*Hobbahk
    Jeon*), 89
BBQ
  BBQ Short Ribs (Mushroom
    Galbi), 237
  Korean BBQ Black Bean
    Burgers, 215–16
  Omma's Korean BBQ Sauce, 45
beverages
  Boricha (Cold Barley Tea), 53
  Date and Ginger Tea, 289
  Sweet Maple-Roasted Corn Tea,
    301
bibimbap (leftover rice), 61, 249
Bindaetteok (Mung Bean
    Pancakes), 81–83
"birthday soup" (*Miyeok Guk*;
    Seaweed Soup), 161
black beans: Korean BBQ Black
    Bean Burgers, 215–16

blackberries: *Dotori Muk* (Acorn
    Jelly) with Blackberry
    Dressing, 95–96
Black Soybean Noodles
    (*Jjajangmyun*), 171–72
blog of author, 17
blueberries: Lemon and Coriander
    Blueberry Muffins, 297–99
Boricha (Cold Barley Tea), 53
Braised Lion's Mane
    Mushrooms, 91
Braised Potatoes (*Gamja Jorim*),
    105–7
Braised Tofu (*Dooboo Jorim*), 267
breads, 54–75
  Dolsot Bbang (Stone Pot Bread),
    61–62
  Milk Bread, 73–75
  Paht Bbang (Red Bean Paste
    Bread), 67–68
  Perilla Leaf Focaccia, 63–65
  Seaweed Sesame Bagels, 69–71
broths, plant based, 29, 43
Brussels Sprout Salad, 135
Buckwheat Noodles, Cold
    (*Naengmyeon*), 177–78
bulgogi
  Bulgogi (Grilled Steak), 235
  Bulgogi Wasabi Melt, 213
burgers and sandwiches
  Bulgogi Wasabi Melt, 213
  Korean BBQ Black Bean
    Burgers, 215–16
  Korean-Style Toast, 217–19

C

cabbage
  Baechu Kimchi (Napa Cabbage
    Kimchi), 117–20
  Carrot and Cabbage Slaw, 217
  Geotjuri Kimchi (Barely Pickled
    Kimchi), 121–23
  Korean Pear Slaw, 137
  Simple Red Cabbage Slaw, 215

cakes
    Chocolate Sweet Potato Cake,
        281–82
    Gochujang-Glazed Persimmon
        Upside-Down Cake, 319
    Mother-In-Law's Éclair Cake,
        307–9
    Omma's Coffee Cake, 317–18
    Paht (Sweet Red Bean) Marble
        Cake, 311–12
Cardamom and Lemon
    Madeleines—The Sexy
    Cookie, 313–15
Carrot and Cabbage Slaw, 217
casserole: Omma's Casserole,
    271–73
challah, 67–68
Chaltteok, Steamed (Sweet Rice
    Cakes), 295–96
Cheesy *Hotteok* (Fried Stuffed
    Pancakes), 220–21
chocolate
    Chocolate Chip *Paht* (Sweet
        Red Bean) Cookies, 303
    Chocolate-Covered Shortbread
        Sticks, 305–6
    Chocolate Persimmon
        Cupcakes, 283–85
    Chocolate Sweet Potato Cake,
        281–82
    Mother-In-Law's Éclair Cake,
        307–9
Chong Gak Kimchi (Ponytail
    Kimchi), 127–28
Chunjinam Hermitage, 19
coconut aminos, 25
Coffee Cake, Omma's, 317–18
Cold Buckwheat Noodles
    (*Naengmyeon*), 177–78
cookies
    Cardamom and Lemon
        Madeleines, 313–15
    Chocolate Chip *Paht* (Sweet
        Red Bean) Cookies, 303
coriander: Lemon and Coriander
    Blueberry Muffins, 297–99
corn: Sweet Maple-Roasted Corn
    Tea, 301
"cream of mushroom" sauce,
    271–73
Cucumber Kimchi, 115

cupcakes: Chocolate Persimmon
    Cupcakes, 283–85
Curried *Tteokbokki* (Rice Cake)
    Skewers, 225–27

D
danmuji, 202
Dashi, Mushroom, 39
dashima (kelp)
    powder, 119
    sheets, 29
Date and Ginger Tea, 289
desserts. *See* sweets
doenjang (fermented soybean
    paste)
    about *doenjang*, 25–26
    Doenjang Chigae, Spicy
        (Fermented Soybean Stew),
        153
    as dressing option, 110
    Roasted *Doenjang*-Glazed
        Onions, 87
Dolsot Bbang (Stone Pot Bread),
    61–62
donuts, 291–93
dooboo
    about, 230, 253
    Dooboo Jeon (Tofu Cakes), 101
    Dooboo Jorim (Braised Tofu),
        267
    Dooboo Kimchi (Tofu and
        Kimchi), 207–8
    Mapo Dooboo (Tofu), 269–70
    Soondooboo Chigae (Silken Tofu
        Stew), 157
    See also tofu
Dotori Muk (Acorn Jelly) with
    Blackberry Dressing, 95–96
doubanjiang (fava bean paste), 269,
    270
Dressed Kale (*Kale Moochim*), 85
dressings
    doenjang and *gochujang* used for,
        110
    Spicy *Gochujang* Dressing, 51
    Spicy Soy Sauce Dressing, 49
dumplings
    Mandoo (Dumplings), 251–52
    Tteok-Mandu Guk (Rice Cake
        Soup with Dumplings), 149

E
Éclair Cake, Mother-In-Law's,
    307–9
egg replacer
    about, 33
    Gyerranmari (Korean-Style
        Omelet), 97–99
    Korean-Style Toast, 217–19
    Omurice (Omelet Rice), 263–65
Egg Rolls, Omma's, 203–5

F
family of author
    and author's first marriage, 143
    and death of Hahlmuhnee,
        13–15
    and dumpling making, 251
    escapes from North Korea,
        11–12, 277–78
    grandmothers (*see* Hahlmuhnee;
        Seoul Hahlmuhnee)
    hunger experienced by, 18,
        277–78
    immigrant story of, 11
    and kimchi, 111–12
    and Korean War, 12, 18, 79,
        277–78
    and mealtimes in author's
        youth, 9–10, 13, 14–15, 18
    and memories of SPAM, 20
    and Omma in nursing school,
        57–59
    parents (*see* Appa; Omma)
    as refugees, 12, 79–80, 277–78,
        321–23
    and rice market, 37
    and "rice rage" of father, 38
    trips to Korea, 198–99, 320–24
    and vegan journey of author,
        17–18, 19–21, 103
fava bean paste (*doubanjiang*), 269,
    270
Fennel Doenjang Guk (Fermented
    Soybean Soup), 151
fermented soybean paste
    (*doenjang*), 25–26
Fermented Soybean Soup (*Fennel
    Doenjang Guk*), 151
Fermented Soybean Stew (Spicy
    Doenjang Chigae), 153

fernbrake (*gosari*): *Yukgaejang* (Spicy Scallion and Fernbrake Soup), 145–47
"Fishy" Sauce, 47
flax eggs, 33
focaccia, 63–65
fried rice
    Kimchi Bokkeum Bap (Fried Rice), 255
    Omurice (Omelet Rice), 263–65
Fried Stuffed Pancakes
    Cheesy *Hotteok*, 220–21
    Sweet *Hotteok*, 223–24

G

Gamja Guk (Potato and Leek Soup), 163
Gamja Jorim (Braised Potatoes), 105–7
Gamja Tang (Potato Stew), 159
garlic
    Kkanpoongi (Spicy Crunchy Garlic Wings), 239–41
    Kkanpoong Tofu (Spicy Crunchy Garlic Tofu), 243–44
garraetteok. *See* rice cakes
Geotjuri Kimchi (Barely Pickled Kimchi), 121–23
ginger: Date and Ginger Tea, 289
gochugaru, 28
gochujang
    about, 26–27
    as dressing option, 110
    Gochujang-Glazed Persimmon Upside-Down Cake, 319
    Lasagna with *Gochujang* Red Sauce, 259–61
    Spicy *Gochujang* Dressing, 51
gosari: *Yukgaejang* (Spicy Scallion and Fernbrake Soup), 145–47
Grilled Steak (*Bulgogi*), 235
gyerranmari
    Korean-Style Omelet, 97–99
    Korean-Style Toast, 217–19

H

Hahlmuhnee (paternal grandmother), *10*
    and corn tea, 301

death of, 13–15
family photos, *11, 12, 15*
fleeing North Korea, 11–12
and gosari, 145
kimbaps of, 201
and kimchi, 111–12
and mealtimes in author's youth, 9–10
See also Seoul Hahlmuhnee
Hobbahk Jeon (Battered Squash), 89
hotteok
    Cheesy *Hotteok* (Fried Stuffed Pancakes), 220–21
    Sweet *Hotteok* (Fried Stuffed Pancakes), 223–24

J

jackfruit: *Kkanpoongi* (Spicy Crunchy Garlic Wings), 239–41
Japan, 11, 12, 56
Japchae (Korean Glass Noodles), 179–81
Jeong Kwan sunim, 19–20, 151
jjajang, 27
jjajangmyun
    about, 168
    Jjajangmyun (Black Soybean Noodles), 23, 27, 171–72
    popularity of, 168
jujubes (Korean dates), 289
juuk (rice porridge), 257

K

Kahl-Guksoo (Knife-Cut Noodles), 173–75
kale
    Kale and Ramen Salad, 129–31
    Kale Moochim (Dressed Kale), 85
kelp (*dashima*)
    powder, 119
    sheets, 29
Kimbap (Seaweed Rice Roll), 201–2
kimchi
    about, 110, 113
    and author's family history, 111–12

Baechu Kimchi (Napa Cabbage Kimchi), 117–20
Chong Gak Kimchi (Ponytail Kimchi), 127–28
Cucumber Kimchi, 115
Dooboo Kimchi (Tofu and Kimchi), 207–8
and "Fishy" Sauce, 47
Geotjuri Kimchi (Barely Pickled Kimchi), 121–23
Kimchi Bokkeum Bap (Fried Rice), 255
Kimchi Chigae (Kimchi Stew), 155
Kimchi Guksoo (Kimchi Noodles), 183
Mool Kimchi (Water Kimchi), 125
Kkanpoongi (Spicy Crunchy Garlic Wings), 239–41
Kkanpoong Tofu (Spicy Crunchy Garlic Tofu), 243–44
kkenip (perilla leaves)
    Kkenip Buchimgae (Perilla Leaf Pancakes), 103–4
    Perilla Leaf Focaccia, 63–65
    Pickled Perilla Leaves, 133
Kkwabaegi (Twisty Sugar Donuts), 291–93
Knife-Cut Noodles (*Kahl-Guksoo*), 173–75
Kong Namul (Bean Sprout) Consommé Ramen, 189–91
Korea
    author's visits to, 19, 198–99, 245, 295, 320–22
    bakeries in, 56, 73, 295
    and family history of author, 11–12, 18, 79–80, 277–78, 279
    and Korean War, 12, 18, 79, 277–78
    toast cafes in, 217
Korean BBQ Black Bean Burgers, 215–16
Korean Glass Noodles (*Japchae*), 179–81
Korean Pear Slaw, 137
Korean Potato Salad with Scallion Aioli, 139
Korean-Style Omelet (*Gyerranmari*), 97–99

Korean-Style *Suppli* (Rice Balls), 209–11
Korean-Style Toast, 217–19

L

Lasagna with *Gochujang* Red Sauce, 259–61
leeks: *Gamja Guk* (Potato and Leek Soup), 163
lemon
  Cardamom and Lemon Madeleines, 313–15
  Lemon and Coriander Blueberry Muffins, 297–99
lion's mane mushrooms, braised, 91

M

Madeleines, Cardamom and Lemon (The Sexy Cookie), 313–15
main dishes, 228–73
  Bulgogi (Grilled Steak), 235
  Dooboo Jorim (Braised Tofu), 267
  Kimchi Bokkeum Bap (Fried Rice), 255
  Kkanpoongi (Spicy Crunchy Garlic Wings), 239–41
  Kkanpoong Tofu (Spicy Crunchy Garlic Tofu), 243–44
  Lasagna with *Gochujang* Red Sauce, 259–61
  Mandoo (Dumplings), 251–52
  Mapo Dooboo (Tofu), 269–70
  Mushroom *Galbi* (BBQ Short Ribs), 237
  Mushroom *Juuk* (Rice Porridge), 257
  Omma's Casserole, 271–73
  Omurice (Omelet Rice), 263–65
  Power Bowl, 249
  Tangsuyuk (Sweet and Sour Mushrooms), 245–47
  Tofu Hot Pot, 253
Mandoo (Dumplings), 251–52
maple: Sweet Maple-Roasted Corn Tea, 301
Mapo Dooboo (Tofu), 269–70

Marble Cake, *Paht* (Sweet Red Bean), 311–12
marinade, 45
measurements used in recipes, 23
Milk Bread, 73–75
miso, 26
Miyeok Guk (Seaweed Soup), 161
Mool Kimchi (Water Kimchi), 125
Mother-In-Law's Éclair Cake, 307–9
muffins: Lemon and Coriander Blueberry Muffins, 297–99
mung beans: *Bindaetteok* (Mung Bean Pancakes), 81–83
mung bean sprouts: Stir-Fried Mung Bean Sprouts, 93
Mushroom Dashi
  about, 39
  and *Fennel Doenjang Guk* (Fermented Soybean Soup), 151
  and *Kimchi Guksoo* (Kimchi Noodles), 183
mushrooms
  about, 29, 31, 39
  Braised Lion's Mane Mushrooms, 91
  "Fishy" Sauce, 47
  Mapo Dooboo (Tofu), 269–70
  Mushroom *Galbi* (BBQ Short Ribs), 237
  Mushroom *Juuk* (Rice Porridge), 257
  Omma's Casserole, 271–73
  Tangsuyuk (Sweet and Sour Mushrooms), 245–47
  See also Mushroom Dashi
My Lovely Sam Soon, 313

N

Naejangsan National Park, 199
Naengmyeon (Cold Buckwheat Noodles), 177–78
napa cabbage
  Baechu Kimchi (Napa Cabbage Kimchi), 117–20
  Geotjuri Kimchi (Barely Pickled Kimchi), 121–23

noodles and pastas, 164–93
  about, 166
  Angry Penne Pasta, 185
  Japchae (Korean Glass Noodles), 179–81
  Jjajangmyun (Black Soybean Noodles), 171–72
  Kahl-Guksoo (Knife-Cut Noodles), 173–75
  Kimchi Guksoo (Kimchi Noodles), 183
  Kong Namul (Bean Sprout) Consommé Ramen, 189–91
  Naengmyeon (Cold Buckwheat Noodles), 177–78
  Sujebi (Spicy Torn Noodles), 187–88
  Tteokbokki Arrabbiata, 193
North Korea, 11, 12–13, 18, 21, 80, 321. *See also* Korea

O

oat milk, 31
omelets
  Gyerranmari (Korean-Style Omelet), 97–99
  Omurice (Omelet Rice), 263–65
Omma (mother), 80
  and author's first marriage, 143
  and author's vegan journey, 20, 103
  BBQ sauce of, 237
  birth of, 12
  and birth of author, 161
  casserole of, 271
  and chocolate sweet potato cake, 281
  coffee cake of, 317–18
  and dumpling making, 251
  egg rolls of, 203
  emigration to U.S., 57
  family photos, *12, 13, 58, 59, 278, 320*
  hunger experienced by, 277–78
  and mealtimes in author's youth, 9–10
  nursing education of, 57–59, *57*
  and parents' flight from North Korea, 277–78

and recipe development of
author, 163
ricotta cheesecake of, 317
and sweet potatoes, 79–80
and torn noodle soup, 187
trips to Korea, 320–24, *322*
youth as refugee, 12, 80,
321–24, *323*
Omma's Casserole, 271–73
Omma's Coffee Cake, 317–18
Omma's Egg Rolls, 203–5
Omma's Korean BBQ Sauce, 45
Omurice (Omelet Rice), 263–65
onions: Roasted *Doenjang*-Glazed
Onions, 87
oyster mushrooms: "Fishy"
Sauce, 47

P

paht (sweet red bean paste)
about, 32–33
Chocolate Chip *Paht* (Sweet
Red Bean) Cookies, 303
Paht (Sweet Red Bean) Marble
Cake, 311–12
Paht Bbang (Red Bean Paste
Bread), 67–68
Pecan *Paht* Pie, 287
pancakes
Bindaetteok (Mung Bean
Pancakes), 81–83
Cheesy *Hotteok* (Fried Stuffed
Pancakes), 220–21
Kkenip Buchimgae (Perilla Leaf
Pancakes), 103–4
Sweet *Hotteok* (Fried Stuffed
Pancakes), 223–24
pantry items, 23–33
dashima, 29
doenjang, 25–26
dried mushrooms, 29, 31
egg replacer, 33
garraetteok, 32
gochugaru, 28
gochujang, 26–27
jjajang, 27
paht, 32–33
plant milk, 31–32
sesame oil, 27–28
soy sauce, 24–25

pears
Korean Pear Slaw, 137
Naengmyeon (Cold Buckwheat
Noodles), 177–78
Pecan *Paht* Pie, 287
Penne Pasta, Angry, 185
perilla leaves (*kkenip*)
Perilla Leaf Focaccia, 63–65
Perilla Leaf Pancakes (*Kkenip
Buchimgae*), 103–4
Pickled Perilla Leaves, 133
persimmons
about, 276, 283
and author's Hahlmuhnee, 277,
279
and author's husband, 283
Chocolate Persimmon
Cupcakes, 283–85
Gochujang-Glazed Persimmon
Upside-Down Cake, 319
Pickled Perilla Leaves, 133
pies: Pecan *Paht* Pie, 287
plant milk, 31–32
Ponytail Kimchi (*Chong Gak
Kimchi*), 127–28
potatoes
Gamja Guk (Potato and Leek
Soup), 163
Gamja Jorim (Braised Potatoes),
105–7
Gamja Tang (Potato Stew), 159
Korean Potato Salad with
Scallion Aioli, 139
Power Bowl, 249

R

radishes
Chong Gak Kimchi (Ponytail
Kimchi), 127–28
Mool Kimchi (Water Kimchi),
125
ramen
Kale and Ramen Salad, 129–31
Kong Namul (Bean Sprout)
Consommé Ramen, 189–91
red bean paste. *See paht*
rice
about *bap*, 36
basic rice recipe, 41
bibimbap (leftover rice), 61, 249

Kimchi Bokkeum Bap (Fried
Rice), 255
Omurice (Omelet Rice), 263–65
Power Bowl, 249
Rice Porridge (Mushroom
Juuk), 257
rice balls, Korean-Style *Suppli*,
209–11
rice cakes (*garraetteok*)
about *garraetteok*, 32
Curried *Tteokbokki* (Rice Cake)
Skewers, 225–27
Steamed *Chaltteok* (Sweet Rice
Cakes), 295–96
Tteokbokki Arrabbiata, 193
Tteok-Mandu Guk (Rice Cake
Soup with Dumplings),
149
rice rolls: *Kimbap* (Seaweed Rice
Roll), 201–2
Roasted *Doenjang*-Glazed
Onions, 87

S

salads
Brussels Sprout Salad, 135
Kale and Ramen Salad,
129–31
Korean Pear Slaw, 137
Korean Potato Salad with
Scallion Aioli, 139
Pickled Perilla Leaves, 133
See also dressings
sandwiches and burgers
Bulgogi Wasabi Melt, 213
Korean BBQ Black Bean
Burgers, 215–16
Korean-Style Toast, 217–19
scallions
Korean Potato Salad with
Scallion Aioli, 139
Yukgaejang (Spicy Scallion and
Fernbrake Soup), 145–47
seaweed
about *dashima*, 29, 119
Kimbap (Seaweed Rice Roll),
201–2
Miyeok Guk (Seaweed Soup),
161
Seaweed Sesame Bagels, 69–71

Seoul Hahlmuhnee (maternal grandmother)
  and buffet chicken wings, 239
  death of, 278–79
  and death of Hahlmuhnee, 13–15
  and dumpling making, 251
  family photos, *12, 278, 279*
  fleeing North Korea, 277–78
  hunger experienced by, 18, 277–78
  and meat, 18
  persimmon tree of, 279
  produce grown by, 18–19, 89
  and torn noodle soup, 187
sesame oil, 27–28
sesame: Seaweed Sesame Bagels, 69–71
shiitake mushrooms
  about, 29, 31
  "Fishy" Sauce, 47
  Mapo Dooboo (Tofu), 269–70
  Mushroom Dashi, 39
  Mushroom *Juuk* (Rice Porridge), 257
  Tangsuyuk (Sweet and Sour Mushrooms), 245–47
shortbread sticks, chocolate-covered, 305–6
side dishes, 76–107
  about *banchan*, 78, 249
  Bindaetteok (Mung Bean Pancakes), 81–83
  Braised Lion's Mane Mushrooms, 91
  Dooboo Jeon (Tofu Cakes), 101
  Dotori Muk (Acorn Jelly) with Blackberry Dressing, 95–96
  Gamja Jorim (Braised Potatoes), 105–7
  Gyerranmari (Korean-Style Omelet), 97–99
  Hobbahk Jeon (Battered Squash), 89
  Kale Moochim (Dressed Kale), 85
  Kkenip Buchimgae (Perilla Leaf Pancakes), 103–4
  Roasted *Doenjang*-Glazed Onions, 87
  Stir-Fried Mung Bean Sprouts, 93

Silken Tofu Stew (*Soondooboo Chigae*), 157
skewers: Curried *Tteokbokki* (Rice Cake) Skewers, 225–27
slaw
  Carrot and Cabbage Slaw, 217
  Korean Pear Slaw, 137
  Simple Red Cabbage Slaw, 215
slurping, 9
Soondooboo Chigae (Silken Tofu Stew), 157
soups and stews, 140–63
  about, 142
  broths, plant based, 29, 43
  Fennel Doenjang Guk (Fermented Soybean Soup), 151
  Gamja Guk (Potato and Leek Soup), 163
  Gamja Tang (Potato Stew), 159
  Kahl-Guksoo (Knife-Cut Noodles), 173–75
  Kimchi Chigae (Kimchi Stew), 155
  Kong Namul (Bean Sprout) Consommé Ramen, 189–91
  Miyeok Guk (Seaweed Soup), 161
  Soondooboo Chigae (Silken Tofu Stew), 157
  Spicy Doenjang Chigae (Fermented Soybean Stew), 153
  Sujebi (Spicy Torn Noodles), 187–88
  Tteok-Mandu Guk (Rice Cake Soup with Dumplings), 149
  Yukgaejang (Spicy Scallion and Fernbrake Soup), 145–47
soy curls: *Bulgogi* (Grilled Steak), 235
soy milk
  about, 31
  Milk Bread, 73–75
soy sauce
  about, 24–25
  Spicy Soy Sauce Dressing, 49
SPAM, 20
Spicy Crunchy Garlic Tofu (*Kkanpoong Tofu*), 243–44

Spicy Doenjang Chigae (Fermented Soybean Stew), 153
Spicy *Gochujang* Dressing, 51
Spicy Scallion and Fernbrake Soup (*Yukgaejang*), 145–47
Spicy Soy Sauce Dressing, 49
Spicy Torn Noodles (*Sujebi*), 187–88
spinach: *Japchae* (Korean Glass Noodles), 179–81
sprouts
  Kong Namul (Bean Sprout) Consommé Ramen, 189–91
  Stir-Fried Mung Bean Sprouts, 93
squash: *Hobbahk Jeon* (Battered Squash), 89
Steamed *Chaltteok* (Sweet Rice Cakes), 295–96
Stir-Fried Mung Bean Sprouts, 93
Stone Pot Bread (*Dolsot Bbang*), 61–62
street food. *See* bar and street foods
substitutions, note on, 23
Sujebi (Spicy Torn Noodles), 187–88
Suppli, Korean-Style (Rice Balls), 209–11
Sweet and Sour Mushrooms (*Tangsuyuk*), 245–47
Sweet *Hotteok* (Fried Stuffed Pancakes), 223–24
Sweet Maple-Roasted Corn Tea, 301
sweet potatoes
  Chocolate Sweet Potato Cake, 281–82
  Omma's memories of, 79–80
  Power Bowl, 249
sweet red bean paste. *See paht*
sweets, 274–319
  about, 276
  Cardamom and Lemon Madeleines—The Sexy Cookie, 313–15
  Chocolate Chip *Paht* (Sweet Red Bean) Cookies, 303
  Chocolate-Covered Shortbread Sticks, 305–6

Chocolate Persimmon Cupcakes, 283–85

Chocolate Sweet Potato Cake, 281–82

Date and Ginger Tea, 289

Gochujang-Glazed Persimmon Upside-Down Cake, 319

Kkwabaegi (Twisty Sugar Donuts), 291–93

Lemon and Coriander Blueberry Muffins, 297–99

Mother-In-Law's Éclair Cake, 307–9

Omma's Coffee Cake, 317–18

Paht (Sweet Red Bean) Marble Cake, 311–12

Pecan *Paht* Pie, 287

Steamed *Chaltteok* (Sweet Rice Cakes), 295–96

Sweet Maple-Roasted Corn Tea, 301

T

tamari sauce, 24, 25

Tangsuyuk (Sweet and Sour Mushrooms), 245–47

tangzhong, 73

tea
    Boricha (Cold Barley Tea), 53
    Date and Ginger Tea, 289
    Sweet Maple-Roasted Corn Tea, 301

Toast, Korean-Style, 217–19

tofu
    about, 230, 253
    Dooboo Jeon (Tofu Cakes), 101
    Dooboo Jorim (Braised Tofu), 267
    Dooboo Kimchi (Tofu and Kimchi), 207–8
    Fennel Doenjang Guk (Fermented Soybean Soup), 151
    Kimchi Chigae (Kimchi Stew), 155
    Kkanpoongi (Spicy Crunchy Garlic Wings), 239–41
    Kkanpoong Tofu (Spicy Crunchy Garlic Tofu), 243–44
    Mandoo (Dumplings), 251–52
    Mapo Dooboo (Tofu), 269–70
    Omma's Egg Rolls, 203–5
    Power Bowl, 249
    Soondooboo Chigae (Silken Tofu Stew), 157
    Spicy Doenjang Chigae (Fermented Soybean Stew), 153
    Tofu Hot Pot, 253

tomatoes: Lasagna with *Gochujang* Red Sauce, 259–61

torn noodle soup (*Sujebi*), 187–88

tteokbokki (spicy rice cakes)
    Curried *Tteokbokki* (Rice Cake) Skewers, 225–27
    Tteokbokki Arrabbiata, 193
    Tteok-Mandu Guk (Rice Cake Soup with Dumplings), 149

Twisty Sugar Donuts (*Kkwabaegi*), 291–93

U

Upside-Down Cake, *Gochujang*-Glazed Persimmon, 319

V

vegan journey of author, 17–18, 19–21

Vegetable Broth, 29, 43

Vietnam War, 14, *14*

W

Water Kimchi (*Mool Kimchi*), 125

wings: *Kkanpoongi* (Spicy Crunchy Garlic Wings), 239–41

Y

Yukgaejang (Spicy Scallion and Fernbrake Soup), 145–47

Z

zucchini
    Hobbahk Jeon (Battered Squash), 89
    Lasagna with *Gochujang* Red Sauce, 259–61